PUBLIC ENEMIES, PUBLIC HEROES

PUBLIC ENEMIES,

PUBLIC HEROES

Screening the Gangster from
Little Caesar to *Touch of Evil*

JONATHAN MUNBY

The University of Chicago Press • Chicago and London

JONATHAN MUNBY is a Lecturer in American Studies at Lancaster University.

The University of Chicago Press, Chicago 60637
The University of Chicago Press, Ltd., London
© 1999 by The University of Chicago
All rights reserved. Published 1999
08   07   06   05   04   03   02   01   00   99   1   2   3   4   5

ISBN: 0-226-55031-1 (cloth)
ISBN: 0-226-55033-8 (paper)

Figure 1 is reproduced courtesy of the Museum of the City of New York. Figures 2–16 are reproduced courtesy of BFI Films: Stills, Posters and Designs.

Library of Congress Cataloging-in-Publication Data

Munby, Jonathan.
    Public enemies, public heroes : screening the gangster from Little Caesar to Touch of
    Evil / Jonathan Munby.
        p.   cm.
    Includes bibliographical references and index.
    ISBN 0-226-55031-1 (cloth : alk. paper).—ISBN 0-226-55033-8
    (pbk. : alk. paper)
        1. Gangster films—United States—History and criticism.   I. Title.
    PN1995.9.G3M86   1999
    761.43′655—dc21
                                                                        98-22151
                                                                        CIP

⊗ The paper used in this publication meets the minimum requirements of the American
National Standard for Information Sciences—Permanence of Paper for Printed Library
Materials, ANSI Z39.48-1992.

For Karen

Contents

4
Ganging Up against the Gangster
Censorship, the Movies, and Cultural Transformation,
1915–1935   83

5
Crime, Inc.
Beyond the Ghetto/Beyond the Majors in the Postwar
Gangster Film   115

6
Screening Crime the Liberal Consensus Way
Postwar Transformations in the Production Code   144

7
The "Un-American" Film Art
Robert Siodmak, Fritz Lang, and the Political Significance of Film
Noir's German Connection   186

Epilogue
From Gangster to Gangsta
Against a Certain Tendency of Film Theory and History   221

Appendix
Production Code Administration Film Analysis
Forms, 1934–1957   *227*

Illustrations

Acknowledgments

I am indebted to many for their support in the development of this book. While it is impossible to do justice to all, there are some I would like to acknowledge individually.

Lary May and George Lipsitz gave me the intellectual and institutional sustenance without which this project could never have been realized. Their unrelenting encouragement and critical appraisal has been an inspiring example of guidance and comradeship.

Thanks must also go to Richard Maltby, who has been generous in exchanging ideas over an area of shared interest—and who can take much of the blame for starting me on the academic road. Any deficiencies and errors along the way are, of course, entirely mine.

This book originated in a dissertation, and David Noble, Paula Rabinowitz, Richard McCormick, Jack Zipes, Richard Leppert, and John Mowitt have all left their imprint on this work as teachers, readers, and friends with mutual scholarly investments. It would also be amiss not to acknowledge the importance of the peer group support I received in executing earlier versions of the manuscript—especially the encouragement gleaned from the American Studies dissertation reading group at the University of Minnesota. Our monthly gatherings over pizza and beer at the Mays' residence boosted flagging minds and bodies.

Parts of this book are based on previously published articles. A version of chapter 3 appeared as "*Manhattan Melodrama*'s 'Art of the Weak': Telling History from the Other Side in the 1930s Talking Gangster Film," *Journal of American Studies* 30, no. 1 (1996): 101–18; and a section of chapter 7 appeared as "The Noir's German Connection," *Iris* 21 (spring 1996): 74–88. Critical appraisal of ideas contained in these articles by the editors of both journals has been greatly appreciated.

At a more recent stage, Robert Sklar, Jeffrey Richards, and Lynn Dumenil have provided invaluably detailed feedback that has been augmented by the enthusiastic and sensitive work of my editing team at the University of Chicago Press: Doug Mitchell, Leslie Keros, Matt Howard, and Richard Audet.

As a recipient of the University of Minnesota's Harold Leonard Memorial Film Fellowship, I was able to conduct extensive research in the Production Code Administration files (with the aid of Sam Gill) at the Academy for Motion Picture Arts and Sciences in Los Angeles. A University of Minnesota Teaching Exchange Award (from the Department of German), with the Humboldt University in Berlin, and a graduate fellowship to the Graduiertenkolleg at the University of Siegen, sponsored by the Deutsche Forschungsgesellschaft, enabled research on exiled German filmmakers in the Bundesfilmarchiv and the Stiftung Deutsche Kinemathek.

John and Lilian Munby, apart from being my earliest scholastic role models, have been paragons of parental patience and support. Finally, I am most indebted to Karen Jürs-Munby for her companionship and intellectual input throughout this endeavor. I dedicate this book to her.

Introduction

Screening Crime in the USA

An Undervalued Symbiosis

This book is a case study of how the gangster film as a controversial mass cultural form mediated perhaps the most profound period of crisis and transformation in twentieth-century United States history, from the Depression to the Cold War. As an account of the American gangster film's changes over this period, this work is also, and necessarily, a history of the attempts to censor this particular form of production. Perceived as transgressive, the gangster film was subjected to continual moral and political censure. This is the story of how the concerted efforts to contain the subversive potential of this Hollywood film form were resisted and countered.

The gangster film's relation to the custodians of American virtue and politics between 1930 and 1960 was both symbiotic and antagonistic. That is, while at first glance most gangster narratives could be seen to advance the moral message "crime doesn't pay," this is not enough to account for the appeal of this film cycle to audiences. Equally, it is clear that Hollywood's watchdogs were not convinced that this message properly compensated for all the transgressive competing meanings that characterized the gangster film. At one level the gangster film typified Hollywood's traditional acquiescence to external authorities, but at others (and more significantly) it clearly violated an established policy of moral accommodation. How, why, and with what consequence are of central interest here. And this interest extends not just to reevaluating the historical significance of the

1

American gangster film, but to interrogating some of the base assumptions we have about mass culture's ideological allegiancies.

Writing in the 1940s about his American experience, C. L. R. James, the radical culture critic, stated that the gangster film expressed the most enduring social and ideological currents of his age.[1] The same could be said of the gangster film today, especially as it has been deployed to dramatize the blasted hopes of African Americans incarcerated in the ghettos of the nation's deindustrializing cities. The original gangster came of age at the same time as America's arrival as a modern industrial and urban nation. As a key part of a growing mass culture, gangster narratives addressed the consequences of modernization, mediating the relationship of modern Americans to an increasingly anachronistic national idealism. Gangsters captured the antagonistic imagination of a population afflicted first by the repressive order of Prohibition and then by the devastating consequences of the Wall Street Crash.

In their confrontations with increasingly desperate and discredited forms of institutional power, gangsters posed awkward questions about the line that separated legitimate from illegitimate Americans. In turn, the gangster film rose to be one of the most disputed mass cultural objects, continually subject to the interferences of different regulatory interests seeking to contain its seditious propensity (something most recently manifest in the demand to censor "gangsta" rap by moralizing panic-mongers).

Unlike other central national myths, such as the cowboy and the Western outlaw, the gangster never allows an escape from the problems of the here and now. He is not so much about the past or an alternative landscape as he is about the inescapable truths of the urban present. While gangsters certainly draw on an old-stock (or "nativist") tradition of social banditry and primitive rebellion that can be traced from the American frontier and the American revolutionary fighting for independence from British rule, they are particularly products of a modern urban-industrial and demographically divided society. Moreover, as a key component of the movie industry, the gangster represented the unacceptable face of a growing and transforming mass culture.

If anything, gangsters, as urban ethnic rebels, were in conflict with

---

1. C. L. R. James, *American Civilization*, ed. Anna Grimshaw and Keith Hart (Oxford: Blackwell, 1993). See especially the chapter "Popular Arts and Modern Society," which hinges on the volatile status of the gangster film.

older notions of American outlawry. As Robert Warshow has articulated, gangsters express "that part of the American psyche which rejects the qualities and the demands of modern life, which rejects 'Americanism' itself."[2] While some gangster films of recent years, such as *Bugsy* (1991), place the gangster within a nostalgic costume drama, other films, such as *New Jack City* (1991) and *Menace II Society* (1993) (made by African Americans), preserve the gangster's uncomfortable proximity to present "raced" inequities. The black "gangsta" films of today draw on the power of 1930s "classic" prototypes, which addressed similar problems of an American ethnic lower class struggling to overcome problems of cultural and economic ghettoization.

The distance between the promise of inclusion and the reality of exclusion for European immigrants at the turn of the century has eerie parallels with the postwar African-American story. The contrast between the beckoning words by Emma Lazarus that grace the foot of the Statue of Liberty ("Give me . . . your huddled masses") and the alienating experiences of first Ellis Island and then the city slum has analogues in the journey from the South to the North that similarly failed to deliver postwar blacks from the "idiocy of rural life" and its slavery associations to the promised land of the modern city. The recourse to gangster imagery by African Americans is more than a reflection of the "criminal" reality of ghetto life. It has a deeper symbolic worth in connecting today's disenfranchised with a tradition of dissent. In the words of C. L. R. James, the significance of the gangster to Americans is that he is a "derisive symbol of the contrast between ideals and reality."[3] As such, the enduring nature of this national myth lies precisely in its adverse power to dramatize an American idealism at odds with itself.

OVERVIEW

In arguing for the American gangster film as a particular and important point of resistance to the concerted efforts to contain Hollywood's transgressive potential, this work is divided into two parts. The first (chapters 1 through 4) attends to how the first talking gangster films constituted a way of articulating discontent with the post–Wall Street

2. Robert Warshow, "The Gangster as Tragic Hero," *Partisan Review* 15, no. 2 (February 1958).

3. James, *American Civilization*, p. 127.

Crash (dis)order of things from the specific space and vantage of the United States' urban ethnic working class. In the process, I concentrate on the interests of censorship in policing this first cycle of gangster films, and how this affected the shape and content of gangster films themselves. The second part (chapters 5 through 7) examines the mutations the gangster film underwent consequent to changes in cultural, economic, and censorship priorities brought on by World War II. While the gangster was stripped of his ethnic ghetto markings, the 1940s and 1950s cycle of gangster films raised new tensions with those trying to set wartime and postwar political agendas, tensions that culminated in direct political intervention in the business of making movies.

Hollywood's gangster films changed over time subject to the multiple determinations of generic evolution, moral intervention, and the need to remain topical in a rapidly changing world. The term "cycle" (which was also the contemporaneous term adopted to describe the gangster films of the time) does justice to the idea that while these films shared generic conventions, they were also part of a socially volatile formula in flux. When considered primarily as representatives of a "genre" rather than a cycle, however, the value of individual gangster films can be reduced to measuring only the degree they exemplify the attributes of a formula cinema and thus guarantee the stability and predictability of the Hollywood system.

As chapters 1 through 3 reveal, the primary significance of the early 1930s film gangsters was that they were the first who could speak. With the advent of sound the gangster came to express the desires of the culturally and economically ghettoized in an ethnic street vernacular. Not only this, but in the context of the Depression the 1930s gangster film's mass distribution led to its cross-class and cross-ethnic appeal, helping foster the nation's collective identification with the desires of "new" Americans for a fairer share of the American pie.

The reality of the ethnic gangster's national appeal was met by increased panic among civic and moral guardians. To the representatives of a declining Anglo-Saxon Protestant order, gangsters had always embodied the twin threats of America's arrival as a modern industrial nation. On one hand, they represented the forces of urban envelopment and the destruction of civic idealism. On the other, they testified to the radical demographic transformation of the American population. In the context of Prohibition (1920–1933), pre-Crash (1929) silent-era gangster films (as well as popular press representations) were part of a general middle-class moral crusade to both redeem and stigmatize the ethnic ghetto. The latter was subjected in fiction and on film to the conventions of moral "uplift" narratives. This translation of ghetto realities into a Victorian nativist middle-class fantasy of "how the other half lives" was, equally, a way of defusing the unsettling forces of immigration, industrialization, urbanization, and consumerism. All these forces were perceived as corroding the essentially Anglo-Saxon Protestant vision of an "authentic" American civic culture. The post-Crash talking gangster, however, emerged to challenge such strategies of containment and exclusion on the part of moral and cultural stewards.

The fact that the gangster's rise to national popularity in the early Depression years coincided with the introduction of sound to the movies has all but been ignored in film scholarship. When the gangster eventually spoke, he relocated the desires of his community in a specific body politic and in a particular social space. The talking gangster, as it were, took advantage of one of the few places granted in the culture for the representation of lower-class ethnic American life. A space of cultural containment and ideological legitimation was turned into something more rebellious. What had once been a way to manage the crisis features of America's entry into modernity was transformed into a way to produce crisis.

In their blatant disregard for Prohibition and ironic mimicry of the laissez-faire capitalist "road to success," ethnic urban gangsters directly confronted the key moral and economic precepts associated with an ailing nativist order. In the context of the Depression, the gangster's challenge was only intensified. Once a means to demonize the ethnic underclass, the post-Crash talking gangster film only put more panic into the panic-mongers, helping to fuel a restrictive resolution in 1931 and aid in the formation of the Production Code. In spite of much acquiescence to hostile moral custodians, the talking gangster film became one of the objects of the Code's first enforcement when a moratorium was declared on all gangster film production in 1935. In the process, the gangster film was publicly and permanently marked as something bearing a seditious import, exposing the dark side of Anglo-America.

Chapter 4 documents that the story of the gangster film's endurance in spite of attempts to suppress it involves an analysis of the function of the Production Code Administration. The inception of a full Production Code in the early 1930s was the latest moment in what had been a long history of the American cinema's negotiation with censorship. In fact, a strong case has been made that the significance of the Production Code itself has been overvalued, for Hollywood's commercial imperative had always dictated the avoidance of controversial subject matter. Generally, illicit or taboo issues had been recast to suit the combined needs of satisfying an undifferentiated mass audience on one hand, and appeasing the wrath of moral interest groups on the other. Throughout the pre-Code era, the risk of upsetting the audience was as big a concern with the studios as the fear of inciting antimovie legislation. In this sense, it could be argued that the inception of a detailed Code constituted not so much a watershed in the moral monitoring of movies as a refinement and tightening of long-established rules of conduct that accommodated both economic and moral sensibilities.[4]

This having been said, the drafting of a formal Code and establishment of an administering body were motivated out of unique circumstances and did reflect some significant changes in moral stewardship of the movies. The fact that those primarily responsible for forging the Code in the aftermath of the Wall Street Crash were Catholic rather than Protestant reformers begs some important questions. Traditionally, the antimovie lobby had been dominated by representatives of old-stock Protestant America. It is no accident that following the Crash, and with the onset of the Depression, Catholics took occupation of the moral high ground (vacated by a finally bankrupt old order) as arbiters of the most powerful mass entertainment medium of the day. And this changing of the moral guard was not trivial.

Protestant censorship groups had taken particular objection to Hollywood as an agent not only of moral, but cultural, corruption. The movies were deemed synonymous with the contaminating forces of urban growth and immigration. While the Catholic church may have shared a concern with Protestants about Hollywood as a vehicle

4. Richard Maltby points out that the Code has been mistaken as a "watershed" document that separates an era of "tumult" from an era of "order." Such a vision tends to obscure the fact that Hollywood had always ordered its priorities around the accommodationist principle of avoiding controversy. This was primarily because raising the hackles of moral custodians had economic repercussions, leading to demands for film cuts or even film boycotts. And as Ruth Vasey highlights, Hollywood, in marketing its products for an undifferentiated global audience, implicitly steered itself in a conservative moral course. Needing to reach markets abroad as well as at home, the world according to Hollywood was not likely to offend. Richard Maltby, "The Production Code and the Hays Office," in Tino Balio, ed., *The Grand Design: Hollywood as a Modern Business Enterprise, 1930–1939* (Berkeley and Los Angeles: University of California Press, 1995), pp. 37–72; Ruth Vasey, *The World According to Hollywood, 1918–1939* (Exeter: University of Exeter Press, 1997). See also Lea Jacobs, *The Wages of Sin: Censorship and the Fallen Woman Film, 1928–1942* (Berkeley and Los Angeles: University of California Press, 1997).

of moral lapse, quite obviously it could not share in the nativist's negative cultural perspective of the movies; the Catholic constituency was fundamentally urban, and very much part of those forces the old-stock antimovie lobby most feared.

Catholic leaders were more prepared to work with rather than against Hollywood in finding a way to satisfy business and moral needs through internal regulation. Studios wanted to prevent external censorship groups from interfering in the business of making, distributing, and exhibiting their products. This did not mean, however, that the Production Code was toothless. Studios were forced to make compromises over their more candid representations of sex and crime. The so-called fallen woman film and the first talking gangster films were subject to the first enforcements of the Code. Most dramatically, in a quid-pro-quo gesture, Will Hays (head of the Motion Picture Producers and Distributors of America) declared his moratorium on gangster film production in 1935 to demonstrate that the Code could be an effective instrument of Hollywood self-regulation and to offset the demand to establish an external federal censorship agency.

Following Hays's prohibitive edict of 1935, the studios found (once again) a way to continue to meet audience desire for the gangster by adjusting the formula. While the gangster formula would have had to change for many reasons (such as formal exhaustion and the need to meet changes in the world of the audience), censorship had always played a crucial role in determining the nature and meaning of the gangster's mutations.

As chapter 5 contends, the changes brought on by the circumnavigation of censorship strictures facilitated the development of yet another "dissident" crime cycle, the so-called film noir of the 1940s and early 1950s. The combination of moral and political pressure on one hand, and infrastructural changes on the other, led to the fostering of the crime film in the growing area of B and independent movie production. The increasingly preponderant fascination with crime on the American screen after World War II was understood in its day not as something new or discontinuous with Hollywood's traditions, but as a rejuvenation of the illicit themes and issues associated with the earlier Depression-era gangster cycle. The postwar crime cycle we now call film noir was received as an awkward reminder of problems whose resolution had been postponed by the need to prosecute the war. Though clearly belonging to an aesthetically distinctive style of cinema, postwar crime films were understood contemporaneously as refinements on a repressed but established formula.

While the postwar gangster film was different from its progenitors in many important ways, it was still perceived as not only belonging to a tradition but also perpetuating a legacy of dissidence (something made possible in the more permissive realm of B and independent studio production). Detailing the way these films were received and monitored reveals many parallels with the pre-war discussion of the moral and cultural impact of the gangster cycle. In accordance with changes brought on in the mid- to late 1930s, the postwar gangster film no longer centered on the issue of lower-class ethnic aspiration. It did, however, continue to dispute the terms of economic and cultural success. These terms had, of course, changed since the early 1930s. The war had facilitated the revival of big business and had also provided a (temporary) way for Americans of all castes and creeds to join together in fighting the common enemy.

The postwar gangster film increasingly focused on problems of adjustment to peacetime prerogatives and the new political and economic order. Narratives built around the metaphor of return proliferate. Taken as allegorical structures for the GI returning home to find it irrevocably altered, 1940s gangster plots addressed the changed terms of American life. And the postwar crime cycle's particular attention to the dismal fate of foot soldiers in anonymous gangster syndicates passed cynical comment on the disempowering features of corporate culture.

Chapter 6 shows that for the self-appointed guardians of America's postwar destiny, the gravitation of Hollywood back to negative representations of the American way (or rather the adjustment of Hollywood to candid representations of dissillusion with the new American way) was very disappointing. During the war, and under the auspices of the Office of War Information, Hollywood had been turned into a powerful propaganda weapon. Following the war, Hollywood saw more profit in adjusting to the desires of an unsettled audience than in continuing to toe the jingoistic line.

In returning to its noncommital, commercially driven ways, Hollywood became the center of a brewing storm about its political direction. The outpouring of dark, pessimistic, and criminal visions of late 1940s America upset a variety of political and moral monitors. The Code continued to censure anything that looked like a 1930s gangster film. But in the process it failed to police other kinds of gangster films. The State Department voiced its own concern that Hollywood was feeding the wrong impression of the United States to the world at the very moment that the film industry should have been supporting America's rise to global protector. More sinister were the objections of the hard-line anti-Communists, who had seen their first attempts to root out supposed Reds from Hollywood in 1938 aborted by the war. In 1947 the House Committee on Un-American Activities, led by J. Parnell Thomas, embarked on a crusade to exorcise Hollywood's "un-American" demons spawned by the industry's purported allegiance to New Deal ideology.

While the new head of the Motion Picture Producers and Distributors of America, Eric Johnston, did not share the same political disposition of men like J. Parnell Thomas, he felt that Hollywood should be harnessed to a constructive political agenda (advancing the cause of liberal consensus in this case). In sum, the postwar crime cycle was taken as evidence of an ideologically dysfunctional Hollywood. At its most extreme, Hollywood's lack of commitment was interpreted as "un-American."

Chapter 7 attributes the ideological scepticism and political aesthetics of the postwar gangster film to the influence of emigrés on postwar Hollywood. Crucial to understanding how the gangster film was reinvigorated as a potent vehicle of social criticism is a generation of German and central European filmmakers who, in their exile from fascism, found a Hollywood calling in refining the American gangster film. And the final part of this book attends to why exiled directors such as Fritz Lang and Robert Siodmak found in Hollywood's gangster film formula an optimal way to express their despondency and anxiety over the postwar American order. Their experience in the declaredly modernist cinema of Weimar Germany equipped these directors particularly well in fashioning an appropriate representation of concerns that characterized the disoriented postwar American world. How ironic that exiles from fascism would come to find themselves embroiled in the climate of yet another political purge, in the form of McCarthyism (Fritz Lang would find himself blacklisted).

THEORETICAL STAKES

In documenting the gangster film's battle with the nation's moral and political stewards between 1930 and 1960, this study provides a means to reassess the political value ascribed to Hollywood by cultural historians and film theorists. To reveal how this kind of mass representation has held an enduring appeal for disenfranchised social groups as a privileged site of sociocultural disputes with discriminatory forms of authority is also to redress tendencies to dismiss commercial cinema all too easily as "co-opted" or as a weapon of the "captains of consciousness." More specifically, my examination of the gangster film's symbiotic relationship with institutional censorship (based primarily on research in Production Code Administration censorship files) forces us to reevaluate the ideologically reactionary status film scholarship has generally assigned to "classical Hollywood narrative" or "genre cinema." The latter theoretical paradigm has helped not only those critics arguing for a theory of "mass culture as mass deception," but those making claims for the exceptionalism of certain Hollywood film forms, especially the visually dark and fatalistic 1940s crime film cycle that has been posthumously categorized as film noir.

Film noir's significance has been understood in terms of its departure or exception to Hollywood norms that were established in the so-called genre cinema of the 1930s. Not only has this fostered a notion of film noir as a "break" with tradition, but it has concomitantly serviced a forgetting of the 1940s crime cycle's link with the 1930s classic gangster film and thus to a tradition of dissent. That is, the scholastic tendency to celebrate 1940s crime films as aesthetically experimental and deviant has only reinforced the notion that 1930s Hollywood cinema was without radical potential stylistically and ideologically. My work, however, documents continuities between 1930s and 1940s gangster films, not to establish that the 1940s crime cycle was in fact as normative as its 1930s forbears, but to reveal how 1940s deviance (attributable to its apparently alien/modernist aesthetic treatment of the problems of bourgeois life and identity) was deeply indebted to a socially antagonistic cinematic tradition allied to lower-class and ethnically marginalized American interests in the 1930s.

Studies of mass culture have generally advanced the argument that something called hegemony dictates the flow of ideas between dominant groups and the so-called masses. Censorship studies are one rare area that has sought to identify the mechanisms that actually control and determine this exchange, which mediate dissent and the problem of competing interests, and which link state, economic, and cultural prerogatives. Like other work in this area, this study is concerned with censorship as a form of direct action or intervention by particular parties. I, too, am invested in revealing the stakes religious, political, and corporate powers have had in attempting to silence Hollywood.

This study, however, is not content to settle on a strictly "prohibitive" definition of the significance of censorship. In examining the symbiotic relation of the American crime film to censorship between 1929 and 1958—from the Crash and birth of the first controversial talking gangsters to the putative swansong of film noir, *Touch of Evil*—it is clear that something dynamic took place. Censorship effected counter-actions that produced significant changes and mutations over time of both censorship agendas and the form of the crime film itself. In other words, I am ultimately interested less in confirming the ultimate victory of censors than in accounting for why censorship is never a completed project. Following the fate of Hollywood's crime film as a primary object of censure over an extended period of profound transformation in the United States has exposed the way that yesterday's hegemony cannot be today's, and that yesterday's counter-hegemony remains a source of dissent even when its social basis disappears.

My claims affect, then, not only the assumptions we have about mass culture's ideological allegiances, but how we need to review the kind of historiography that has been built around such assumptions. Theories of film noir's exceptionalism to some otherwise axiomatic rule about mass cinema have only aided and abetted the establishment of a master narrative about the postwar triumph of corporate capitalism and the ideology of liberal consensus. The latter's victory, so the story goes, was dependent on a mass culture whose role a priori was to defuse rebellion, suture contradiction, and maintain authority.

My research on the gangster film, however, reveals how such a story has tended to devalue the aleatory and overvalue the co-opting features of Hollywood cinema. The academic consensus on the inherently reactionary ideological value of the American commercial cinema has encouraged a form of critical-historical amnesia over the policing of Hollywood.[5] And the general reticence to acknowledge the history of struggle involved in trying to make Hollywood toe any ideological line has, ironically, been exacerbated precisely by the film scholarship that actually concentrates on censorship. The latter tends

5. See Robert Ray's *A Certain Tendency of the Hollywood Cinema, 1930–1980* (Princeton: Princeton University Press, 1985) for a systematic account of classic Hollywood's conservative ideology. In spite of his argument that the Hollywood film is an "overdetermined" form, it is strange that Ray offers no treatment of the role of censorship as one of those many determining influences on Hollywood. While Ray avoids indulging those who simplistically oppose mass cinema's vices to counter cinema's virtues in exposing the ideologically reactionary tenets of Hollywood's "normal" procedures, he tends to severely limit Hollywood's capacity for dissidence. The latter is only a marginal phenomenon (a deviation from the norm that titillates), experienced more often than not as a form of camp intertextual irony. Perhaps the consideration of censorship of the American film industry begs too many questions of those offering variations (no matter how nuanced) on the critical consensus that Hollywood is "always already" reactionary?

to confirm that Hollywood's volatile features were indeed successfully defused by the formation of a Code Administration.[6]

In claiming that a "classic Hollywood genre" could assert itself counter-hegemonically, I am challenging some of the key tenets that underpin the theory of "classic" Hollywood narrative economy. To uncover the extent of the stakes involved in the censorship of the gangster film means, effectively, to abandon much of what film and culture studies scholarship has taken to be axiomatic about classic Hollywood's sociocultural function.

The most famous post-Crash/pre-Code talking gangster films, *Little Caesar* (1930), *Public Enemy* (1931), and *Scarface* (1932), have been subsumed as cornerstones of the sound era's "genre" system. The latter covered the period from 1930 to the postwar 1940s, the so-called studio era when the "talking picture" achieved maximum popularity. Both Andrew Bergman and Robert Ray argue that the "classic" gangster film helped consolidate a sophisticated narrative system of representation that guaranteed the continuity of the film industry through a period of profound sociocultural upheaval. Part of the gangster film's significance lay in its co-optation of turbulent sociohistorical realities to the needs of generic reproduction. This parasitic relation to the realm of the audience's lived experiences was a product of the film form's obligation to supposedly "timeless" thematic and formal paradigms that predate silent-era film narratives and have their roots in an American mythological order first established in nineteenth-century literature.[7]

Andrew Bergman, for example, describes *Little Caesar* as a desperate reaffirmation of the Horatio Alger story. The gangster film

6. Gregory Black's *Hollywood Censored: Morality Codes, Catholics, and the Movies* (Cambridge: Cambridge University Press, 1994) is a case in point. As an empirical account of how moral interest groups came to interfere in "classic" Hollywood, Black's study provides invaluable insight into how a minority group gained a disproportionate say in controlling the most influential mass medium of its day. Black's conclusion that the appointment of leading Catholic moral guardians to head the enforcement of a moral agenda within Hollywood via the Production Code constituted the victory of conservative regulation is, however, less convincing. Certainly, the attempt at promoting a reactionary political agenda was there, but the degree of its success has to be measured by criteria other than the fact of censorship alone. The constant need to monitor Hollywood's products, as well as the concomitant awareness on the part of moviemakers that they had to circumnavigate the strictures of the Production Code, point to a more dynamic system of negotiation and counter-action than Black's perspective allows. And as other censorship scholars, such as Richard Maltby, Ruth Vasey, and Lea Jacobs, have argued, the Code of 1934 was only the most recent moment in an evolving system of regulation. See note 4 above.

7. Andrew Bergman, *We're in the Money: Depression America and Its Films* (New York: Harper & Row, 1972) and Ray, *A Certain Tendency of the Hollywood Cinema, 1930–1980.*

constituted a way to rescue the residue of a controlling American myth of individualistic capitalist enterprise, with its rags-to-riches narrative pattern, in the climate of economic catastrophe. Such an assertion of an original American story, Bergman argues, belies the material circumstances of the Depression, which ought to have undermined such traditional myths. Equally, for Robert Ray and Thomas Schatz, the "classic" gangster film was a way to dress up older outlaw myths in modern clothes, a way to enable the traditional frontier mythology to remain unscathed and unaltered by the onslaught of a transforming and crisis-ridden social sphere.[8]

Accordingly, the gangster films of the early 1930s have been interpreted as "disguised Westerns" that replay the oppositions and problems endemic to that genre. The gangster film's most notable inheritance from traditional outlaw mythology was its splitting of audience identification between the center of narrative interest, the individual outlaw/gangster, on one hand, and the center of moral interest, the official community, on the other. In essence, the gangster replayed seemingly eternal American dichotomies between the values of individualism and the values of civic responsibility. Understood as a prime Hollywood genre, the 1930s gangster film is said to typify the function of classic narrative economy to the extent that it sought to resolve these enduring antagonisms between individualism and community, and rebellion and conformity, without disturbing the status quo.

In the context of Depression America, this has been interpreted as a way of having your cake and eating it too. The gangster film is taken to be emblematic of an entire system that took advantage of pervasive Depression propensities to be suspicious of "governmentality" and make them service, paradoxically, ideals of continuity rather than change. The established mythological order (that known body of narrative conventions and the national ideology it supported) gained strength, so the argument goes, as a guarantee of stability in the face of unpredictable sociohistorical transformations. The reactionary dynamic that effaced the social in the name of myth is explained as a property of Hollywood's obligation to itself rather than any manipulative political agenda.

Hollywood was invested in preserving ways of telling stories that were ultimately conducive to its need to guarantee a return on the large

---

8. Thomas Schatz, *Hollywood Genres: Formulas, Filmmaking and the Studio System* (New York: Random House, 1981).

monetary capital invested in individual film products, which encouraged a tendency to standardize plots and to repeat tried and tested formulas. To this extent, the economic necessity to guarantee box-office returns led to a tendency to guarantee the continuity of *cultural* capital invested in an established narrative and mythological order.

The consequent insight that Hollywood films are not simply mechanical reflections of "reality," but *mediations* affected primarily by internal narrative rules and stylistic conventions, is invaluable. This has led, however, to an ahistorical notion of Hollywood cinema as ultimately sealed off and isolated from the influences of the social realm, and has fueled an argument that "classic" Hollywood is ideologically committed to the maintenance of the status quo.[9]

Such monolithic interpretations of Hollywood's ideological function have been countered by a flip version that tends to overvalue the notion of genre "subversion." Both theories are marked by their ahistorical notions of the text and its reception. More nuanced has been the kind of ideology critique advanced by critics associated with the film journal *Screen* during the 1970s, such as Stephen Heath and Stephen Neale.[10] This approach is often tantamount to a more sophisticated version of Frankfurt School monolithic culture theory, but it remains the best conceptualization of the function of deviancy within genre-based cinema. As Barbara Klinger explains:

> The critical assumptions that measure the subversiveness of a genre, based on its anti-classical formal attributes, selectively overstate the radical valency of conventional signifiers and underestimate the means through which supervising systems negotiate a normative function for even the most excessive, foregrounded, deformative textual tendencies.[11]

That is, Hollywood's classical textual system (genre) is precisely constructed out of the "volatile combination of disequilibrium (excess, difference) and equilibrium (containment, repetition)." To this extent,

9. For an example of this monolithic approach to genre cinema, see Judith Hess Wright, "Genre Films and the Status Quo" in Barry Keith Grant, ed., *Film Genre Reader* (Austin: University of Texas Press, 1986), pp. 41–49. Her critique is directly influenced by Frankfurt School scholar T. W. Adorno's seminal chapter "The Culture Industry," in *Dialectic of Enlightenment* (which he co-authored with Max Horkheimer), trans. John Cumming (New York: Seabury Press, 1972).

10. Stephen Neale, *Genre* (London: British Film Institute, 1980) and Stephen Heath, "Film and System," *Screen* 16, no. 1 (Spring 1975) and no. 2 (Summer 1975). Both discuss the problem of genre "subversion" as an attribute that is system-generative.

11. Barbara Klinger, "'Cinema/Ideology/Criticism' Revisited: The Progressive Genre," in Barry Keith Grant, ed., *Film Genre Reader* (Austin: University of Texas Press, 1986), p. 89.

disequilibrium should not be conceived of as a "partisan component of the subversive text, but as an essential functioning element of the overall system." [12] In this sense, the subversion/tradition or rupture/ norm relation is precisely constitutive of the "classical" system—a law of genre that always turns transformation into a reproductive regulatory power. There is thus no "real" rupture or deviation, for every genre film is dependent for its difference (and thus existence) on the tradition it is seen to twist or from which it departs. There is only mutation, which instead of threatening the system serves to generate and maintain it.

To argue that mutation is genre's generative attribute, its primary constitutive law, is one thing. To assert, then, that this can only function in the name of a reactionary and nontransformative ideology is another. There is a tendency to equate uncritically textual system with social system as though they are self-identical realms. Just because the text/ideology relation renders deviation normative does not ipso facto mean that genre ensures social stasis. Rather, as a legitimation apparatus in a purportedly "democratic" capitalist society, the commercial cinema is forced to extend its containing net to include rather than exclude elements that open up social norms to critique.

There is no doubt that the films we generically label Western, Gangster, and Musical wielded tremendous influence in shaping audience dispositions toward authority during the 1930s and 1940s. It hardly needs stressing that mass mediation is a most crucial place in the constitution of subject-power relationships in twentieth-century society. A conception of "genre as closed system" is inclined, however, to project mass film spectators in a remarkably passive and undifferentiated relationship to the entertainment they consume. And while it is true that "classic" 1930s Hollywood was apt to encode the world and its audience's place in it according to its own rules and logic of self-preservation, it does not follow that the audience always employed consonant and universally predictable decoding practices. Nor does it follow that what a movie encoded was necessarily reactionary. Even an established mythology depends for its meaning on the historical context of its reception. As I shall argue in the case of the talking gangster film, the myth of individual success means one thing in a time of economic boom and another in Depression. Not only this, but such a myth resonates differently with different parts of the population.

12. Ibid., p. 88.

All of which is not to deny that the commercial cinema's immense appeal during the Depression must have depended on its general ability to lend order to the chaotic and contradictory features of Depression-era America. The movies' imposition of teleological certainty (the insistence that irresolvable social problems could at least be given fictional resolution on screen) must have had a strong appeal in the 1930s. Bergman insists, for example, that in spite of Depression realities, *Little Caesar*, far from dismantling traditional stories, "only reinforced some of the country's most cherished myths about individual success. The outlaw cycle represented not so much a mass desertion of the law as a clinging to past forms of achievement." [13] The suggestion here is that the 1930s gangster film embodied a key feature of "genre": its self-interested ability to guarantee continuity and stasis. The gangster typified genre cinema's implicit allegiance to the lingua franca, an established "official" language or dominant regime of myths and cultural codes.

However, the severity of contemporaneous objections to the gangster cycle (which culminated in the moratorium of 1935) seems somewhat inconsistent with such a perspective. If the post-Crash talking gangster only "reinforced" older success mythology and governing laws, why did it warrant censure? Genre theory cannot answer this question because it tends to seek out unchanging elements that unite a body of films and to uncover an enduring structure that is somehow immune to history. Consequent analyses of the gangster film are apt to prioritize continuity over change, and similitude over difference.

This has had curious repercussions in accounting for the significance of the triumvirate of gangster classics, *Little Caesar, Public Enemy*, and *Scarface*. These three have been singled out in film criticism and have been taken to be emblematic of the gangster as a whole in the early 1930s. Yet the more interesting point is that these three films have probably selected themselves as "classics" because of the way they *stand out* rather than fit into the bulk of gangster film production at the time. They are so clearly different to what had come before. They represented a break with conventional modes of representing "the other half" on screen. To censors, the classic three were highlighted as signs of sedition, signs of a system in flux rather than signifiers of genre consolidation. And it is these features (of anomaly, difference, and deviation) that I shall argue better explain why the early 1930s gangster film was singled out for censorship, censorship

13. Bergman, *We're in the Money*, p. 7.

being part of a quest to enforce the conformity that genre theorists tend to assume is definitive of "classic" Hollywood cinema.

Significantly, it is the cultural historian rather than the film studies scholar who has highlighted the more seditious features of Hollywood's gangster. Situating the gangster film in the context of the Depression, Richard Pells, for example, interprets the gangster as "a parody of the American Dream . . . a psychopathic Horatio Alger . . . a reproach to both the principles of the market place and the reigning values of American life."[14] In this sense, I prefer to adopt the terminology of the times in understanding individual 1930s gangster films as part of a volatile *cycle* rather than as "classic" reactionary consolidations of genre.

In examining how and why the gangster film helped spawn two of the more significant attempts to regulate Hollywood's powers of mass persuasion—the inception and first enforcement of the Production Code in the early 1930s and the infamous House Committee on Un-American Activities' inquisitions from 1947 to 1953—this study suggests that the purported "certain tendency of the Hollywood cinema"[15] to recuperate dissidence might be less an attribute endemic to the American mass cinema itself than an outcome of a critical vision projected by a "certain tendency of film scholarship."

14. Richard H. Pells, *Radical Visions and American Dreams: Culture and Social Thought in the Depression Years* (Middletown, Conn.: Wesleyan University Press, 1973), pp. 271–72.

15. The term is Robert Ray's, drawn from his book of the same title, which defines Hollywood's politics of noncommitment as essentially reactionary. Ray, *A Certain Tendency of the Hollywood Cinema, 1930–1980.*

1

The Gangster's Silent Backdrop

Contesting Victorian Uplift and the Culture of Prohibition

On July 15, 1935, Will Hays, head of the Motion Picture Producers and Distributors of America (MPPDA), declared a moratorium on all gangster film production in Hollywood. Hays was acting in his capacity as the figurehead of the newly founded Production Code Administration (PCA), Hollywood's system of internal self-regulation and censorship. The Production Code had only recently become an enforceable entity in 1934, and its first wholesale enforcement came at the cost of the post–Wall Street Crash talking gangster.

Gangster films, like other film forms that dealt with tendentious topics, had never not been subject to moral policing. The influence of such surveillance had traditionally made itself apparent in the films themselves.

While the gangster film had been subject to previous attempts to suppress it, most notably in an October 1931 resolution from the Association of Motion Picture Producers, Hays's declaration in 1935 constituted the first generalized clampdown. Previous gangster films, especially *Scarface* (made in 1931), had had their release delayed until cuts and additions had been made to secure that the film incorporated sufficient moral compensation for its indulgences in vice. Even though *Scarface*'s producer (Howard Hughes) and director (Howard Hawks) resisted the intrusion of censorship, an accommodation was made, and the movie was eventually released in

1932.[1] By 1935, however, the principle of accommodation gave way to a moratorium, albeit one that the studios would manage to circumnavigate. What made the declaration of 1935 significant was that it exposed the degree to which an established system of moral compensation had broken down in Hollywood.

This moratorium was motivated ostensibly by the concurrent media fascination surrounding the outlaw-gangster John Dillinger's escapades and his death in 1934. Fear about the romanticization of Dillinger in particular proffered yet another opportunity to demand the suppression of the general representation of gangsters. If custodians of American virtue had hoped that the end of Prohibition in 1933 ought to have spelled the end of the gangster's raison d'être, Dillinger granted him a stay of execution.

The backlash to Dillinger, then, had its roots in an earlier concern about the spectacular rise to popularity of a particular gangster type and his story, best embodied in the now "canonized" films *Little Caesar* (1930), *Public Enemy* (1931), and *Scarface* (1932). Central to the appeal of these gangster films of the early 1930s (as I shall discuss in detail in the next chapter) was their candid dramatization of the contradictory nature of the ethnic urban working-class American experience.

Much more than his predecessors, this post-Crash gangster was distinguished first and foremost by his ethnicity. Rico Bandello (gangster-protagonist of *Little Caesar*), Tommy Powers (*Public Enemy*), and Tony Camonte (*Scarface*) were definitively "hyphenated" Americans. They played out the violent dilemma of living in two worlds and yet not belonging fully to either. Tommy Powers was an Irish-American gangster played by an Irish-American actor, James Cagney. Rico Bandello and Tony Camonte were two Italian-American gangsters played by Jewish-American actors, Edward G. Robinson and Paul Muni, respectively. This suspended or "split subject" status was a repressed feature of silent-era gangster films and underworld literature. Until the advent of the post-Crash talking gangster films, the underworld melodrama encoded the world of the "other" as the dark opposite of "official" society. From *The Musketeers of Pig Alley* (1912) (the first gangster feature film) to *The Lights of New York* (1928) (the

---

1. See Richard Maltby, "Tragic Heroes? Al Capone and the Spectacle of Criminality, 1947–1931," in *Screening the Past: The Sixth Australian History and Film Conference Papers*, ed. John Benson, Ken Berryman, and Wayne Levy, (Melbourne: La Trobe University Press, 1995).

first talking gangster film) the screen gangster narrative had mediated fears about the nation's urbanization and modernization primarily in terms of a binary system of oppositions inherited from a traditional frontier mythology.

The Lights of New York (the first all-talking feature film ever made), for example, uses sound to consolidate the theme of country innocence versus city decadence. Small-town mainstreet USA is pitted against the cacophony of big-city streets, a gangster milieu marked by Brooklyn accents, all of which helped stigmatize ethnicity as the unacceptable facet of a new modern and urban culture that threatened to eradicate the ideals of small-town rural America. That is, such a film, as Eugene Rosow points out, fitted into the prescriptions of a "nativist backlash," that "cultural climate which nurtured the mythic gangster."[2] The 1920s were marked by the Klan's activities, Prohibition, moral crusades, the anti-immigration acts of 1921 and 1924, and the first Red Scare. In conflating new Americans with the corrosive "un-American" forces of the city, the image of the ethnic-as-gangster certainly helped sustain such anti-urban and anti-immigrant sentiments.

Accordingly, it could be argued that in the pre-Crash era gangster film, the gangster's ethnicity (where it was featured) was significant only to the extent that it could help confirm the logic of a divisive and exclusionary national ideology. Being Italian, Irish, Polish, or Jewish only helped to clarify the boundaries that separated the realm of legitimate values from the illegitimate. In other words, ethnicity, far from threatening to upset traditional mythology, only served to strengthen it. Moving the frontier to the city initially helped keep old-stock culture on the right side of the street.

The gangster story had been traditionally told from a socially reforming point of view. Taking their cue from the perspective established most powerfully in the photojournalism of Jacob Riis, in the teens and twenties gangster films represented gangsterdom as evidence of a degrading and evil modern world in need of "uplift." Riis's *How the Other Half Lives* was a vehement and highly influential piece of social realist reform literature augmented by illustrations and halftones based on his extensive photodocumentation of the slums of New York. His later work featured properly reproduced photographs that,

2. Eugene Rosow, *Born to Lose: The Gangster Film in America* (New York: Oxford University Press, 1978), pp. 103–104.

Bandits' Roost (1890). Ghetto denizens as loitering menace in need of "uplift" in the reform photography of Jacob Riis.

The reforming perspective of "the other half" is extended to the silent screen in
D. W. Griffith's *The Musketeers of Pig Alley* (1912), the first gangster feature film.

in combination with his images for newspapers, depicted the full scale
of urban depravity at the turn of the century.[3]

Riis's fascination with the hapless and destructive nature of ghetto
life (its inhabitants cast as victims or gangsters) overlooked the more
positive capacities of slum dwellers. Informed by Riis's socially reforming sensibilities, these images, while bringing attention to the ap-
palling conditions that defined ethnic lower-class existence in the city,
also reinforced the line that separated the world of virtue from the
world of vice. Riis's "staging" of the ghetto as a sinister underworld
fed a nativist middle-class fantasy about those who lived on the wrong
side of town. One of his more famous images, *Bandits' Roost*, testifies
to a mixture of fear and fascination that is central to Riis's photographs of the denizens of the back alley. Featuring an alley lined with

3. *How the Other Half Lives* was first published in 1890 and then again in 1901. Riis also
supplied photographic images for later works such as *The Children of the Poor* (1892) and *The
Making of an American* (1901). He was a police reporter for the *New York Tribune* and worked
for *The Evening Sun* and the Associated Press, through which he gained a mass reputation as a
zealous social reformer.

men dressed in rough attire and sporting derby hats who look un-smilingly and directly at the camera, this image, while pretending to be a captured natural moment, was in fact arranged and staged. We look not at the world as seen by the so-called bandits, but at a projection dictated by the middle-class perception of the slum dweller as threat.

In 1912 D. W. Griffith's *Musketeers of Pig Alley* perpetuated this view, turning the still image into a moving one. The story was derived from contemporaneous newpaper headlines about the shooting of Herman Rosenthal, a gambler, in what the title cards referred to (after Riis) as "New York's other side." Filming on location and using local street toughs, Griffith attempted to extend Riis's perspective in his desire for a social realism that would also feed the demand for reform. The gangster's world is replete with bars, alleys, dance halls, guns, cops, loyal sidekicks, and rival gangs.[4] Behind the veneer of realism lies a whole host of conventions that would come to dominate the gangster cycle.

Once established as popular with film audiences, these conventions became the staple way of seeing and representing the ethnic urban lower classes. Such a view initially did not conflict with that of the Protestant reformer. Fear of these films rested, instead, on these films' potential for the glamorization of crime and sex, not on their representation of ethnicity.

The gangster melodramas of the silent era saw the world from the perspective of middle-class protagonists who strayed from the virtuous path and crossed the tracks to "slum it" in the ghetto where they were burned by avaricious prostitutes, conquered by pimps, and lost their money to the gambling racket. Clearly, a reforming morality was an integral part of these dramas, even as these movies titillated a public fascination for illicit and taboo subject matter. And the enduring question for Protestant reformers suspicious of Hollywood was whether the "uplifting" moral message succeeded in outweighing the other ways these movies attracted audiences. A concomitant problem with the racket film of the 1920s was the way it paraded the new materialism across the screen. The gangster film was a vehicle where the new consumer culture found its most exciting expression. The gangster was someone who had thrown off the straitjacket of bourgeois moral rectitude and had set about the business of selling pleasure.

---

4. See Eugene Rosow's discussion of the significance of *Musketeers of Pig Alley* as the first of its kind. *Born to Lose,* pp. 67–70.

This world of fulfilled desires contrasted strongly with the "official" doctrine of deferred gratification and hard work. The gangster, in bucking Prohibition, embodied not only a desire for material improvement but a desire for freedom from many established forms of legislative and moral constraint. The gangster became increasingly identified with a new realm of (hetero)sexual freedom as "real man" incarnate. Films such as *The Exciters* (1923), *While the City Sleeps* (1928), *Come Across* (1929), and *Alibi* (1929) cast the underworld as a realm of seductive licentiousness and linked the consumption habit with sex. All these films told the story of middle-class society women who are irresistibly drawn across the moral tracks by gangster manhood.[5]

While these films encoded gangsterdom as an exciting taboo world, they did not ultimately disturb fundamental oppositions that guaranteed the bourgeois order. For example, the 1920s silent gangster (unlike the "classic" talking gangster) did not threaten idealized definitions of manhood. Rather, he inscribed masculinity within established heterosexual norms (either as an updated noble sexual savage or a chivalrous dandy). Neither did the silent gangster threaten ideals of success. If anything, he encouraged reverence for business. In general, the silent gangster replayed age-old (Oedipal) oppositions between the demands of civic responsibility and the desires for individual self-advancement.

If the 1920s gangster film had any political edge to it, this lay in its implicit encoding of capitalism-as-racket; in revealing the liaisons between capitalists and gangsters, and politicians and gangsters; and in breeding contempt for a corrupted judicial system. A film such as *The Racket* (1928) took this as far as possible in exposing the way Chicago politicians (and even federal prohibition agents) were in cahoots with gangsters. As such, even the more controversial silent representations of the underworld had nothing directly to do with representing the concerns of the immigrant ethnic community.[6] Primarily, the screened underworld functioned as a bourgeois trope, or reforming corrective, designed to discipline cravings to consume and morally police the limits of ambition.

5. Ibid., p. 92.

6. Purportedly, the most notable exceptions to this tendency were *The Racket* (1928) and *Underworld* (1927). Both films point forward to a less moralizing gangster melodrama with a shift in narrative perspective. They featured gangsters as romantic heroes and abandoned the need to attribute their behavior to a patronizing social rationale. That is, these films did not accommodate the need to deal with the causes of crime, nor did they endorse the usual reforming perspective. Instead life in the criminal environment is rendered from the gangster's point of view.

Robert Ray goes further in arguing that the gangster film only ostensibly related to the changing "real" world and actually played out the familiar oppositions that had come to structure much of traditional American (western) mythology: country (smalltown) versus city, individualism versus community, self-interest versus social responsibility, corruption versus virtue, desire versus deferment of gratification, leisure versus work, sexual expression versus moral rectitude.[7] In essence, the terms of the urban ethnic ghetto's entry into mass representation were initially determined and shaped by long-established metaphors held to be more definitive of Americanness than any lived reality.

While Ray argues that this process was typical of the 1930s "classic" gangster film, his analysis actually better describes the 1920s gangster film; even then there is room for debate about just how successfully the 1920s gangster film serviced old-stock nativist frontier mythology and bourgeois mores. By contrast, *Little Caesar, Public Enemy,* and *Scarface* no longer cast ethnicity as the taboo "other" of "true" America. Essential to the drama of these gangster films is precisely the accentuation of hyphenated identity as a competing authentic American condition. As I shall detail later, these films played out ethnic lower-class resentments about being subject to nativist ideals of "naturalization" and "Americanization."

Policing the silent movie gangster, then, fitted into a larger frame of predominantly old-stock concerns about the changing character of American life and identity. As such, in the 1920s custodians of America's moral backbone tended to be cultural guardians at the same time. This is exemplified in the way that the imposition of Prohibition, designed to enforce moral temperance, coincided with anti-immigration legislation.

In 1921 the first of the Immigration Acts was passed, designed to halt the flow of immigrant labor into the United States. In the same year the Daughters of the American Revolution (DAR) published their *Manual for Citizenship.* Compiled in 1920 and modeled on the "Guide to the United States for Immigrants" (published by the Connecticut DAR), the *Manual* was (and continues to be) furnished to the Naturalization Courts for free distribution to foreign-born prospective United States citizens "or for use in Americanism classes for the foreign-born." Symptomatic of this manual's defense of an Anglo

---

7. Robert B. Ray, *A Certain Tendency of the Hollywood Cinema, 1930–1980* (Princeton: Princeton University Press, 1985), pp. 74–77.

definition of Americanness is its strict proclamation "Printed in English Only."[8]

The institutionalized rhetoric of "naturalization" and "Americanism" dates back to the founding fathers and their desire to ground a definition of the "true" and "authentic" American citizen on the demographic configurations of their day. As Stephen Steinberg has highlighted, at its inception the United States was indeed ethnically and religiously homogeneous, which enabled the establishment (relatively free of contradiction) of an Anglo-Saxon Protestant political and cultural hegemony over American life. This authority, however, came increasingly under duress with the onset of massive immigration between 1820 and 1930, in which 32 million Europeans of largely peasant and non-Anglo-Saxon Protestant background came to staff the United States' industrial revolution.[9]

The state and the industrial and cultural elite set about a process of "Americanization." This was designed to forge not only a good citizenry rooted in the old-stock definition of the "true" American but to legitimate structures of subordination at the workplace and in the culture at large. Implicit to the program of Americanization was not simply the fashioning of a melting pot ideology in which the mixing of the ethnic working class would magically conjure up a citizen whose identity cohered with the nativist model.[10] Rather, this policy established very specific power relations between "authentic" versions of American life and apparently "false" ones. A hierarchy of value was established in which the *distance* between the ideal version of the American self and the reality of ethnic working-class identity was underscored. The policy of Americanization involved the "naturalization" of old-stock nativism as normative, all of which aided a corresponding naturalization of ethnic labor's status as a second-class (only "potentially" American) citizenry.[11]

---

8. National Society Daughters of the American Revolution, *DAR Manual for Citizenship* (1987) (originally compiled by Mrs. John Laidlaw Buel in 1920).

9. Stephen Steinberg, *The Ethnic Myth: Race, Ethnicity, and Class in America* (Boston: Beacon Press, 1989).

10. James R. Barrett, in "Americanization from the Bottom Up: Immigration and the Remaking of the Working Class in the United States, 1880–1930," *The Journal of American History*, 79, no. 3 (December 1992), attends to differences between what WASP elites and native middle-class Americans did to immigrant workers, and what immigrants did for themselves in adjusting to the terms of the host culture.

11. Gary Gerstle has highlighted just how central this battle over the terms of Americanism was to ethnically divided working-class communities during the 1920s and 1930s. His study reveals how the conflict between a "traditionalist" notion of Americanism (rooted in a "nostal-

This alienation of self was exacerbated by the terms of bourgeois capitalism.[12] That is, the uprooting of the southern and central European peasantry to make up for America's lack of population (lack of workers to realize industrial capitalism's growth) involved not only a system of specific cultural reprogramming but subjection to the more global forces of modernization. The peasant arriving in America confronted the transforming forces of both old-stock cultural dominance, on one hand, and a bourgeois capitalist society in which one was hailed as a "modern individual" on the other. Both these forces fostered a situation in which the members of the ethnic working class found themselves under pressure to adopt an alien identity quite removed from their lived experiences. To be a "modern individual" meant belonging to an undifferentiated and idealized notion of community. For members of the ethnic lower class, the result was the devaluation of (even estrangement from) the actual content of their social lives. Instead, these "potential" Americans were expected to acculturate toward an abstract American identity whose character had been determined somewhere else.

At one level, this abstracted understanding of the ideal or generic citizen was seductive. Theoretically, a society built on the principle of equality had to rid itself of class and ethnic distinctions. Or, put differently, the establishment of a community in which all are equal and all have "rights" depends necessarily on the establishment of an ideal and abstract subject. In the late nineteenth- and early twentieth-century United States, however, what might have passed as generic subjecthood elsewhere in the industrializing world came dressed in specifically nativist clothing. The apparently abstract modern individual in the American context (this moral individual of public identification, the civic sphere, and bourgeois social power) could never assume an abstract mask. In the United States, *embourgeoisement* necessarily involved the program of Americanization on behalf of a particular ethnocentric order.

---

gia" for a return to the virtues of republican, small-town, white, Anglo-Saxon, Protestant America) on one hand and the forces of the new Americanism (of modernization, diversity, and progress) on the other deeply affected the political attitudes of working-class Americans. Gary Gerstle, *Working-Class Americanism: The Politics of Labor in a Textile City, 1914–1960* (Cambridge: Cambridge University Press, 1989).

12. As Derek Sayer puts it, the capitalist mode of production seeks to abstract the "juridical person" as the "imaginary member of an illusory sovereignty . . . deprived of his real individual life and endowed with an unreal universality." Derek Sayer, *Capitalism and Modernity: An Excursus on Marx and Weber* (London: Routledge, 1991), p. 86.

In talking about the more general mechanisms of capitalism and modernity, Derek Sayer articulates this tension as follows: "Bourgeois social power claims to represent all, but grants admission only to the selected."[13] This "illusion" of equality, however, was hard to maintain in the American situation, for America's demographic explosion was composed out of *transplanted* populations ruled by heterogeneous traditions and languages. Unlike most industrializing European nations America had no homogeneous cultural or language base out of which to extract the "modern individual." As a result, it was confronted by the problem of having to submit those things definitive of society that other nations could take for granted (such as a shared language, history, culture, and land) to a program of "naturalization."[14]

In this sense, the volatile tension endemic to capitalist society in general—its promise of equality versus its endless deferment of delivering on that promise—was complicated in the United States by the contest over the definition of the "true" or "authentic" American. This returns us to the DAR's *Manual for Citizenship*, a document that brings this constellation of forces to the surface and helps to further frame the multiple challenge the talking ethnic gangster offered authority. I quote the DAR's commentary added to "The Oath of American Citizenship (Taken When Naturalized)":

> This Oath of American Citizenship you take is a solemn statement that you call upon God to witness, that you absolutely give up of your own free will your citizenship in any other country and your allegiance to any foreign ruler whose subject you have been. You promise on your honor that you will support and defend the Constitution and laws of the United States against all enemies. You do this of your own free will, keeping back nothing in your mind.
>
> If you take this Oath with the intention to deceive, you are a traitor to the country you have adopted.
>
> If you take this Oath in true faith you are a true citizen of the United States of America.
>
> You are not an Italian-American.
>
> You are not a Spanish-American.

13. Ibid.

14. As Eric Hobsbawm has articulated, European nations reinvented themselves in the nineteenth century—literally inventing traditions and rewriting the historical record in ways that could consolidate and naturalize ideals of nationhood and subjecthood. E. J. Hobsbawm and Terence Ranger, eds., *The Invention of Tradition* (Cambridge: Cambridge University Press, 1983). But the point remains that such guarantees of nationalism, state boundaries, and terms of citizenship rested on a degree of preexisting consensus about cultural belonging and identity that was constantly undermined and defamiliarized in America by massive immigration waves.

You are not a German-American, nor any other kind of a hyphenated American. YOU ARE AN AMERICAN.
There is no prouder title than "Citizen of the United States of America." It is now yours. YOU ARE AN AMERICAN.

In this invocation of some abstract yet authentic American we find a crucial problem that reemerges within the gangster narrative. Ultimately, in spite of the distinctions established between WASP identity and the cultural "others," the process of Americanization held out the promise of inclusion (assimilation) rather than exclusion to the (European) foreign-born.[15] The question for the centers of economic and cultural power, then, was how to regulate the nature of this inclusion in ways conducive to the ruling order of things. This "top-down" attempt to administer cultural otherness sought to deny the actuality and particularity of being a *hyphenated* American. Instead a more abstract, idealized, and formal definition of public identity (simply "American") was sanctified. This, as I have stressed, is simultaneously the project of bourgeois capitalist subjecthood.

To summarize, the talking ethnic gangster film's emergence in the immediate post-Crash years comes on the back of an era most marked by a contest over American ideals.[16] Not only do we have the 1921 and 1924 Immigrations Acts as evidence of the stress the new American had brought to bear on ruling definitions of Americanness, but we have the whole context of America's retreat into a politics of isolation. America turned inward to deal finally with the consequences of industrial modernization. The era featured a nativist backlash and a Red Scare that also had a role to play in articulating the differences between American and un-American ideals.

It was a period framed by the Volstead Act (Prohibition, 1920–1933), which was a "top-down" attempt to police the excessive potential of consumer capitalism on the part of the puritan ethic. While it was a time in which the forces of WASP hegemony directly interfered with the private sphere of everyday life, it was, conversely, an age of

15. Steinberg makes an important distinction between European ethnic immigrants and racial minorities vis-à-vis Americanization: "Immigrants were disparaged for their cultural peculiarities, and the implied message was, 'You will become like us whether you want to or not.' When it came to racial minorities, however, the unspoken dictum was, 'No matter how much like us you are, you will remain apart.'" *The Ethnic Myth*, p. 42.

16. The defense of "traditionalist" or nativist versions of Americanism was at its most intense in the 1920s. See Gerstle, *Working-Class Americanism*, and Joseph R. Gusfield, *Symbolic Crusade: Status Politics and the American Temperance Movement* (Urbana: University of Illinois Press, 1963), for more extended discussion of this.

minimum interference in the practices of big business. The policy of laissez-faire led to a paradoxical tension between a morally irresponsible use and distribution of economic resources and a moralization of the domestic realm.[17]

Historians of early twentieth-century American working class leisure practices have highlighted just how significant the realm of consumer entertainment was for the exercise of subaltern desires for a better life. This complex alliance between the needs of consumer capitalism and working class leisure practices led to a concerted attempt on the part of a residual old-stock cultural elite to "gentrify" the entertainment industry and make the objects of entertainment safe for bourgeois consumption.[18] This attempt to hold the transfiguring potential of consumerism (and its harnessing of working-class expression) in check (or at least to mold these to suit the requirements of embattled social reformers) found its most absurd manifestation in the form of Prohibition. Here was a moral law that had as its specific target the working class. The Volstead Act was a material policy born out of the philosophies of Taylorism, scientific management, and social engineering, all designed to rationalize not only work but the laborers themselves. Not only did alcohol directly threaten the productive efficiency of the worker, but, more significantly, the institutions associated with alcohol (bars, dance halls, theaters, working men's clubs) represented the space of "free" time, that area most at odds with the policing intentions of economic and cultural guardians.

In short, Prohibition was an attempt to control the new consumer culture in terms of the puritan ethic. At the same time, the growth of the leisure sphere (especially through the expansion of time enabled by the electrification of the night) was a new space of economic possibilities. American entrepreneurs were not going to miss their chance

17. For further work and differing perspectives on the project of ethnic working-class Americanization, see Mike Davis, *Prisoners of the American Dream: The Failure of the American Left* (London: Verso, 1990), which critiques working-class ethnic division as a recipe for an effective antiunionism by corporate power interests; and Gary Gerstle, *Working-Class Americanism.*

18. For the development, institutionalization, and function of popular culture practices in sociocultural transformation during the first thirty years of this century in America, see Roy Rosenzweig, *Eight Hours for What We Will* (Cambridge: Cambridge University Press, 1985); Kathy Peiss, *Cheap Amusements: Working Women and Leisure in Turn-of-the-Century New York* (Philadelphia: Temple University Press, 1985); Lary May, *Screening Out the Past: The Birth of Mass Culture and the Motion Picture Industry* (Chicago: University of Chicago Press, 1983); and Lewis Erenberg, *Steppin' Out: New York Night Life and the Transformation of American Culture* (Chicago: University of Chicago Press, 1984).

to exploit the commercial potential of new forms of entertainment. Thus cultural practices initially condemned as the root of moral transgression increasingly gained legitimacy as elements of a growing consumer capitalist market.

In the "roaring" 1920s "leisure" became an integral part of middle-class American life. While the reasons for this are multiple, one particularly salient argument sees this growth in appetite for leisure as a function of the rationalizing forces of the workplace. As these forces stripped workers of any sense of personal autonomy all the more completely (and the more this became the pervasive character of work across *all* classes with the growth of a corporate culture), the more vital a role leisure came to play as an antidote to the subjection of the workplace. The groups most experienced and most attuned to dealing with the frustrations of disenfranchisement and rationalization were, of course, the racial and ethnic urban working class.

It's no accident then that jazz and cinema, two modes of entertainment originating in the cultural margins, should come to occupy such a *central* place in 1920s culture. It could be argued that such cultural practices were examples of "compensation," designed to defuse frustrations with the conditions of the status quo. At the same time, the fact remains that these cultural practices were rooted in the lower-class experience of the contradictions of modernity, and gave a concrete and collective articulation to otherwise abstract and atomized anxieties about ruling societal conditions.

Accordingly, we might characterize the 1920s as a time when middle-class American reticence about the culture of the lower social echelons receded dramatically. Both at the level of leisure practices and at the level of cultural politics there was a growing public recognition of the need to include the ethnic working class in the definition of Americanness. At the same time this recourse to the cultural "other" had to be effectively policed, for not only did the entertainment industry provide an arena for the articulation of subaltern desires, but it lent sanction to these desires in the process.

Prohibition embodied all that was contradictory about this attempt to have it both ways on the part of old-stock authority. For thirteen years Prohibition affected all areas of American society. It was an act born out of anxieties about consumerism's corrosion of the puritan work ethic and the public good. As I have outlined, however, this fear cannot be separated from a concomitant fear of the "new" and hyphenated American. The combination of these fears was embodied precisely in the gangster. If leisure had been stigmatized as the realm of the "other" (as an amoral sphere populated by the wrong kind of Americans), here was that realm's most feared representative. Yet, for the realm of leisure, the most rapidly expanding part of American life, the gangster emerged as a culture hero. Here was someone who had the tenacity to buck the system. The ethnic gangster as boot-legger, as the boss of America's urban nightlife, as a fashion leader, and as a capitalist opportunist was nativism's nemesis.

Prohibition drew a battle line between old and new in which what had once been generally perceived as illegitimate and culturally mar-ginal moved to the center of life. Precisely what it was designed to keep in check, it generated: namely, the popularization of the ethnic urban "underclass" (a mix of working class and criminal underworld). And the stigmatizing of "leisure" as morally corrupting only exacer-bated its appeal as an excitingly new social space. In turning leisure and pleasure-mongering (which included the very practice of movie-going) into something consonant with the cultural "other," WASP moral and civic guardianship only increased the growing distance be-tween a rarefied nativist idealism and the concrete reality of American everyday life. Consequently, Prohibition catalyzed a growing coalition of interests between the cultural margins and the expanding middle class.

Lary May, in dealing with the Hollywood of the 1920s, sees the movement of the cinema as a cultural institution out of the ethnic urban ghetto and onto Main Street as part of a transformational pro-cess, one inflected by a pervasive "progressivism." That is, the film narratives are dominated by a moralizing impulse that tempers the corrosive capacities of both consumerism (of which the cinema was an integral part) and alternative versions of Americanism to old-stock authority. The stars of the day, such as Douglas Fairbanks Sr. and Mary Pickford (Anglo-Saxons), became models of moral consumers, embodying a way of managing and rationalizing the contradiction consumerism posed to an American civic idealism rooted in the pre-industrial values of a small-town producer-based society.[19]

Throughout the 1920s a fundamental instability was growing be-tween, on one hand, an increasingly anachronistic and visible elite fighting a rearguard action to fashion capitalism after its own image,

19. See May, Chapter 5, "Revitalization: Douglas Fairbanks, Mary Pickford and the New Personality," *Screening Out the Past*, pp. 96–146.

and, on the other hand, rival cultural groups using the expanding leisure industry to voice their demands "bottom-up" for proper representation. The tensions between Anglo-America and the "new" Americans that had first emerged following World War I, and that had been kept in check throughout the 1920s by the forces of a nativist backlash (of which Hollywood had been no small part), took on a new character after 1929. The Wall Street Crash undermined the fundamental grounds on which both the bourgeois and WASP social order rested for their legitimacy. Hollywood's traditional resolutions of American cultural contradictions, which invariably endorsed a nativist (socially and morally reforming) perspective, lost much of their currency. New stories and new resolutions would have to be forged for a new era.

What I have discussed here is the vital pre-history of key sociocultural tensions that inform both the production of the 1930s gangster film and the conditions of its reception. Given the right conditions such as the Crash produced, these tensions could finally break Hollywood's obligation to the aesthetics of reform. It is only in this way that we can see the significance of the post-Crash early 1930s gangster film as part of an ongoing cultural and political battle, a contest in which America's ethnic polyglot reality fought back against its traditional casting as the villainous un-American "other."

Key to this argument for the 1930s gangster film's significance is the one major characteristic that distinguished it from its prototypes: sound. The injection of sound into the gangster melodrama added a new layer of signification that altered the perspective from which urban stories were told. City noise, the sound of cars, trams, buses, factory machines, and sirens and the cacophony of crowds on the street, helped dramatize the urban realm in a new way. And the fact that the gangster could talk was no trivial matter. For what made *Little Caesar, Public Enemy,* and *Scarface* so different from anything that had come before was that their protagonists spoke in ethnic urban vernacular voices.

Sound was something that threatened to change Hollywood's hegemonic allegiances. As Ralph L. Henry, a reformer-educator, anguished in 1929:

> What is going to happen to the English-speaking language and to American culture generally once every small-town movie house is equipped to reproduce night after night the language which the current cult of realism . . . will demand of successful screenplays? . . . Alongside the comic strips, the movies up to the present have . . . not

ranked with the illiterate or foreign home environment, with street and playground associations, with the vaudeville shows, or with cheap books and magazines which make for the degeneration of the language and the consequent lowering of the general cultural standard.[20]

This notion that the talking picture had the power to "debase" not just established moral standards, but cultural ones too, was to make the talking gangster film such a problematic entity in Depression-era America.

It is not accidental that the talking gangster film gained notoriety between two key events, the Wall Street Crash of 1929 and the death of John Dillinger in 1934 (which, as I have outlined, precipitated the Hays Code moratorium on gangster film production in 1935). The period 1930 to 1933 constituted the last years of Prohibition and the now discredited Republican regime that supported it.

In 1932 Franklin Delano Roosevelt rode to victory in the presidential election promising a New Deal for America. His triumph depended on making a clear break with everything associated with previous administrations. While this was primarily achieved via a commitment to pursue an entirely new economic planning policy, it was also important that Roosevelt disassociated himself from the Protestant old guard within the Democratic party. And key to this was his decision to shift from being an advocate of Prohibition to supporting a repeal platform.[21]

By 1932 it made sense to ride the "wet" plank. Not only did this help in garnering support from voters, but it was vital in securing nomination as a presidential candidate within the Democratic party. This had not been the case during the 1928 campaign, when the party had presented itself as a deeply divided organization over the issue of Prohibition. Being for or against Prohibition was to take a cultural stand. The old guard of the Democratic party was "dry" and Protestant in cast, features embodied in William Jennings Bryan and

---

20. Ralph L. Henry, "The Cultural Influence of the 'Talkies,'" *School and Society* (February 1929), as printed in Gerald Mast, ed., *The Movies in Our Midst: Documents in the Cultural History of Film in America* (Chicago: University of Chicago Press, 1982), pp. 292–293.

21. For a fuller treatment of the significance of the change in the Democratic party's political culture during this time (from dominance by Protestant reformers such as McAdoo and Bryan to representing a coalition of inter-ethnic, urban, Catholic, and repeal interests), see David Burner, *The Politics of Provincialism: The Democratic Party in Transition, 1914–1932* (New York: Knopf, 1967); Allan J. Lichtman, "Critical Election Theory and the Reality of American Presidential Politics, 1916–40," *American Historical Review*, 81, no. 1 (February 1976), pp. 317–348; and Lizabeth Cohen, *Making a New Deal: Industrial Workers in Chicago, 1919–1939* (Cambridge: Cambridge University Press, 1990).

William McAdoo. Significantly, the first challenge to this within the ranks came from Al Smith, a devout Catholic who was fiercely proud of his urban ethnic lower-class roots in the Irish section of New York's Lower East Side.

Al Smith's identity had uncanny parallels with the "classic" gangster's, which extended to his open bucking of the Volstead Act. In 1928, riding a "wet" plank, Al Smith won the Democratic nomination for president. However, the divisions over rival party leaders' ethnic and class affiliations had been exacerbated by bitter feuding over the issue of Prohibition. American voters were presented with an image of a party in inner turmoil, and Al Smith lost the election.

The shift had been made, however, and by 1932 savvy presidential advisors had no hesitation in insisting that a "wet" ticket was the only ticket. Smith's stance had been influenced by the success of Anton Cermak in winning the mayoral office of Chicago. As Lizabeth Cohen highlights, at the end of the 1920s

> workers became drawn into an interethnic Democratic machine in Chicago under the leadership of Anton Cermak that connected them not only to a unified Democratic Party on the city level, but also to the national Democratic Party. The issue that made Cermak's political career, and drew Chicago's diverse ethnic communities together behind him and the national Democratic candidate in 1928, Alfred E. Smith, was Prohibition.[22]

Repeal was a key part of any politician's campaign in gaining the urban working-class ethnic vote. These voters, who inevitably formed the majority of the metropolitan electorate, conceived of Prohibition as an attack on immigrant cultural traditions. In the big city, at least, defiance of the Volstead Act had become a prerequisite to electability.[23] And just as the Democratic party saw the need to exploit anti-Prohibition and urban ethnic sentiment, so too did Hollywood with its production of gangster films. The fact that the political recipe for success seemed to mirror Hollywood's in the early 1930s points to the complex interrelationship between changes in mass media sensibilities and politics at the time.

The period of Prohibition had also been the quintessential context responsible not only for the growth of gangsterdom but its cultural sanction. An antagonistic popular disposition toward Prohibition had been most publicly fostered by gangsters real and fictional. While this

22. Cohen, *Making a New Deal*, pp. 254–55.
23. Ibid., pp. 210–11.

antagonism reached its peak in the post-Crash period of 1930 to 1933, the ground had been prepared in the late 1920s by the tabloid fascination with the ethnic gangster. Eugene Rosow's historical study of the gangster film reveals that between 1925 and 1929 the gutter press found its favorite front-page news in the activities of Al Capone, Lucky Luciano, and Meyer Lansky.[24] This attention helped shape a new culture hero who depended for his identity precisely on his bucking the temperance system and the civic and moral interest groups that backed this system.

What scholars like Rosow have failed to develop, however, is that the gangster was interesting not just because he was a bootlegger, but because he was an urban *ethnic* type as well.[25] He championed the desires for public recognition of an under- and misrepresented part of American culture, the ethnic urban popular classes. In this way the opposition between the advocates and enemies of Prohibition was recast as a struggle between an ethnic urban working class and a recalcitrant dominant old-stock order. Although a criminal and an ethnic to boot, someone like Al Capone gained credibility as a new national hero in the context of Prohibition, a piece of legislation universally despised across class and ethnic lines. Capone bucked not only the law but the entire system of nativist middle-class idealism rooted in commitment to the work ethic and the deferment of gratification. The gangster's popularity reached new heights in the aftermath of the Wall Street Crash, an event that removed the economic platform on which Prohibition's credibility had rested.

In many ways, then, the first talking gangster films of the early 1930s appeared during a relative power vacuum. Their emergence coincided with a crisis-ridden period of profound and traumatic political, economic, social, and cultural transformation. And it is this coincidence that invites an analysis of the role Hollywood's gangster played in mediating such dramatic change. As Robert Sklar points out:

> Among intellectuals and in centers of political power, the importance of cultural myths to social stability was a seriously debated topic. The Depression had shaken some of the oldest and strongest

24. See Rosow, *Born to Lose,* and David Ruth, *Inventing the Public Enemy: The Gangster in American Culture, 1918–1934* (Chicago: University of Chicago Press, 1996), for a detailed examination of the media fascination and exploitation of the gangster image over this period.

25. Rosow notes that Hollywood gangsters became identified as immigrants in the late 1920s, and locates this within the context of a nativist backlash to immigration. Having said this, Rosow interprets the ethnic marking of the gangster as a debilitating stigma and doesn't attend to the more volatile and emancipatory features of casting the gangster as an ethnic type.

American cultural myths, particularly the middle class homilies about the virtue of deferred gratification and assurance that hard work and perseverance would bring success. . . . The widespread doubt about traditional American myths threatened to become a dangerous political weakness.[26]

In the context of the Great Depression, Hollywood found itself at the center of a debate about its sociocultural responsibilities. Integral to the gangster film is precisely a dramatization not only of myths of capitalist success but of the struggle of the ethnic urban working class to gain legitimate representation in a culture dominated by Anglo-Saxon Protestant mythology. For my purposes, this struggle is the starting point of any analysis that seeks to explain what the stakes were in censoring the gangster film. It is the terrain that best explains the fascination of these films for contemporaneous audiences and why this fascination came to be perceived as dangerous by the centers of political power.

26. Robert Sklar, *Movie-Made America: A Social History of American Movies* (New York: Random House, 1975), pp. 195–96.

2
The Enemy Goes Public

Voicing the Cultural Other in the Early 1930s
Talking Gangster Film

Little Caesar (1930), *Public Enemy* (1931), and *Scarface* (1932) have been hailed as the key examples of the so-called classic American gangster film. As starring vehicles for Edward G. Robinson, James Cagney, and Paul Muni, respectively, these films introduced Americans to actors who, regardless of the countless other roles and types they played, became synonymous with the screen gangster. Yet the most significant aspect of these generic and typological milestones has all but been ignored in film scholarship: namely, that these films featured gangsters who could speak. More important, they spoke a street vernacular in the accents of groups designated as cultural "others."

Edward G. Robinson, James Cagney, and Paul Muni were stars of a stock entirely different from what had come before. Most obviously, they were *not* Anglo-Saxon Protestants. Edward G. Robinson's real name was Emmanuel Goldenberg, and Paul Muni's real name was Friedrich Muni Meyer Weisenfreund. Both were New York Lower East Side immigrant Jews who had gained their formative theatrical experiences on the Yiddish stage. James Cagney was also a city boy from the Lower East Side (of Irish Catholic stock) who had honed his performance skills on the vaudeville stage, and who prided himself on having learned Yiddish in order to survive in the ghetto street culture.[1] This collusion of real and cinematic identity had everything

---

1. Evidence of Cagney's streetwise bilingualism is articulated in his film *Taxi!* (1932), in which he uses his Yiddish to help solve a difference of opinion between a Jewish fare and a taxi

to do with the refinement of the gangster as an "authentic" American type.

In catering to an audience experiencing the radical upheavals brought on by the Depression, Hollywood found success in developing its social realist dimensions. The fact that the sound era was ushered in during a turbulent social, economic, and cultural climate only exacerbated shifts in Hollywood style. Sound aided in providing franker representations of everyday life more adequate to America's changed realities. Some trends of the late 1920s were especially enhanced, such as a gravitation toward more candid or "adult" treatment of sex and crime.[2] The impulse toward a more "social realist" or documentary treatment of life was particularly well served by the early 1930s talking gangster film and the new "social problem" cycle (epitomized by *I Am a Fugitive from a Chain Gang* in 1932).

Even the seemingly "escapist" 1930s musical is grounded in the problems and desires of everyday folk during the Depression; characteristically, the plots of the early 1930s musical concentrated on the "backstage" collective efforts of the complete cast in making a show, in the making of illusions. This direct attention to the concerns of workaday existence was no longer subordinated to the goals of "progressivism" and "moral uplift," no longer easily subsumed (or silenced) by the conventions of traditional mythology and the aesthetics of reform that dominated the silent era. Such framing conventions gave way to a different and more candid view of life at the bottom of

driver. For Cagney's self-understanding as a hyphenated American in Anglo America, see his two autobiographical works: James Cagney, *Cagney by Cagney* (Garden City, N.Y.: Doubleday, 1976) and Douglas Warren with James Cagney, *James Cagney: The Authorized Biography* (New York: St. Martin's Press, 1983). See also Robert Sklar's *City Boys: Cagney, Bogart, Garfield* (Princeton: Princeton University Press, 1992), a biographical account of the "city boy" star and Hollywood's nationalization of the metropolitan type.

2. See Lea Jacobs on continuities and developments in risqué representations of female sexuality that in some ways echo patterns of the gangster film in the context of sound and the Crash. *Wages of Sin: Censorship and the Fallen Woman Film, 1928–1942* (Berkeley and Los Angeles: University of California Press, 1997). Lary May's discussion of changing patterns of late 1920s Hollywood representation suggests lines of continuity and change that may well have been accelerated by the economic catastrophe. *Screening Out the Past: The Birth of the Motion Picture Industry* (Chicago: University of Chicago Press, 1983). Ruth Vasey provides a rich account of how the introduction of sound caused Hollywood problems in meeting the needs of its massive non-English-speaking market. *The World According to Hollywood, 1918–1939* (Exeter: University of Exeter Press, 1997). An argument could be advanced that in its initial reorientation to sound, Hollywood seemed uncertain about how to avoid upsetting foreign audiences, something that probably exacerbated its commitment to risqué domestic subject matter that it knew would draw at the home box office, and that the industry may have traditionally avoided or tempered for fear of moral censure.

the social ladder. No longer simply objects of someone else's story, the poor and the criminal were granted a say in stories narrated from *their* perspective.

Cagney, Robinson, and Muni did not descend from schools of "high" acting. All three came out of popular and ethnic theatrical traditions. This, in tandem with the fact that they were all once Lower East Side kids, granted them a biographical proximity to the gangster roles that made them Hollywood stars. While the gangster melodrama had always gestured toward social realism, it is highly intriguing that these particular actors got their break when they did, playing the roles they did.[3]

While gangsters had been able to talk since 1928, the success of Cagney, Robinson, and Muni was a post-Crash phenomenon. This had much to do with the framing context of economic catastrophe, and the widespread collapse of confidence in established American verities that came with the disaster. Such circumstances enhanced the appeal of stories and characters that debunked older Hollywood fantasies and gestured toward a grittier truth.

A major interference with this search for a newer "truth" about American identity was the stigma of having to anglicize one's name as an ethnic actor (something reflective of the ongoing xenophobic character of idealized American identity). To some extent, the costs of "making it" in America for the ethnic actor paralleled those of the gangster characters they portrayed. Anglicizing one's name betrayed the quintessential problem facing these actors with hyphenated identities as Jewish- and Irish-Americans. Like the protagonists they portrayed, Robinson, Cagney, and Muni were involved in a struggle with an old-stock mainstream.

Key to their success was the way they brought a tough talking street vernacular to the screen with the introduction of sound. That this should have precipitated their rise to national prominence, however, cannot be attributed to the question of vocal delivery alone; these new gangster stars who emerged after the Wall Street Crash captured and dramatized a general disillusionment with the pre-Crash order of things.[4]

3. The idea of casting "real" ghetto denizens in gangster films was as old as the first gangster feature, *The Musketeers of Pig Alley* (1912), which featured the "Snapper Kid" played by an actual street hoodlum.

4. One could examine the degree to to which there was a more widespread disenchantment with older Hollywood types. An analysis of *Variety* lists of the top ten male and female box-office stars and top movies of 1928, 1929, 1930, and 1931 reveals that the high-society comedy

Douglas Gomery has highlighted the key role sound played in the economic consolidation of the major studios, especially in the period from 1928 to 1929.[5] Economic mergers and collusions between studios and sound engineering companies (such as AT&T and RCA) enabled the formation of cartels that drove smaller concerns to the wall. When the majors decided to make the change to talking pictures, they took a remarkably short time to overcome the myriad difficulties of converting studio stages into sound stages, of creating a vocal star system, and of wiring their theaters for sound. As Gomery points out, synchronized sound had been a possibility almost since the inception of the movies. He argues that the change to sound came when it did because of a planned strategy on the part of larger companies that had been contingent on the securing of patents. Indeed, the move to sound proved to be the economic making of the majors, as they all saw their profits soar. Yet Gomery's detailing of this collusion of economic interests is only a partial story—one that ignores the mitigating social changes that loosened the grip of established "silent" reform aesthetics on the American cinema, paving the way for a culture disposed to talking pictures (especially ones that featured gangster protagonists who bucked the Prohibition order).

Gomery's "top-down" story of economic cartels dictating the evolution of Hollywood has been supported by critics such as Mary Ann Doane, who have interpreted the "marriage" of sound and image within such vertically integrated capitalist institutions as an ideologically reactionary recipe. She argues that the use of sound in Hollywood helped intensify its reproduction of a seamless and natural image of the world.[6] Soundtracks helped smooth over the fragmentary forces of cutting, imposing continuity of diegesis over the discontinuous features of cinematic montage. This naturalization of the film artifice is interpreted less as something that aids social realism than as something that ultimately affirms bourgeois ideology: for, so the argument goes, to erase the signs that movies are man-made con-

---

disappears, while the gangster film and social problem film gain in popularity. Equally, certain silent stars fade (such as Mary Pickford, Douglas Fairbanks, Gloria Swanson, and Clara Bow) while others (such as Cagney, Muni, and Robinson) begin to shine.

5. Douglas Gomery, "The Coming of Sound: Technological Change in the American Film Industry," in *Film Sound: Theory and Practice*, ed. Elisabeth Weis and John Belton (New York: Columbia University Press, 1985), pp. 5–24.

6. Mary Ann Doane, "Ideology and the Practice of Sound Editing and Mixing," in *Film Sound*, pp. 54–62.

structs is to keep audiences blind to the fact that what they are viewing is the product of work and ideological decisions.

However, as I shall now detail, giving the gangster a voice begged questions of what had been formerly taken for granted in Hollywood's representations of the ethnic urban lower class. The talking gangster openly broached the issues of class and cultural exclusion that had frustrated his ambition (and that had been "naturalized" in the silent-era gangster). Moreover, in light of the universal afflictions the Depression brought to American society, the ethnic gangster's struggles with economic and cultural disenfranchisement resonated with a growing *national* condition. The gangster's tough vernacular voice only enhanced his status as an outspoken representative of the vox populi. The growing change in the perception of these once "othered," "ghetto-ized," and "unnatural" Americans was accelerated by a cinematic culture now wired for sound, one disposed, finally, to listen to formerly silenced voices.

LITTLE CAESAR: "IT'S AN ITALIAN PICTURE"

As the first of its kind to gain public renown, *Little Caesar* occupies a significant place as a watershed gangster film. *Little Caesar* has been interpreted primarily as a parody of the success mythology typified in the popular Horatio Alger rags-to-riches stories.[7] And there is much that is compelling about attributing the success of this film to its desperate invocation of ambition in a Depression climate of defeat and unemployment. In dramatizing one man's ruthless desire to "make it" in America, *Little Caesar* both appeals and repels. Sympathy for the protagonist as someone prepared to battle the Depression is mixed with distaste for his methods. Rising and falling, the gangster passes ironic comment on the violent and corrupting terms of once sacrosanct beliefs in individualism and capitalist success. Such themes had

7. The very first chapter of Andrew Bergman's *We're in the Money: Depression America and Its Films* (New York: Harper and Row, 1971), is entitled "The Gangsters" and starts with the sentence "*Little Caesar* wasted no time"—by which he means that the gangster film was really the first to address the realities of the Depression. Having noted that this crime cycle was to cause "consternation among civic pressure groups," Bergman barely touches on the role of sound in raising moral alarm bells. His interest in the gangster controversy centers on its pastiche of Algerism and Andrew Carnegie's *The Road to Business Success, An Address to Young Men*. See also Richard H. Pells, *Radical Visions and American Dreams: Culture and Social Thought in the Depression Years* (Middletown, Conn.: Wesleyan University Press, 1976), for an adumbration on the gangster as parody of the American Dream.

become increasingly definitive of the late 1920s gangster film, and it is clear that the circumstances of the Crash lent even more sanction to the cycle's scepticism about the American Dream.

What makes *Little Caesar* different, however, is not just the coincidence that the gangster's story is narrated in the aftermath of the Crash. Rather, this gangster is significant because he speaks. After all, *Little Caesar* was more than just a fine gangster film; it was the first great gangster *talkie*. And this gangster spoke Italian American (actually, the situation is more complicated—we have a Jewish-American actor imitating an Italian American). The gangster's voice adds a layer of signification that further complicates the nature of the gangster's relation to established success mythology. It is not just that *Little Caesar* is a dark allegory of Algerism; whenever the gangster speaks he reveals that this American's story is delivered from a very specific cultural space. His accent frames his desire for success within a history of struggle over national identity.

When civic pressure groups responded to the gangster film, they couched their objections in terms of a moral paradigm (e.g., how such films glorified the criminal and would adversely influence the young). This moral dressing, however, ultimately disguised a more complex fear of cultural "otherness" for gangsters gained popularity not simply because of the stories they told, but how they told them. It wasn't some abstract notion of the criminal that was celebrated, but the gangster as Robinson (or Cagney or Muni) portrayed him. Robinson, for example, could never shake off his characterization of Little Caesar, precisely because the role and the actor were inseparable. It wasn't just anyone who could play the gangster most effectively; he had to be from a very specific part of American society. Thus, what gangster films popularized was not only a critical disposition toward the law but national identification with an ethnic urban type.

In the case of *Little Caesar* the irreverence for law becomes bound up with a complicated relationship with the language of officialdom and the dominant old-stock culture. The quest to be "legitimate" for this gangster is not simply a question of building a front to disguise the essentially immoral nature of capitalist enterprise. No, it is this and more: it is simultaneously a quest to gain cultural acceptance into the upper echelons of "society."

Little Caesar tells the story of a hoodlum seeking to make it in the big time—"to be somebody." This somewhat abstract quest taps into a more general collective desire for upward mobility fostered in age-old American myths (such as that inscribed in the Horatio Alger rags-to-riches narratives). Little Caesar's dreams are fostered by a newspaper exposé of a famous big-city gangster, Legs Diamond. Out in the countryside (of small-town "burgs"), Little Caesar sees no future in small-time gas station heists and sets his sights on the city. He moves then from the country to the city, a symbolic passage from innocence into corruption, a foreshadowing, as it were, of his fall from grace. Again, this narrative configuration echoes a constant preoccupation in American mythology, that of the loss of a "virgin state" or Eden out of which we have been cast.

The rise of the machine, of the big city, represents some kind of deviation from a truer path back to the garden. This ur-narrative patterning of American thought has been named as the "American Jeremiad" by Sacvan Bercovitch, who sees it as an informing structure pervasive in much of nineteenth-century American literature.[8] In his discussion of American intellectual history David Noble extends this insight, identifying the ways in which a paradigm of declension or lament has informed American historiography. This history's "story" tells us how capitalism and modernity have led America astray from its original promise to achieve a republican small-town producer-based civic society peopled by Anglo-Saxon Protestant artisans and yeomen. The question for jeremiad historians, then, has been how to rationalize this fall from grace, how to fabricate a new narrative (historiography) that can make industrial capitalism service a return to prelapsarian origins.[9] Such an historiography is thus marked by its clinging to some essentially WASP definition of "true" or ideal Americanness.

To some extent, we can read *Little Caesar* in this light. W. R. Burnett, upon whose novel the film is based, prefaced his book and the movie with a quotation from Machiavelli: "The first law of every being is to preserve itself and live. You sow hemlock and expect corn to ripen." In an interview Burnett described his use of the quotation as follows: "It meant, if you have this type of society, it will produce such men." He described Little Caesar as "a gutter Macbeth—a composite figure that would indicate how men could rise to prominence or money under the most hazardous of conditions, but not more hazardous than the Renaissance." At this abstract or universal level

---

8. Sacvan Bercovitch, *The American Jeremiad* (Madison: University of Wisconsin Press, 1978).

9. David Noble, *The End of American History: Democracy, Capitalism, and the Metaphor of Two Worlds in Anglo-American Historical Writing, 1880–1980* (Minneapolis: University of Minnesota Press, 1985).

Burnett was looking for a "type" who could embody the "tragic flaw" of "overriding ambition." [10] *Little Caesar* indeed tells the story of a man who rises ruthlessly to the top from nothing, only to die in the gutter. And in this sense, *Little Caesar* is indeed a critique of the corrosive features of modern capitalist society and its (lack of) mores, a critique that shares much with the paradigm of the jeremiad.

This is actually much clearer in Burnett's later gangster narrative, *High Sierra* (1941), which starred Humphrey Bogart as Roy Earle, a figure modeled on one of America's most celebrated gangsters, John Dillinger (a hero of dust bowl Depression America, not a figure drawn from the 1920s city). Compared to Robinson, Bogart was a star without strong ethnic markings, who could more easily fit into a nativist version of American history. Bogart's Roy Earle was reminiscent of his earlier role as the anachronistic gangster fugitive, Duke Mantee, in *The Petrified Forest* (1936), both of whom represented a completely different kind of gangster than Robinson's Little Caesar. As Burnett confirms:

> You see there's a confusion here: Dillinger and Roy Earle, such men are not gangsters, organized crime, mafioso. They were a reversion to the western bandit. They had nothing in common with the Italian, Irish, or Polish hoodlums in Chicago. An entirely different breed, and Roy Earle was a perfect example.

In response to the question "What are [these gangster types] symbolic of?" Burnett's answer is telling: "Old America, rural America, and a simpler time." [11]

This is a crucial distinction, for it points back to particulars in *Little Caesar* that belie its being read simply as a general allegory for the corrosive features of capitalism and modernity. Such an allegory (as featured in *High Sierra*, with its protagonist's flight to the natural landscape of the mountains away from the complications of modern life) implicitly confirms the virtues of a premodern (prelapsarian) moral landscape. In *Little Caesar*, the protagonist is comfortable in the modern urban world. This big-city gangster is definitively not symbolic of "old America." His is a new story that departs from an older nativist narrative structure and its conventions. As Burnett emphasizes about *Little Caesar*'s dialogue:

10. Pat McGilligan, *Backstory: Interviews with Screenwriters of Hollywood's Golden Age* (Berkley and Los Angeles: University of California Press, 1986) p. 57.
   11. Ibid., p. 67.

I had a literary theory about dialogue. This was in the twenties. Novels were all written in a certain way, with literary language and so much description. Well, I dumped all that out; I just threw it away. It was a revolt, a literary revolt. That was my object. I wanted to develop a style of writing based on the way American people spoke—not literary English. Of course, that the Chicago slang was all around me made it easy to pick up.[12]

This stress on veracity of language was designed to tranform the conventional view of crime and the criminal:

Ultimately, what made *Little Caesar* the smack in the face it was, was the fact that it was the world seen through the eyes of the gangster. It's a commonplace now, but it had never been done before then. You had crime stories but always seen through the eyes of society. The criminal was just some son-of-a-bitch who'd killed somebody and then you go get 'em. I treated them as human beings.[13]

According to Burnett, to provide a picture of the criminal as a human being (rather than reducing him to a literary device or cipher), the writer had to see the world through the social "other's" eyes. And this had radical consequences for the gangster myth. No longer was the underworld story to be told exclusively from the socially reforming nativist perspective. As Burnett emphasizes about *Little Caesar:* "It's an Italian picture."[14] It is this filling out of the ethnic point of view that made *Little Caesar* significantly new.[15] The coupling of ethnic vernacular identity with the underworld is important, not so much as a consolidation of the cycle's rules but as something that ruptured older conventions.

Caesar Enrico Bandello enters the big city and the Club Palermo. He rises through the ranks of the gang, assumes its leadership, and eventually gets to control a huge urban territory. As he rises, his material circumstances improve. He moves out of the dingy Club Palermo into more baroque surroundings. He adorns himself with the signifiers of social success: smart suits, cigars, diamond rings, marble tables, classical realist paintings, cars. Yet the running joke is

12. Ibid., p. 58.
13. Ibid.
14. Ibid.
15. Strangely, film scholarship has been quite limited in its understanding of the quality of being Italian or Irish as a gangster attribute. The tendency is to see ethnicity as an iconographic device that helps further consolidate the line separating legitimate from illicit activity. That is, ethnicity aids in the solidification of convention—not its breakdown.

that he and his compatriots of Italian extraction, while they can accumulate the outward signs of "making it," have no way to actually
appreciate the artifacts they have collected. For example, the only
value Little Caesar can attribute to a painting he sees in Big Boy's
office is a financial one. He judges this not on the basis of the painting
itself but on the fact that it has a huge gold frame. This lack of "culture" emphasizes the continual gap between legitimate and illegitimate social realms. At the same time, Little Caesar's desires for the
signs of official society signify his yearning for cultural inclusion and
acceptance.

This vernacular view of the sociocultural elite invites contradictory
interpretation and is a common theme in all three of the gangster
films I want to deal with here. When Little Caesar is given a party by
his gang to honor his rise to prominence, we are provided with a parodic simulation of a high-society banquet. The gang is appropriately
dressed but has no sense of the protocol or language that is appropriate to such an occasion. No one can give an eloquent speech, the banquet disintegrates into a food fight, and the gift the gang gives Rico
turns out to be stolen: seemingly, those who can only ape "society"
are really only apes after all.

A patronizing view of the ethnic underworld, one that "naturalizes" the ethnics' second-class-citizen status, certainly seems to be
encouraged. Their poverty, as it were, becomes equated with cultural
inadequacy. The grounds for ethnic disenfranchisement thus shift
away from inequitous societal causes and onto the groups themselves.
Several elements, however, undermine the seductiveness of this reading. Once we relocate *Little Caesar* in the context of 1930, and once
we look at how Robinson plays out his role, we can recover a competing version of ethnic portrayal that would have been available (and
probably more persuasive) for contemporary audiences.

Little Caesar played on the hyphenated American's frustrated desire for cultural and economic inclusion. The possibility for upward
mobility within the social structure was implicit to the immigrant's
position in American society. While southern European immigrants
were positioned low on the sociocultural ladder, they were, from the
outset, included within the dynamic industrialized and modern centers of the economy. As Stephen Steinberg puts it, even though European ethnic immigrant groups initially started at the bottom of the
economic and social pyramid and "were disparaged for their cultural
peculiarities . . . the implied message was 'You will become like us

The banquet scene in *Little Caesar* (1930). Going "legit"—ethnic gangsters betray their desire for cultural acceptance in trying to emulate the ways and protocols of high society.

whether you want to or not.'"[16] Yet *Little Caesar* reveals the way in which the rewards for assimilation (simulation/aping) are ultimately withheld.

The project of assimilation encouraged a splitting of identity among groups targeted for top-down "Americanization." Ethnic immigrants certainly had a sense of ethnic origin. As a transplanted popular class, however, subjected to the forces of modernization and Americanization, they found little beyond the ghetto itself that would support and solidify any old-world sense of roots. Rather, the experience of deracination might be a better way to conceptualize the immigrant ethnic experience—that is, alienation from both roots in the old world and the projected future in the new. *Little Caesar,* as an urban production coming in the wake of the Crash and designed for metropolitan audiences, plugged straight into this realm of contradiction.

16. Stephen Steinberg, *The Ethnic Myth: Race, Ethnicity, and Class in America* (Boston: Beacon Press, 1989), p. 42.

The question it raised on behalf of the disenfranchised was "Why haven't we been granted access to power?" Rico plays out the role of the entrepreneur but is condemned to do so from the wrong side of the tracks. He wants "in" to the official culture (a promise that is held out to all ethnic immigrants) but ultimately is only allowed to mimic legitimacy.

In the context of 1930 the "legitimate" culture was itself under duress. Through its direct association with economic catastrophe and the enforcement of the unpopular Volstead Act, "official" society became increasingly susceptible to a "bottom-up" critique. *Little Caesar*'s box-office success has to be understood in this context: as a film that, in light of the Crash and the repressive order of Prohibition, dramatizes the deferment of capitalism's promises from the perspective of the vernacular American subject. Little Caesar, Tommy Powers, and Tony Camonte all attempt to execute those otherwise deferred promises of upward mobility and cultural inclusion within the existing social structure. As films that found their audiences in the Depression metropolis they testified to the polyglot American reality that was increasingly at odds with the rarefied discourse of official society.

Little Caesar's Italian fraternal gang represents ethnic community as the "real" realm of social relations, which is condemned only to mimic the rarefied rules of the legal norm. The gang and the urban territory it rules are ultimately simulations of an "idealized" normative America. The fact that Rico speaks a street slang ties him to a "real" world against which norms and ideals are measured as ultimately unattainable.[17] As the banquet scene reveals, the protocol of apparently "normative" society is absurdly detached from the realm of ordinary people. In 1930 (a post-Crash and pre–Prohibition repeal context), an audience composed largely of lower-class to lower-middle-class urbanites would have laughed at the ridiculous insistence that Americans should kowtow to such an artificial social code. A "banquet" replete with alcohol would have not only signified inequitous class division but drawn attention to the hypocrisy of Anglo-American elitism. Given the film's overall thematic pre-occupation

---

17. I put the term "real" here in quotation marks because I am well aware that these films are involved in negotiating a new body of aesthetic rules and codes to signify a break with older notions of an "authentic" or "real" America. The question for me is how ethnicity came to be essential to the new patterns of "verist" signification, against which the older encodings of American reality and experience could be perceived as "false" or ideologically inscribed as "exclusionary."

with cultural exclusion from the point of view of the ethnic, this scene could only have delivered an ambivalent message about class and ethnic distinctions.

PUBLIC ENEMY: "HE'S NOT THE MARRYING KIND"

Public Enemy's narrative is an attempt at documentary realism that follows a real chronological "historical" time frame and tries to locate its protagonist in a real social space. The film starts in 1910 with the gangsters as kids growing up tough in an Irish ghetto behind the Chicago stockyards. The kids get involved with organized crime and with making a profit out of bootlegging in the Prohibition era. The social realism here constitutes an attempt to dramatize the role "environment" plays in the manufacturing of criminality. Like Little Caesar, Tommy Powers (James Cagney) wants to "make it" out of the ghetto. He too has an estranged relationship to official society.

The film opens with a disclaimer couched in the rhetoric of the officiating culture. In acquiescence to civic pressure and censorship, *Public Enemy* (like *Little Caesar* and *Scarface*) is prefaced by a warning that it seeks to "depict an environment," not "to glorify the gangster." It sought to explain him as a social problem that needed a solution. Such an imposed frame narrative was the product of negotiations with civic and moral interest groups who were seeking to establish federal censorship of Hollywood. Fears about Hollywood's contributions to the general breakdown of social mores that had been spawned in the 1920s took on even more intensity in the aftermath of the Crash. More significantly, if this fear was directed at issues of sex and nudity during the 1920s, it found a new target in the glorification of lawlessness in 1930. Here was the most obvious sign of Hollywood's capacity to facilitate social degeneration. Furthermore, to valorize gangsterdom and bootlegging in the context of the early Depression years could only intensify such objections.

To temper things, Hollywood introduced a form of self-censorship that suited, ultimately, its own interests. The gangster film disclaimer was the most obvious example of this. The rhetoric of civic responsibility comes to form a frame narrative, as it were, which attempts to impose a preferred reading on the rest of the text. Such an imposition, however, had to compete with a range of other meanings, including precisely a rejection of moral and civic norms. The view of the social order from the perspective of "the other side" is encoded from the first by the opening credits. These introduce us to the players replete with ghetto costumes and ethnic nicknames. This is followed by an establishing shot that moves us literally across the railroad tracks and locates the story in a space behind the city stockyards. This conflict between the moral disclaimer and the opening credits and shots fore-shadows the battle of opposing sociocultural perspectives that is definitive of the early 1930s gangster film.

A central dramatic interest in *Public Enemy* is the relationship between Tommy and his brother Mike. Their fraternal fallout is a reworking of the Cain and Abel story (a motif that would come to characterize a whole generation of gangster films, including one I discuss in detail later, 1934's *Manhattan Melodrama,* and, more famously, 1938's *Angels with Dirty Faces*). It is important to these films that the opposition of "good" brother/"bad" brother is not a mechanical one. While his brother is good, Tommy carries the burden of dramatic interest as the hero. It is not that Tommy is bad, but that he is rightly cynical about the ruling definitions of good behavior and good citizenry. From his position in the social order it makes no sense to stick one's neck out for God and Country. Mike enlists to fight in World War I; Tommy thinks he's crazy. Mike works a legitimate job as a ticket collector on the trams; Tommy sees this as self-exploitation. Mike attends night school in an attempt to improve his social and economic lot; Tommy's reaction is that Mike is only "learning how to be poor."

Tommy's solutions lie in departing from the prison of normative behavior by refusing to ape the host culture. He gains his power and agency in differentiating himself from his brother's way of seeing. When Prohibition is enforced, Tommy takes advantage of the situation. He joins ranks with a brewery owner, Mr. Leehman, who encodes sartorially and vocally the features and affectations of an assimilated ethnic (in this case a Jew, the name Leehman being loosely associated with one of New York's most famous wealthy Jewish families, Lehman) and who has "made it" and wants his name kept out of things.[18] The hypocrisy of this stance is underscored in Tommy's irreverent gestures toward the owner. Cagney lampoons the owner's limp handshake and ironically mimics Leehman's affected Anglo voice. In the process, the cowardice of having "others" do your dirty work is recast as the defining relation between ethnic poor and nativist elite.

As the aping-nativist absentee owner of one of the ghetto's major

18. I am grateful to Paula Rabinowitz for this insight into Leehman/Lehman as a signifier of Jewish success and assimilation.

employers, Leehman encodes the complicated power relations of ghetto culture. The hypocrisy of the situation is drawn to the surface as Prohibition forces Leehman into an unholy alliance with ethnic hoodlums of both Irish and Jewish stock (one of the gangsters is "Nails" Nathan, "born Samuel," who is particularly tough on Leehman's reticence to join ranks). Leehman's loss of agency is the lower-class ethnic's gain. The blurring of the boundary between the lowly ethnic and nativist "wannabe" is underscored in this scene as former employees suddenly find an opportunity to become partners, and the former owner suddenly finds himself in union with gangsters.

Earning big money through the bootlegging racket, Tommy undergoes a sartorial transformation and, like a good son, offers his mother a share of the profits. But his brother Mike won't have it. He won't take dirty "blood" money from a bootlegging gangster. This attitude, however, has already been exposed as hypocritical. In an earlier scene when Mike rejects an offering of bootleg beer because it is the product of blood and murder, Tommy responds, "You didn't get those medals holding hands with the Germans." Unlike his brother, Tommy sees that moral and civic rectitude will condemn him to (rather than lead him out of) cultural and economic poverty.

Rejected by his brother and consequently estranged from his mother, Tommy is set adrift in gangland. His antagonistic status as a social misfit grants him an attractive agency (his name is, after all, Tommy Powers) to do what he likes. Yet it damns him, too. Cut off (or liberated?) from the security of home (the ghetto-within-the-ghetto), Tommy gets caught in a sociopsychological limbo. He is unwilling to start a family of his own. As his sidekick partner states, "He's not the marrying kind." Furthermore, his sexuality becomes thematized as problematic. This is partly a symptom of Cagney's "man-boy" portrayal of Tommy.[19]

This image is enhanced in his awkward relationship with women. Tommy loathes domesticated "sappy" love (which prompts a now famous scene where he smacks a grapefruit into Mae Clarke's face). Yet when he does find someone embodying raunchy sex, Jean Harlow (playing Gwen Allen, a WASPish flapper "slumming it" with the ethnic gangster), she withholds sexual favors. In what constitutes an intriguing fusion of two troublesome film cycles for moral custodians

19. The description is Andrew Bergman's (*We're in the Money*, p. 11), drawing on Lincoln Kirsten's review of Cagney's appeal in 1932 (Kirsten, "James Cagney and the American Hero," *Hound and Horn*, April/June, 1932). He asserts: "Cagney is not a man, but neither is he a juvenile."

in 1931, *Public Enemy* played out the dual concerns of the "fallen woman" and the ethnic urban gangster.

Harlow's portrayal of a self-confident, sexually aware, male-manipulating woman was in keeping with a type central to a cycle of films that enjoyed success and controversy rivaling that of the gangster in the early 1930s. The gangster's anxieties about masculinity were compounded by the presence of confident (and candid) women prepared to use sex as a route to success. In *Public Enemy* it is Gwen who has the mobility to cross the sociocultural lines that have trapped Tommy. Not only is this mobility an attribute of her belonging to the old-stock community (something encoded in her highly mannered speech), but it is also an attribute of her "adult" understanding of sex. Tommy stands comparatively impotent in the face of this empowered womanhood, relating to Gwen more as a substitute for his estranged mother than as a lover.[20]

As such, Tommy becomes, like Tony Camonte (Scarface), a problem for the impetus of "classical" narrative economy. The latter normally seeks resolution in the bourgeois heterosexual couple. Gangster heroes, who are invariably torn between fraternal loyalty (the gang, the partner) and women, end up with confused sexual identities and ultimately resist accommodation to the convention of the happy ending. This is integral to their status as decentered heroes, as agents of narrative displacement. All of this augments the gangster's more obvious status as a social threat and as a representative of the cultural "other." His split identity as Irish and American is heightened by corresponding splits in love loyalties.

This having been said, such splitting does not ultimately serve to pathologize the gangster. That is, this decentering does not compromise the gangster's perspective. The gangster hero was a big box-office draw, and it is clear that far from disturbing audience empathy, the gangster's misfit status was key to his attraction. The gangster wanted out of the ghetto, and that meant out of the moral frame narrative too. His problematic subjectivity was the source of his power because it freed him from the fetters of normative codes. In the end,

---

20. Jean Harlow's best and probably most infamous embodiment of this "adult" type was as the star of *Red-Headed Woman* (1932). See Lea Jacobs' *Wages of Sin* for a full discussion of the moral censure of the fallen woman/gold-digging woman film during the period. *Public Enemy*'s fusion of gangster and fallen woman is a precursor of the recipe that defined the postwar gangster film where gangsters all too often are played for a patsy by gold-digging femmes fatales, such as in *The Killers* (1946).

out of this "environment" we don't get a criminal as such, but a new hero whose way of seeing corresponds more accurately to the problems of modern urban-American everyday life.

What made the early 1930s Hollywood gangster appealing, then, was not the degree to which he reflected the bad side of real gangsters. Rather, the recourse to realism was part of a concerted attempt to address the real social experiences and desires of a Depression- and Prohibition-era audience. Gangster movies stylized gangsterdom (albeit in the name of documentary realism) in order to bring Hollywood closer to its audience. And the proximity of the actor to experience helped ameliorate the gangster's dysfunctional status while intensifying his cathartic powers. The gangster's "problem" was revealed to be not only something shared but a source of inspiration. These films, for example, had a profound influence on 1930s fashion codes and even on the real underworld itself.[21] Showcases for imitators of Cagney and Robinson were held before screenings as part of publicity campaigns for their movies.[22] This extratextual information was bound to mediate audience expectations of who the gangster was: namely, a Hollywood star. Even if the films told a story in which the hero died, the star's extratextual life confirmed the gangster's ultimate ability to exceed even the conventions of death.

Cagney's huge star popularity, for example, testified to a narrative of success (a rise with no fall) that was sponsored by fanzines. As the ethnic urban-ghetto kid who really had "made it," Cagney's biography countered the attempts at this typology's containment on screen. Cagney's Hollywood fame (which constituted a parallel success narrative, as it were) conferred the immortality denied his screen gangster portrayals. It predetermined audience expectation and understanding of who the gangster was and helped the ethnic gangster gain cultural acceptance against the interests of civic pressure groups, a situation that boiled over in the case of the most notorious of the classic gangster films, *Scarface.*

21. See David E. Ruth, *Inventing the Public Enemy: The Gangster in American Culture, 1918–1934* (Chicago: University of Chicago Press, 1996), for a study of mass-media images of the criminal in shaping consumer trends.

22. The film industry's major trade journal *Motion Picture Herald* gave, among other things, advice to exhibitors on how to best promote film products. In the case of the early gangster cycle this often involved holding impersonation shows and awarding prizes to the best imitator. Such events, while self-serving for the studios, quite obviously intensified the rise of the talking gangster star to culture hero.

SCARFACE: "THE WORLD IS YOURS" (ONLY IF YOU CAN "TALK NICE")

To the extent that it is clearly based on the exploits of Al Capone (even including the St. Valentine's Day Massacre), we might call *Scarface* an attempt at documentary expressionism. But rather than pretend to execute an environmentalist (disinterested, objectivist, and historical realist) representation of the world of the criminal "other" (like *Public Enemy*), *Scarface* declares itself as a deliberately subjective and allegorical view of gangsterdom. The mise-en-scène reflects the distorted nature of Tony's subjectivity, and the film is marked quite literally by a cross-motif that signals not only death but the fact that the narrative itself is a manipulation/fabrication. Such expressionist devices exist in tension with the movie's representation of the objectively real escapades of Al Capone. Instead, a heightened realism is effected. This kind of aesthetic experimentation helps service a more general alienation or deracination effect in which Tony is constantly torn between possible identities.

Like *Little Caesar, Scarface*'s narrative is structured around a rise-and-fall motif. The mythology of capitalist opportunity and success is given distinctly public marking in the form of a travel company's neon billboard towering above the urban landscape that announces "The World Is Yours." All sections of the city can see this sign, but its meaning is precisely dependent on which section you come from. For the lower social echelons this sign is not simply a clichéd confirmation of some inevitable American truth; it is a reminder of deferred gratification. Tony, as a lower-class ethnic, no longer wants to be denied what the sign promises. Like both Rico and Tommy Powers, Tony's rise through the gang hierarchy is signaled by an improvement in his sartorial presence and living conditions. Again there is an excessive and ironic character to the gangster's attempt to ape the codes and graces of "society."

Tony buys silk shirts and tailored suits and smothers himself in jewelry. The "moll" he is pursuing, Poppy, remarks that his taste is "gaudy." Tony doesn't understand the term and simply agrees with her. We are invited to laugh at the gangster for his cultural poverty. This point of view, however, is given a twist. Poppy adds the comment that his jewelry and taste are also "effeminate." Once again the status of the gangster's heterosexual masculinity is questioned. Tony's problematic ethnic identity is compounded by his desire for the wrong love object. Just as Rico in *Little Caesar* is ascetic and intensely

Caught between old and new worlds, Tony Camonte (Paul Muni) experiences the rejection of his old-world mother as a prelude to his death at the hands of the defenders of "legitimate" America in *Scarface* (1932).

jealous of Olga (his partner's lover) and just as Tommy Powers in *Public Enemy* cannot make love to Gwen (Jean Harlow), Tony also cannot fit into the heterosexual economy. *Scarface*, building on its predecessors, takes the problem of the gangster's sexuality to a new level of intensity through the suggestion of incest. Tony makes the wrong object choice in falling for his own sister, Cesca (Ann Dvorak). Insanely jealous of the love his partner Guido (George Raft) feels for her, Tony kills him. These intimations of incest corroborate the gangster's problematic function in terms of "classical" narrative economy. The film cannot end with Tony and his sister's love confirmed. Having killed off George Raft, the "good" and "natural" lover, there is no hope of a "classical" resolution in the resanctification of the heterosexual couple.

This decentering of the normative (bourgeois) narrative trajectory is enhanced by strong messages about the gangster's cultural rootlessness. The figure of mother does not operate to secure generational anchoring. Tony is distanced from his mother. She doesn't trust him, seeing him as the "bad" modern seed corrupted by the desire for money. To Tony, "mother" represents the prison from which he wants to escape. Dressed up as an old-world gypsy, she encodes a traditional ethnic past as hopelessly anachronistic. Divorced from this identity Tony strives to conform to the terms of the host culture instead.

This discourse on "going legit" is deepened by the protagonist's avowed intent to pass as a member of the official culture. For Tony, "making it" involves elocution lessons and teaching his mob members to master the devices of modern communication. He doesn't just want cars, suits, and money. He wants a secretary, a telephone, and to be literate. He wants to master a whole range of officiating media. In the key scene where language is thematized, he tries to teach one of his partners how to answer the phone and take a message. This involves a range of protocol problems, not least of which are his partner cannot pronounce the word "secretary" and cannot write. Tony wants his secretary to "talk nice." However, his secretary ends up swearing at the phone and threatening to "smash" the caller's face in. While there is comic irony directed at the gangsters here, it dramatizes a crucial issue for all hyphenated Americans. Questions of literacy and elocution are understood as questions of power. Tony's desire to rid himself so completely of signs of his ethnicity (his vernacular markings) comes down to a matter of speech. And nowhere is this issue so marked in the film as in its added scene.

Scarface's producers came under pressure to add a scene featuring a moral diatribe by a press representative and moral custodians against the gangster. It was hoped that this would help temper the movie's encouragement of sympathy for such criminals. *Scarface* was prohibited from release until censors' demands were met. The theme of incest was problematic enough, but worse still the film seemed to condone Tony's behavior. The film simply glorified the gangster and offered no moral lesson. Structurally, this arose, as I have argued, from the problem of having a decentered hero as the primary figure for audience identification. The gangster was defined by his distinction from moral norms. This differentiation was underscored and made sympathetic by the reduction of the moral economy to a subplot in the form of Guido and Cesca's affair.

To rectify this, censors demanded that scenes be added to balance (compensate) the perspective. After protracted argument producer Howard Hughes gave way to the intervention, which involved not only adding scenes but cutting a major (and violent) action sequence. What resulted, however, was not a successful (re)moralization of the plot. Rather, for reasons I shall now adumbrate, this ideological interference became visible and audible as such. The major added scene occurs halfway through the film. It features the office of a newspaper publisher. This "official" mise-en-scène is populated by key figures from civic enforcement and pressure groups. The latter's cultural prejudice is marked first by accent and second by the content, style, and vocabulary of the spoken communication. These figures of official society deliver their moral diatribe about gangsterdom in distinctly Anglo tones.

Stylistically, the scene interrupts the film's general diegesis (which is not surprising since the film's director, Howard Hawks, refused to participate in the shooting of added scenes). The camera remains fixed and static, filming from a stable establishing-shot distance. The scene is brightly and flatly lit. All of this is entirely out of character with the rest of the film's use of extreme high- or low-camera angles and chiaroscuro low-key high-contrast lighting. In short, the rest of the film encodes an absolutely different kind of mood and subjectivity. The added scene with its pretence to an "objective" realism ends up appearing as heavy-handed aesthetic interference with the film's otherwise "expressionistic" mode. Put another way, the "addedness" of this scene is its most noticeable characteristic.

Most obviously, the objective gaze of the added scene is intended to underscore the "naturalness" of the scene's moralizing content. The whole scene at the level of voice and mise-en-scène, however, appears as a gross aberration. As an interruption in the film's stylistic consistency and narrative flow, the scene appears artificial and ideologically imposed. Because the film has already thematized the issue of language exclusion, the Anglo tones of the added scene are seen and heard to preach from an offscreen space. Simply put, the scene appears precisely to be a crude attempt to police the meaning of the film. Audiences did not pay to be preached at by civic interest groups. In this act of censorship the language of officialdom identifies its ideological allegiancies very clearly. The consequence of this could only have been to distance the audience from the moral point of view. Paradoxically, the only benefactor from this kind of censor intervention could have been the gangster himself.

As Richard Maltby points out, while this scene was added, others were cut—most notably a now celebrated extended action sequence that featured a violent car chase and the St. Valentine's Day Massacre.[23] Such cuts can be read as an attempt to literally "arrest" the subjective movement of the film, which is confirmed when the film cuts to the chief police detective's office before the segue to the newspaper office. Here the mise-en-scène assumes an objective cast, and the narrative montage and movement are suspended for preaching words. First, the chief detective gives a speech about the difference between the modern gangster and the traditional Western outlaw. In response to a minion's claim that the gangster is a "colorful character," he protests:

> Colorful? What color is a crawling louse!? Say listen, that's the attitude of too many morons in this country. They think these big hoodlums are some sort of demi-gods. What do they do about a guy like Camonte? They sentimentalize him. Romance. Make jokes about him. They had some excuse for glorifying our old Western bad men. They met in the middle of the street at high noon and waited for each other to draw. But these things sneak up and shoot a guy in the back and then run away.

There is then a fade to black (the only such fade in the film) and then a fade-in to the door of The Evening Record on which is stenciled "Mr. Garston—Publisher." From behind the door we hear the voices of the complaining civic interest groups: "Our groups are opposed to your policy, Mr. Garston. Your paper should be an influence against the gangster . . . you're glorifying him by giving him all this publicity." The publisher is sitting behind his desk ringed by representatives of various moral and civic interest groups. The publisher's authority is underscored not only by his central position within the

23. In the restored version of the print (from which most film scholars make their generalizations) the added scene's intrusion is even more overt. The added scene comes on the back of a completely different use of sound as a sophisticated device of narrative acceleration. Filmed from the perspective of a mobile camera and dolly shots, the scenes leading up to the added scene are set to the rhythm of car chases, police sirens, and machine guns. The scenes are subjectively marked by a pervasive cross-motif (the expressionistic sign of death) achieved through the mannered use of light, shadow, screens, and signposts. Richard Maltby makes the added and invaluable point that because of censorship the *Scarface* that contemporaneous audiences saw was very different from the restored version that genre theorists assume was exhibited. This fact has obvious repercussions for scholars interested in the reception of gangster films and in making generalizations about the ideological function of gangster films *en tout*. See Richard Maltby, "Tragic Heroes? Al Capone and the Spectacle of Criminality, 1947–1931," in *Screening the Past: The Sixth Australian History and Film Conference Papers*, ed. John Benson, Ken Berryman, and Wayne Levy (Melbourne: La Trobe University Press, 1995).

frame and this ring of chairs, but by the way all his responses seem aimed directly at the camera. His demagogic status is confirmed at a critical moment when he is given the blocking directive to stand up in the middle of the circle and deliver his speech top-down to the seated representatives. In defense of his newspaper he states that the papers aren't to blame, but the government:

> Instead of trying to hide the facts, get busy and see that laws are passed that'll do some good. . . . Pass a federal law that puts the gun in the same class as drugs and white slavery. Put teeth in the deportation act. These gangsters don't belong in this country. Half of them aren't even citizens.

Cut to a civic representative of ethnic (Italian) stock, replete with heavy accent, who says: "Thatsa true. They bring nothin' buta disgrace to my people." The blocking arrangement means that the ethnic has to "look up" at the Anglo publisher, visually underscoring his verbal deference. The scene ends with the publisher calling for the instigation of martial law.

The xenophobic proportions of this scene are tied to its aesthetic presentation as interference in the film's diegetic flow, its meanings marking themselves as top-down and artificially imposed. The verbal calls for "deportation" and "martial law" are bound to scenes that betray themselves as "time out" from the action but offer no pleasure in the process. Anti-immigrant sentiment is tied to the interests of a dominant Anglo culture that manifests itself as a policing agency that interferes directly with the pleasure of the narrative's unfolding, as well as interfering with the film's vernacular or street syntax. As such, the aesthetic discontinuity produced by the added scene only marks the opposition between gangsterdom and "official" society in a way that backfires on the interests of censorship.

THE GANGSTER'S DIALOGICAL PRINCIPLE

The talking gangster's desire is to turn the world over. This quest, while it is certainly violent, is framed by circumstances that lend it a degree of sanction. Most obviously, his activities are mitigated by the context of class and cultural subordination. The talking gangster is at war with a form of cultural apartheid. While he ultimately fails in his own attempt to win acceptance, his story bespeaks a need to counter established forms of intolerance.

This gangster is a champion of dialogue in a world grown weary by the impositions of what we might call a "monological" old-stock order. The latter, from its position of dominance, had always viewed the process of acculturation as one in which "others" learned their language. The talking gangster, in his attempt to follow this edict, brings with him a more tolerant ability to learn more than his own language. Ironically, he is punished for daring to try to pass for a member of legitimate society. This contradiction not only makes the gangster a tragic hero, but it draws attention to fundamental differences between the narrow perspective of the cultural elite and the more heterogeneous view of "others."

The history of race and ethnic representation in America has been characterized by an Anglo-white dominant culture seeking both ways to define itself and to legitimate its right to dominance. Essential to this task has always been the manufacture of images of otherness. Such manufacturing has created an awkward interdependence between subordinate and dominant cultures. The paradox is that while the dominant order seeks to render its challengers invisible and inaudible, it requires for its very constitution the continual production of representations of and dialogue with the "other."[24]

As was the case with early images of the ethnic urban lower classes, the American "other half" was reduced to the status of a degrading object, which reinforced the authority and superiority of the onlooking culture. Yet, the speaking gangster exploited this subordination against the grain. Little Caesar, Tommy Powers, and Tony Camonte all expose the collusion between language and social power, and gain our sympathy in the process.

The early 1930s ethnic gangster is excessively star- rather than

---

24. As one of the foremost theoreticians of language and power, Mikhail Bakhtin, has asserted, there is an "absolute aesthetic need of man for the other." The sense of the self as complete can only be achieved through someone else's gaze:

> In life we do this at every moment: we appraise ourselves from the point of view of others, we attempt to understand the transgredient moments of our very consciousness and to take them into account through the other . . . ; in a word, constantly and intensely, we oversee and apprehend the reflections of our life in the plane of consciousness of other men.

That is, at a larger political level, the concept of otherness has often been co-opted to the self-defining needs of a dominant order—an order that depends for its dominance on repressing the dialogical truth of its own constitution—in representing itself "monologically." Tzvetan Todorov, *Mikhail Bakhtin: The Dialogical Principle*, trans. Wlad Godzich (Minneapolis: University of Minnesota Press, 1984), p. 94.

genre-dependent. He gains his life antagonistically to known conventions (the gangster hero gains his distinction through differentiation from his silent prototype, from his sidekick-partner, and from his ethnic "roots"). The Tony/Guido (Muni/Raft) partner conflict in *Scarface*, for example, dramatized precisely this departure from previous incarnations. George Raft's role as Guido, the suave dandy, constitutes a holdover from older pre-Crash gangster stereotypes. He harks back to a period in the early and mid-twenties when movie gangsters were conceived of as dapper rogue sophisticates, with names like "The Peacock," "Dapper Dan," and "Fancy Charlie." [25] This residual convention, however, is sidelined as the domain of a minor character whose chivalrous affection for a woman (the conventional "love story") becomes a subplot to the main interest (Tony's incestuous desires). The biographical proximity of Cagney, Robinson, and Muni to their roles helped these gangsters speak less as characters in someone else's story than as authors of their own tales. And their dynamic vernacular performances contest successfully the continual attempts at their moral containment. The authoritarian impositions of censorship only serve to increase our perception of the gangster as victim of persecution.

This is underscored in the problem of killing off the gangster. All three gangster films discussed here have tacked-on endings that are glaringly discontinuous with the narrative trajectory. *Little Caesar* features the protagonist falling victim not to an empowered rival but to the machinations of an old lady. After falling on hard times, he ends up being drawn out of hiding to be gunned down by the police. He dies asking the rhetorical question, "Mother of Mercy, is this the end of Rico?" Of course not, this is just the beginning for Robinson's gangster portrayals and the beginning of a major cycle. *Public Enemy*'s Tommy Powers is forced to die even after he has had his redemption scene. This excessive imposition of the gangster death convention is ironically colored in his body's deliverence to his mother's door wrapped up like an Egyptian mummy. (And, as we all know, to the Egyptians death only prefigured an eternal afterlife—in this case an afterlife involving more gangster roles for Cagney.) The ending of *Scarface* features our protagonist suddenly turning yellow, which is entirely out of character with Tony's general portrayal as someone

---

25. See Eugene Rosow's discussion of this representation of gangster manhood, *Born to Lose: The Gangster Film in America* (New York: Oxford University Press, 1978), pp. 103–4.

cool in the face of fire. As such, these films all turn the gangster's death into a question rather than a solution. Audiences were left to ponder why he had to die. Ironically, the improbable character of these gangsters' deaths revealed how attempts to establish closure and reestablish the moral order were seen to be acts of violence and censure.

The talking gangster's resistance to closure (and being silenced) was reinforced by his identity problems, especially those encoded in his voice. The gangster's broken grammar and colorful accent was key to changing the relation between "other" and authorial culture. As I have shown, central to all these films' dramatic interest is a dialogue between the dominant culture's version of the truth and the "other's." What is preserved in the gangster's vernacular voice is then the difference between these cultural identities. Thus, to empathize with the gangster's point of view was to identify with the "not I," with something split and incomplete.[26]

This is an important part of the way ruling perceptual norms were turned over by the talking gangster. Their challenge extends to contesting the organizing principles of genre, which seem misapplied when imposed on the films discussed here. These so-called classics are notable not as symptoms of a genre per se than as anomalies. What censors feared about these gangster films was precisely that they were emblematic of a larger disorganizing and destructive force: not a genre, but a criminal "cycle." This cycle was one in which the fiction of nativism's "natural" right to cultural dominance was exposed not from outside but from within. Ultimately, all the gangster asks is that the culture deliver on its own declared democratic principles. Not only this, but the demand is vocalized from within the machinery of cultural administration—that is, from within the realm of mass cinema.

The framing conditions for a fuller understanding of the particular significance the gangster film held for contemporaneous audiences and censors are complex. As I hope to have demonstrated, sound's introduction to the gangster film was an essential element in lending

---

26. At various levels (speech, narrative structure) these films resist a "dialectics of nature" (which seeks to resolve conflict and difference in the name of some ultimate wholeness), and propose instead a "dialogics of culture" in which a plurality of competing ways of seeing co-exist without fusing. Here I am drawing from Todorov's analysis of Bakhtin's differentiation between dialectic (with its tendency to monologically merge and move toward unity) and dialogue (with its heterogeneous tendency to preserve multiplicity, divisions, and distinctions). *Mikhail Bakhtin*, p. 104.

sanction to the perspective of the ethnic cultural "other" on the American screen. The contentious meaning of these early 1930s gangster films was contingent not only on the time they appeared (on the back of the Wall Street Crash and in the last years of Prohibition) and the medium in which they appeared (the mass cinema), but on the irony of how sound helped expose the cultural prejudice involved in their own censure by civic and moral pressure groups. It is only in this way that we can begin to make proper sense of why external censors, and then internal ones, would force a moratorium on Hollywood's gangster film production.

While the gangster films I have discussed here enjoyed their rise to popularity and controversy in the waning years of Prohibition, the question remains as to what the gangster film would come to signify after the Volstead Act's repeal, and a new political order (the New Deal) had taken positive hold of the nation's destiny. How, in these changed conditions, the cycle could continue to invoke the ire of external monitoring authorities (even after it had been subject to powerful censure) is the subject of my discussion of *Manhattan Melodrama* in the next chapter.

3

Manhattan Melodrama's "Art of the Weak"

Tactics of Survival and Dissent in the Post-Prohibition Gangster Film

*M*anhattan *Melodrama* was released in 1934, a crucial point of transformation for the gangster film (it was the year before Will Hays declared a moratorium on gangster film production) and for the culture at large. Prohibition had been repealed and the New Deal administration had made its first decisive moves in countering the problems of the Depression. Following a censorship resolution in 1931, the talking gangster film had undergone a degree of transition but was still providing compelling stories for ever-interested audiences.[1]

On screen, James Cagney and Capone look-alike Edward G. Robinson had not yet switched sides from gangster heroes in 1930 and 1931 to "G-men" (government men, federal agents) in 1935 and 1936.[2] Offscreen, Al Capone was imprisoned in 1931, Dillinger was

1. An Association of Motion Picture Producers resolution in October 1931 had placed stricter limits on the representation of gangsterdom. Subsequent to this, direct depictions of gangsters' involvement in bootlegging and armed conflict with the police were outlawed. While this certainly affected the scope and style of gangster action, it did not halt production. And as *Manhattan Melodrama* exemplifies, gangster narratives still relayed provocative signals to their audiences. See Richard Maltby's discussion of this resolution in "Tragic Heroes? Al Capone and the Spectacle of Criminality, 1947–1931," in *Screening the Past: The Sixth Australian History and Film Conference Papers,* ed. John Benson, Ken Berryman, and Wayne Levy (Melbourne: La Trobe University Press, 1995).

2. Cagney and Robinson switched sides, as it were, in *G-Men* (1935) and *Bullets or Ballots* (1936), respectively. Paul Muni (eponymous hero of *Scarface*) also underwent an intriguing "conversion" in *Bordertown* (1935), a thinly disguised gangster film, in which he stars as a Chi-

shot dead in 1934. This complicated interweaving of popular culture and social realities, the confusion of real and fictionalized gangster narratives, is exemplified in the case of Dillinger's death. He was shot down by G-men as he left Chicago's Biograph cinema having just seen *Manhattan Melodrama*.

While this last event points indirectly to the fact that the lives of real gangsters often seemed modeled on those of their cinematic representations, it also provokes questions about the role the gangster film played in historical mediation, especially in the context of Prohibition repeal and the onset of the New Deal. Central to *Manhattan Melodrama*'s interest is precisely the discussion of the gangster's continuing sociocultural relevance in a post-Prohibition, New Deal world. What makes *Manhattan Melodrama* such an intriguing entry in the 1930s gangster cycle is the fact that it historically frames the gangster's impending death in terms of the rise of Franklin Delano Roosevelt and the kind of political order he encoded. One of the film's two protagonists, Jim Wade, is an ersatz Roosevelt, whose career mimics the president's as he rises to become governor of New York (Roosevelt's post before becoming president), marrying a woman named Eleanor en route. Such elements would not have been missed by contemporaneous audiences and are vital to understanding more fully what this narrative signified.

The film was directed by W. S. Van Dyke and starred William Powell (Jim Wade) and Clark Gable (Blackie Gallagher) as two foster brothers and Myrna Loy (Eleanor) as their mutual love interest. The film contains two parallel narratives, Jim's and Blackie's, whose paths collide to create irresolvable tensions. Jim's story is that of the Lower East Side kid "making it" on dominant culture's terms as a lawyer, D.A., and governor, representing the interests of the state. Contrastingly, Blackie's story is that of the Lower East Side kid "making it" as part of "the common people" (his words). He must become a gangster in order to do this, something that sets up the film's central contradiction. In spite of setting up this legitimate/illegitimate opposition, the film insists on showing how both foster brothers have integrity and are "on the level." This is achieved primarily through the figure of Eleanor, who oscillates between narratives, falling in and out of love with both (eventually marrying Jim and becoming an incarnation of

---

cano and former hoodlum who tries to make it as a lawyer representing the interests of *el barrio* in Los Angeles. (I discuss this film briefly in the next chapter.)

Eleanor Roosevelt), acting as an internal (within the text) witness to the two men's good characters.[3] Even as the split narrative reflects the impact of censorship (the demand for including compensating moral narratives in gangster plots), it also dramatizes how *Manhattan Melodrama* concerns itself, just like other "classic" gangster films, with disputing the border that separates legitimate from illegitimate cultures and histories.[4]

Jim's world is the formal one, wrapped in the stiff and uncompromising language of the law, which is above society (separated from it). His position is sanctioned as the *only* position from which society can be judged (i.e., he speaks *for* society, not *with* it: a "monological" position, as I have previously described it). As "Mr. Law and Order" (as Blackie calls him) Jim must remain clean of corruption, which, as the film ironically demonstrates, is to remain outside humanity (Jim ends up condemning his own brother to death in the name of the law). By contrast, Blackie's world is rooted in the vernacular, in the popular realm. He admires his brother for having "class written all over him," while he casts himself as "common." The film tries hard to side with Jim. It has to work hard to make Jim's defense of law and order both credible and attractive. By comparison, Blackie's common man nature probably resonated much more with contemporaneous audience experience and the realities of the social realm. Sporting events loom large in *Manhattan Melodrama* as scenes of community mixing. The boxing ring, Belmont racetrack, and the ice-hockey stadium (Madison Square Garden) are marked as places where a collective identity is reinforced in opposition to the isolation Jim experiences. While Blackie lives in this peopled space of interrelations and dialogue, Jim segregates himself behind a law book as a student, in an office as a D.A., delivering monologues in court, alone as the governor.

Exemplary of this tension is the exchange between Blackie and Jim at the Dempsey-Firpo boxing match (the latter emblematic once again of the film's collapsing of boundaries between fiction and reality).

---

3. There is work to be done on Eleanor Roosevelt's symbolizing of empowered womanhood in the context of Depression culture. It is interesting to note that in *Manhattan Melodrama* she comes from the popular, antiestablishment, sexually expressive underworld, all of which lends her a degree of metaphorical power as someone who can speak to the culture of the oppressed.

4. As I have highlighted in the previous chapter, the most famous of the early talking gangster films such as *Scarface*, *Little Caesar* and *Public Enemy* are marked by linguistic games that examine the ethnic attempt to "ape" the master culture. Questions of how to speak, eat, and dress "properly" reveal both the extent to which the ethnic urban lower class is distanced from the mores and codes of "official" culture, and the extent to which those codes are precisely exclusionary and distancing.

Cain or Abel? Jim Wade (William Powell), district attorney at work and play: a man alone and above the people defending the impersonal world of law in *Manhattan Melodrama* (1934).

This chance encounter leads Blackie to ask good-humoredly, "What are you doing up here with all these common people?" Jim asks if Blackie knows some underworld figure who is putting pressure on him as D.A. to relax prosecution against him. Blackie says he knows the man in question but warns Jim "not to play ball with those grafters." He continues, "You're the one guy who's on the level and everybody knows it. And that's what pays off in the end, and you're not gonna let those grafters shove ya behind the eight ball." But the praise only makes sense because it is a code that Blackie also represents, the subterfuge being that in order to be honest within the law you have to adhere to a code embodied in many ways by the strengths of the gangster, a man by definition *outside* the law. Ironically, Jim requires Blackie's endorsement before audiences can empathize with him.

Blackie's fraternal loyalties mean that he is Jim's most fanatical supporter and admirer. And when a gangster holds such an opinion

Cain or Abel? Blackie Gallagher (Clark Gable), gangster at work through play: defending a personal code of justice in *Manhattan Melodrama*.

of a D.A., it is bound to confuse the order of things. Blackie kills the underworld figure who threatens to destroy Jim's chances at being elected governor. When Blackie is eventually brought to trial, Jim successfully prosecutes the case without ever knowing Blackie's motivations for murder. As the death sentence is delivered, the audience knows what Jim does not—that Blackie has sacrificed himself for his brother. What pays off is some notion of integrity, something that both men possess but only one must die for. The boundaries between law and outlaw are further jeopardized by the status and popularity of Gable.

Although Gable had been cast in earlier MGM talking pictures as a gangster-brute, by 1934 he had built on this image to consolidate a growing reputation as a romantic lead who embodied virility and sex appeal. Casting Gable as Blackie Gallagher in 1934 augmented the gangster-type's popular appeal and meant he could not be reduced to

Cain or Abel? Blackie Gallagher (Clark Gable), gangster at play: a man of the people (part of the sporting crowd) in *Manhattan Melodrama*.

being a two-dimensional "bad" guy.[5] Equally problematic is the fact that Powell's character stands, in some instances, for values not dissimilar to those associated with the "classic" gangster.

Previous gangster heroes like Little Caesar (Edward G. Robinson's role in the film of the same name) or Tommy Powers (Cagney's role in *Public Enemy*) shared the same puritan asceticism as Governor Jim Wade. Eleanor asks Jim "Why be a freak? Why not give in like the others do? 'Dip in the gravy' as Blackie says?" Jim explains later on in the Cotton Club that he's "not sure. Maybe ideals have ceased to exist.

5. Before coming to Hollywood, Gable had played romantic leads on stage. His movie career started in the silent era when he was limited to being an extra. In the early talking era he got his break as the villain in a William Boyd Western, *The Painted Desert* (1931). Suitably impressed, MGM signed him and cast him initially in supporting roles as a tough guy or gangster. His route to playing more rewarding romantic lead roles was soon secured by his performance as a gangster with sex appeal (the object of Norma Shearer's desires) in *A Free Soul* (1931).

Maybe they're old and outmoded, like oil lamps and horsecarts. . . . But they're mine and I'm stuck with them." These words echo W. R. Burnett's thoughts on his creation, the gangster Little Caesar, whom he saw as an anachronistic vestige of republican idealism, caught in the midst of consumerist hedonism.[6]

Such a view exists in tension with the gangster's ability to "make it" in the illicit sphere of popular culture, through bootlegging, the numbers racket, nightclubs, and gambling. It is in this new urban leisure realm that the gangster thrives. Both Little Caesar and Tommy Powers want the deportment consumerism will allow: smart suits, champagne (although the gangster himself might not drink, he can indulge others), limousines, jewelry, and so on. However, it is less the money itself than the kind of individualism and enterprise that the popular realm enables that the gangster is interested in.

To this extent, the Cain and Abel metaphor that *Manhattan Melodrama* uses is a way of splitting the traits formerly gathered in one character. This is also a means to defusing the omnipotence and mythological power of the gangster. *Manhattan Melodrama*, however, does not cast Blackie as evil and Jim as good (as I have argued, this Manichean arrangement is confounded by fraternal loyalty and Gable's "intertextual" romantic star persona). If anything emerges as evil, it is the impersonal and rarefied condition of the law (in this film, living up to the law means condemning one's brother). At another level, Jim Wade's ambitions to be governor tie his defense of the law to the interests of the state. His intolerance of the gangster can be clearly allied to the New Deal's insistence on the need to regulate and control the laissez-faire features of capitalism encoded in the illegal activities of the gangster-entrepreneur. The sympathetic treatment granted Blackie testifies to an ambivalent attitude about what state control really signifies (Socialism? National Socialism?). Consequently, the film could be interpreted as a plea for autonomy in the face of too much government. Such a reading would not be out of line either with MGM's conservative leadership (something discussed later on) or with the industry's general objection to federal intrusion on its capitalist (trust) practices.

Having said this, the fact remains that it is ridiculously reductive

6. W. R. Burnett, "The Outsider," in *Backstory: Interviews with Screenwriters of Hollywood's Golden Age,* ed. Pat McGilligan (Berkeley and Los Angeles: University of California Press, 1986), pp. 49–84.

to understand the gangster film as an unambiguous celebration of the freedom of unregulated capitalism. If anything, the gangster's corrupt capitalist practices reveal the exclusionary features of the Alger myth of success. As most gangster films demonstrate, they are less about reinforcing ideals of capitalist success than about the rules and prejudices that bar specific social groups from access to power. *Manhattan Melodrama* is no exception, its bifurcated narrative devoting attention precisely to the prejudicial issues of ethnicity and class that dictate its characters' separate fates. Indeed, the film continues the sonic battle between official voices and the vernacular that is central to the so-called classic talking gangster films, *Little Caesar*, *Public Enemy*, and *Scarface*. The upper-class formality William Powell's "Anglo" voice encodes (corroborated by his use of stilted legal language as a lawyer) exists in dramatic tension with Clark Gable's use of a Lower East Side accent and street vernacular (replete with sports metaphors).

The film starts out in 1904, with a party aboard the steamship General Slocum. Men are dressed in straw boaters and blazers and sport large mustaches, while kids run around making graffiti and drawing likenesses. Both the drawings and the men they depict (who have distinctively haughty Anglo voices) bear marked resemblance to "Teddy" Roosevelt. Following a fire on board, the childhood Blackie (played by Mickey Rooney, an obvious signifier of Irishness) and Jim find themselves rescued by an Italian Catholic priest (Father Joe) but orphaned. Though not brothers, Blackie and Jim are both adopted by a benevolent Jew ("old man" Rosen) who has lost his son Morris in the same accident. When Mr. Rosen asks Blackie and Jim if they want to become his kids, Blackie retorts, "I'm not a Jew and neither is Jim." Rosen replies, "Catholic, Protestant, Jew? What does it matter now?" But it does matter. For ethnic marking is connected to a disempowered lower-class status, something dramatized violently one scene later.

Atop a soap box in Blackie and Jim's Lower East Side neighborhood stands Trotsky. He tells a crowd, which includes Rosen, to "forget the promises of Debs and Bryan," that "the revolution is inevitable," and that it is time for America's working class to act. He prophetically predicts a revolution in Russia, one that will offer an example to Americans. Rosen interjects that he is Russian too, but that in Russia he was persecuted and that is why he came to America. He does not see the need of revolution in a land where everyone has what he calls "opportunity." A man standing next to him accuses him of being a "capitalist stool pigeon" and unceremoniously hits him. Rather than leave us with an affirmative (and reactionary) endorsement of capitalism, the film takes a twist. Violence breaks out, and the police rush in and club people indiscriminately, killing Rosen.[7] Blackie sees this, tells Jim, and swears that some day he will "get even with those cops." The narrative choices are thus set up. Blackie chooses a life of crime, Jim a career in the law.

In light of Mr. Rosen's death at the hands of the police, both choices are informed by an understanding that the law is inadequate and prejudicial. Jim lives to make the law fair, Blackie to buck it. While neither turns into a revolutionary, both do provide histories that undermine an important American creed: namely, the notion that capitalist "opportunity" alone, not government policy, constitutes the most viable solution to inequality.[8]

In giving some space to a fuller representation of law and order (in the character of Jim and his extratextual referent Franklin Roosevelt), *Manhattan Melodrama* departs from its gangster progenitors *Little Caesar, Public Enemy,* and *Scarface.* While the latter provide one protagonist for primary audience identification, *Manhattan Melodrama* provides two. But the differences between gangsterdom and the law, between the excesses of popular culture (gambling, sports, booze, sexually emancipated women) and the asceticism of the sanctity of the state (marriage, sobriety, hard work) represented in Blackie and Jim, are compromised throughout, first by the fraternal love between Jim and Blackie and second by the content of their lives. Blackie's compassion and his accessibility lie in his connection to a world of lived relations. In Jim's rarefied and impersonal realm it is much harder to create sympathy. In fact, the film requires Blackie constantly to tell Jim (and, by extension, the audience) that what Jim is doing is "on the

7. The violence of this death may have been underscored by the casting of George Sidney in the Rosen role. He was most closely associated on screen with his comic role as Nathan Cohen in the popular *Cohens and Kellys* Jewish-Irish comedy series. Audiences used to seeing Sidney in this more jovial part, as recently as late 1933 (*The Cohens and Kellys in Trouble*), may have been doubly disturbed to see him the object of a riot killing!

8. It could be argued that this scene is precisely symptomatic of the way Hollywood reduces and dissolves political difference into a question of personal difference, an example of co-optation and defusing of dissidence. However, my point here is that given this tendency in Hollywood narrative, this film does something else with it. It uses the personalization of conflict (that system of "primary identification" with character rather than political issues) in an aleatory way. While it is clear that the political choices offered do not include something as radical as socialism, neither do they include other more conventional (jingoistic) forms of political allegiance. *Manhattan Melodrama*'s adverse relationship to an array of authorities is typical of Hollywood's gangster film.

level." In effect, the law needs to be sanctioned by the gangster to gain our sympathy. While this works toward giving back the law its legitimacy, this dynamic is ultimately undermined by the need for the gangster to speak in the law's favor.[9]

While the fiction demands some move to formal resolution of narrative (which here entails killing the gangster and reaffirming the need for law), this is hardly satisfactory. In fact, *Manhattan Melodrama* has an open ending: Jim resigns from the governorship of New York, announcing that he has found himself inadequate to the law (having at the last minute striven to commute Blackie's death sentence). As he puts it, he gave in to "emotions." Once again this undermines any sympathy we might have for the law, for we see it as a dehumanizing structure somehow divorced from life. William Powell and Myrna Loy walk out of *Manhattan Melodrama* uncertain of what they will do but with their integrity intact. However, as the narrative has shown, they neither can live up to the law nor down to the popular realm. With this in mind it seems more than coincidence that these two characters under the supervision of *Manhattan Melodrama*'s director, W. S. Van Dyke, should reemerge in *The Thin Man* (MGM, 1934) just three months later as detectives, who by definition are half gangster, half cop.[10] Furthermore, the open ending created by Jim's resignation from the governorship has interesting ramifications with regard to Roosevelt and the New Deal.

As an ersatz Roosevelt, Jim, in deciding to resign, casts a certain doubt on the possibilities of government. This uneasy position with regard to the future is probably a product of two things. First, this film was released in 1934, at a time when the New Deal apparatus was

9. The same might be said of Cagney's and Robinson's reincarnations as federal agents and cops. In the case of *G-Men* for Cagney, and *Bullets or Ballots* for Robinson, it is really their former status as gangsters that lends them legitimacy as cops. In *Bullets or Ballots*, Robinson plays a cop who goes "underground" to penetrate the mob (something made more tenable because of Little Caesar's legacy). Equally, in *G-Men* it is Cagney's upbringing in the underworld (both within the text and intertextually) that allows him to be effective after he joins the FBI. We could add to this list the case of Humphrey Bogart, who played countless "bad guy" gangster roles in the 1930s, and yet emerged in the early 1940s as box-office gold as a romantic lead. His role as Rick in *Casablanca* (1942) is underscored by a shady past. This past refers not simply to his past within the film (his pre-war affair with Ingrid Bergman) but to his 1930s bad-guy image. This image lends Bogart extratextual help in providing his role a mysterious ambivalence (something apparently necessary to make him an effective lead for a 1940s audience).

10. Powell and Loy play out *The Thin Man* series as members of the old-stock upper class. Yet it is essential to these films that these protagonists bear an awkward relationship to their class, resenting its formal codes and often involved in cases that expose the seamy underside of the rich and famous.

in its infancy. Second (and concomitantly), this gangster film was made by MGM. Unlike the primary producer of the cycle, Warner Brothers, MGM had not put its weight behind the Roosevelt administration. Warners had started to make films in which the president was very much the star and in which the New Deal was cast as a way out of Depression (something best evinced in Warner Brother's 1930s musicals, such as *Forty-Second Street* in 1933). By contrast, MGM was probably the most reactionary of the major studios and, as I articulated earlier, was disinclined to endorse an administration that wanted to place fetters on laissez-faire capitalism and to increase the powers of the state.

The history of *Manhattan Melodrama*'s production reveals some intriguing facts in this regard. Although MGM financially backed and released the film, it was produced by Cosmopolitan, William Hearst's producing unit. The media tycoon was to become renowned for his politically conservative views, yet in 1932 he had supported Roosevelt rather than Hoover in the presidential elections.[11] This placed a strain on the relationship of Louis B. Mayer (the staunch Republican head of MGM) and Hearst, which might be reflected in the film's undecided view of Governor Wade's (Roosevelt's) future. The degree, however, to which either Mayer's or Hearst's views were imposed on the film remains a matter of speculation. There were, however, alterations to the script (which was based on an original story by Arthur Caesar entitled "Three Men"), the most drastic of which changed the film's ending. Originally, Governor Wade was meant to retract his offer of resignation in acquiescence to public demand. In his recollection of his work as *Manhattan Melodrama*'s co-screenwriter (along with Oliver H. P. Garrett), Joseph Mankiewicz doesn't attribute this alteration to any interventions by producers.[12]

In fact, despite Mankiewicz's liberal reputation as a founder-member of the Screenwriters' Guild and as the man who later dethroned the conservative anti-Communist Cecil B. De Mille as chair of the Screen Directors' Guild (following a showdown over the taking

11. Gary Carey, *All the Stars in Heaven: The Story of Louis B. Mayer and M.G.M.* (London: Robson Books, 1982), p. 193.

12. Kenneth L. Geist, *Pictures Will Talk: The Life and Films of Joseph L. Mankiewicz* (New York: Charles Scribner's Sons, 1978), pp. 64–69. Mankiewicz does note that W. S. Van Dyke directed only the first half of the film and was replaced by Jack Conway, who is uncredited. Mankiewicz argues this change was not the product of a disagreement over political views. Rather, it was characteristic of producer David O. Selznick, who was out "to destroy the power and concept of the director as the one who makes the film." Geist, p. 68.

of loyalty oaths at the height of the Red Scare), it is just as logical to attribute the script's alteration to his own reservations about political solutions to the Depression.

In 1934, the year of the film's release, Mankiewicz, unlike many of his fellow Screenwriters' Guild members, refused to endorse the candidacy of Upton Sinclair for governor of California (something that adds a further twist to *Manhattan Melodrama*'s ending). Moreover, Mankiewicz seemed quite happy to write anti-Sinclair radio scripts on behalf of the "Stop Sinclair" campaign funded by Louis B. Mayer. When Sinclair won the Democratic party's nomination as a candidate on a platform of what were seen to be utopian socialist ideals, the reactionary forces in California went into a panic, especially the film studio bosses. While Mankiewicz maintained that his prime objection to Sinclair was that "he wanted to raise taxes," this hardly explains his voluntary collusion with Mayer.[13]

Yet, if *Manhattan Melodrama* was indeed affected by the mix of political dispositions associated with its makers and funders (especially the views of those distrustful of the New Deal), this did not lead to a polemically reactionary conclusion. If anything, these politically sceptical forces probably only aided the film's uncommitted conclusion. The film suspends judgment on both the old order and the new, and casts doubt on the efficacy of the law.

In a general sense, *Manhattan Melodrama* tries to maintain that the law remains some incontestable metanarrative to which all of society must ultimately adhere, but it has great difficulty telling us this. A contemporaneous history intervenes, as does the cultural capital invested in the gangster. This is most clear in Jim's summing-up speech in prosecuting Blackie for the murder of two hoods:

> For years the men and women of the country tolerated racketeers and murderers. Because of their own hatred of Prohibition they felt in sympathy with those who broke a law they felt to be oppressive. Crime and criminals became popular. Killers became heroes. But gentlemen, Prohibition has gone, and these gangsters and killers who came with it, must go with it.

Jim's speech acknowledges the link between popular dissent and the gangster. Not only this, it admonishes Prohibition as an oppressive law. Jim attempts to reverse the relationship, then, of the law to oppression and the gangster to emancipation. In the end, the subterfuge

---

13. Nancy Lynn Schwartz, *The Hollywood Writers' Wars* (New York: Alfred Knopf, 1972), p. 36.

remains that for Jim to be successful in this translation of cultural loyalties, he must gain the active cooperation and blessing of the gangster.[14]

In a ridiculous plot twist, Blackie chooses to sacrifice himself for Jim (a fact Jim never realizes until Eleanor tells him at the end). Thus, while Jim believes he (as the law) is the ultimate authority, the audience (through the device of dramatic irony) and Blackie know how this status is under duress. Blackie controls his own fate, and through the power lent him from his previous incarnations, both real and fictional, we realize he is the only one who can write his own coda. His martyrdom might point to how Hollywood ultimately serves the interests of the status quo, but it concomitantly points to how much work hegemony must perform in the process.

This film openly addresses the costs and stakes of erasing the gangster. At one level, as previous gangster films have demonstrated, the gangster typically encodes individualist / laissez-faire capitalist principles. The gangster narrative clearly pits an individualist against the impersonal forces of the state (law and police). Cast this way, the gangster-protagonist's inevitable death at the hands of the state signifies not only that the pre–Wall Street Crash "Algerist" idealism has passed, but that we should be suspicious about what is replacing it. This message, however, is only part of the story.

Like its predecessors, *Manhattan Melodrama* goes to great pains to tie the gangster to a vernacular urban community (as I have already highlighted, Blackie is constantly featured in scenes of collective gathering such as the Dempsey-Firpo boxing match and ice-hockey and racing stadiums). Considered in this light, the gangster's death is testament less to the historical disappearance of Algerism than to the social distance between the rarefied bookish order the law services and the lived realm of human relations the gangster embodies.

As a powerful "chronotope"[15] the gangster combined (not without

14. This is not an unusual way to resolve the gangster dilemma. *Angels with Dirty Faces* (1938) uses a similar device. The priest (Pat O'Brien) uses fraternal loyalites to persuade the gangster (James Cagney) to fake being a coward when he goes to the chair, in order to destroy the Dead End Kids' identification with him. Here, however, in a post-Code gangster film it is less clear whether the gangster genuinely makes a sacrifice. In the end we are left unsure whether he "faked" cowardice or indeed "cracked."

15. Chronotope: "Literally, 'time-space.' A unit of analysis for studying texts according to the ratio and nature of the temporal and spatial categories represented. The distinctiveness of this concept as opposed to most other uses of time and space in literary analysis lies in the fact that neither category is privileged; they are utterly interdependent. The chronotope is an optic

contradiction) two different American "outsiders." On the one hand, he alluded to a folklore tradition of rebellion (through legends of frontier banditry, and the American revolutionary soldier campaigning against the oppressions of colonial British rule). Gangsters such as Dillinger and Bonnie and Clyde, who operated in the landscape of the midwest (the context for their activities being the dust bowl, farm foreclosures, and bank failures), could be subsumed by this tradition. On the other hand, and to more inflammatory effect, the gangster drew on and gave dramatic shape, as we have seen, to the experiences of the newer Americans who made up the nation's ethnic urban lower class. In this era of cultural flux this coalition of "outlaw" and culturally marginal urban identities lent to the gangster's multiple appeal. At the same time, the gangster's popularity in this period set the wheels of censorship enforcement into frantic motion.

    Manhattan Melodrama was a product of a Hollywood more attuned to negotiating the censorship pressures exerted on the gangster film by moral, religious, and cultural agencies. Even as a more "standardized" product, however, the film's commercial success depended on invoking themes and issues associated with its more infamous predecessors. It calls into being the "other" America of the urban ethnic underworld while reminding us, on one hand, that this world's hero, the gangster, is essentially honest and, on the other, that we cannot trust the police and the sanctioned social order they defend. Central to *Manhattan Melodrama* is its strong admonishment of Prohibition as a form of social oppression. To this extent, the film is characteristic of preceding gangster films in that it addresses and supports an audience with what we could call a "counter-hegemonic" disposition. At the same time, as a film that tries to kill off the gangster (to make him "history," as it were), *Manhattan Melodrama* demonstrates the awkward (if not impossible) problem of negotiating censorship, of trying to repress the gangster's more volatile features and make him safe for consumption. In fact, the files of the Production Code Administration (PCA) reveal that the film was indeed deemed controversial by censors. Because *Manhattan Melodrama* was a pre-enforcement film, MGM had to apply for a PCA certificate of approval for the film's rerelease in 1937. Significantly, on this occasion the censors insisted that

---

for reading texts as x-rays of the forces at work in the culture system from which they spring." Caryl Emerson and Michael Holquist, "Glossary," in Mikhail Bakhtin, *The Dialogic Imagination,* trans. Caryl Emerson and Michael Holquist, ed. Michael Holquist (Austin: University of Texas Press, 1981), p. 425.

the speeches about revolution and the police battle with political riot-ers should be cut.

Originally, the censors' main attention in 1934 fell not on the film's obvious but general reflection of the political trajectory of Franklin Roosevelt, but on whether the film cut too close to the bone in terms of certain incumbent political figures in the state of New York such as Fiorello La Guardia and Charles S. Whitney, who might have seen their political careers directly criticized in the plot. La Guardia would have been uncomfortable with the suggestion that his rise to power in New York had been supported by gangsterdom. Whitney would have seen the film as a reflection of how his own political success had been predicated on his successful prosecution of gangland bosses during his tenure as district attorney. Symptomatically, the Code was invested in protecting the industry from those who had power to intervene in film release and distribution, especially in such important box-office states as New York.[16]

The early 1930s gangster film is significant, then, to the extent that it was (along with the sexually controversial "fallen woman" film) the studio system's *enfant terrible*. That is, from within a space of osten-sibly limited aesthetic and co-opted ideological value, these films were consistently (and definitively) able to pose awkward questions about the terms and conditions of living in urban America. While Holly-wood may never have offered itself as a weapon of agitprop, its gang-ster products displayed the extent to which it could foster what Michel de Certeau has termed a "tactical" resistance to power. Defin-ing tactics as "an art of the weak,"[17] he stresses that the "space of the tactic is the space of the other," and as such it "must play on and with the terrain imposed on it and organized by the law of a foreign power . . . it is a maneuver 'within the enemy's field of vision.'"[18]

Compared to this, a "strategy" plans and views the adversary "as a whole" and from a specific locus exterior to the adversary.[19] The fact that Hollywood lacks this "adversarial exteriority" to the status quo is what critics of mass culture (right and left) have generally lamented. For example, launching his critique precisely from a strategic posi-tion, T. W. Adorno concluded that the popular film industry was a

16. MPAA/PCA File *Manhattan Melodrama*, Margaret Herrick Library, Academy for Mo-tion Picture Arts and Sciences, Los Angeles.

17. Michel de Certeau, *The Practice of Everyday Life*, trans. Steven Rendall (Berkeley and Los Angeles: University of California Press, 1984), p. 37.

18. Ibid.

19. Ibid., p. 36.

weapon of mass deception. Because it was part of (and not exterior to) consumerism's "culture industry," Hollywood could never be a vehicle for "real" opposition (i.e., "strategic" use).[20] While such a notion of political opposition has been necessary for the sustenance of political alternatives to a given order (e.g., for party politics, grass-roots organization), it has often led to easy dismissals of, or complete blindness to, "the art of the weak" in their less "strategic" struggles against inequity.

As Warren Susman pointed out in the case of Dwight MacDonald, the leftist intellectualism of 1930s America was strikingly elitist. Its broadside attack on mass culture was rooted in the idea that popular culture "debased" certain cultural values of which the intellectual was a privileged guardian. Radicals in this sense ended up defending a tradition against what were perceived to be the obliterating forces of the present. Consequently, the definition of the radical intellectual in America became more "humanist" than ideological. One's task was to guard certain fundamental universal truths about human nature, not to advance the specifics of a class-based social analysis whose telos was the achievement of an egalitarian society.[21]

While it is important to recognize that Hollywood sought to colonize the experiences of the ethnic urban poor and turn them to a profit in the gangster film, this does not in itself account for the gangster cycle's mass appeal or its wider meanings for contemporaneous audiences. Most obviously, the gangster's popularity was attributed to a generally positive audience disposition toward the gangster. And this existed, as contemporaneous censors protested, in clear contradiction to the film industry's stated defense in making gangster films: that they were conveying the message that "crime didn't pay."

Through this close textual analysis of *Manhattan Melodrama*, I hope to have demonstrated the tendentious ways a gangster film continued to relay doubts about the terms of social and cultural transformation in 1930s America, even after censorship and historical change ought to have diminished its impact. Specifically, I have attended to how the gangster narrative sets up internal choices for the audience that are aided by alluding to collective memories of an oppressive state

20. Max Horkheimer and Theodor W. Adorno, "The Culture Industry," in *Dialectic of Enlightenment*, trans. John Cumming (New York: Continuum, 1972) (original ed., *Dialektik der Aufklärung*, 1944).

21. Warren Susman, "The Nature of American Conservatism," in his *Culture as History: The Transformation of American Society in the Twentieth Century* (New York: Pantheon, 1984) pp. 57–74.

and a sympathetic rebel. As Paul Smith has maintained, a reader "is not simply the actor who follows ideological scripts, but is also an agent who reads them in order to insert him/herself into them—or not."[22] And nowhere is this sense of interpretive choice more clearly revealed and encouraged than in the 1930s gangster film, which consistently undermined the preferred reading of social order and reality. In the historically specific context of the Depression (where capitalism's legitimation apparatus was least effective but most desperately insistent), audiences/readers were in a particularly powerful position to read normative culture "against the grain." And *Manhattan Melodrama* further exemplifies how the early 1930s gangster film, in particular, was a definitively *open* text that took as its very theme the friction between authorized and vernacular versions of American life and history. As such, these films, at both the level of narrative structure and in terms of theme, confronted audiences with dilemmas that were only exacerbated rather than resolved in the gangster's eventual death. Such features illustrate how the gangster film had a propensity to feed rather than placate crisis. And it is only in this context that we can come to a fuller understanding of why the production of this commercially successful film cycle would eventually be subjected to a moratorium in 1935.

22. Paul Smith, *Discerning the Subject* (Minneapolis: University of Minnesota Press, 1988), p. xxxiv.

4 Ganging Up against the Gangster

Censorship, the Movies, and Cultural Transformation, 1915–1935

The 1930s have been characterized as the Golden Decade of formula and genre consolidation. During this period the Western, the Musical, and the Gangster film were given their basic form and thematic content. It was a time when, in spite of economic retrenchment, the big studios consolidated their power, controlling all parts of the industry from production to distribution to exhibition. This stabilization of the studios' economic monopolies was directly related to the standardization of the industry's products, as the studios sought ways to guarantee that films would reach their markets in a time of economic depression. Key to this was the instigation of sound and, in this context, I have discussed the controversial way the talking gangsters rose to popularity in the early 1930s as ethnic urban vernacular heroes who addressed the frustrations and inequities of the times.

Gangster films such as *Little Caesar* (1930), *Public Enemy* (1931), *Scarface* (1932), and *Manhattan Melodrama* (1934) all featured cultural conflicts dramatized as language battles between street talk and official discourse. The gangster film's play with language was only heightened by censorship intrusion because the impositions of censors were aurally marked as Anglophone and nativist. The anglicized sound of moral authority in the gangster film was linked to the first campaigns against the gangster movie, especially its talking incarnations of 1930 to 1931, since these protests were led primarily by those defending white Anglo-Saxon Protestant interests. Objections to the gangster film continued even after concessions were made. In 1935

Will Hays declared a moratorium on all gangster film production to demonstrate that the Production Code Administration (PCA), formed a year earlier, actually had teeth, and to appease those accusing the industry of exploiting the contemporaneous public fascination with Dillinger.[1]

Central to the gangster film's appeal was its criticism of Prohibition, which was in effect from January 16, 1920, until its repeal on December 5, 1933. As gangster films such as *Public Enemy* and *Manhattan Melodrama* dramatized, Prohibition was widely resented across classes, and the gangster emerged as an object of popular fascination and empathy to the extent that, as a bootlegger, he resisted a very unpopular piece of legislation. More significantly, Prohibition, while it indeed affected a broad spectrum of American life, was a censorship act that in many ways extended earlier temperance goals to control the leisure practices of the urban ethnic lower class. Although Prohibition had direct consequences for collective activities centered on alcohol (which included working men's clubs and dance halls), its power did not extend as effectively to the movies. If anything, the movies' attention to "speak-easy" culture in gangster films could only anger advocates of temperance.[2]

The debates over the gangster film in the early 1930s were built on a wider ongoing discussion of the cultural place and function of mass entertainment. An examination of censorship is invaluable in defining the stakes involved in suppressing gangster film production. The almost coincidental demand for an enforceable written Code (1930) and the concerted attempt to prohibit the production of gangster films (first in 1931, and again in 1935) have to be understood in terms of a history of contest and collaboration between moral guardians and the

1. See Richard Maltby's various discussions of this first phase of gangster prohibition from 1930 to 1932, in "The Production Code and the Hays Office," in *The Grand Design: Hollywood as a Modern Business Enterprise*, ed. Tino Balio (Berkeley and Los Angeles: University of California Press, 1995), especially pp. 50–52; "A Short and Dangerous Life: The Gangster Film, 1930–1932," in *Before the Codes 2: The Gateway to Hays*, ed. Giuliana Muscio (Venice: Fabri Editori, 1991), pp. 159–74; "Tragic Heroes? Al Capone and the Spectacle of Criminality, 1947–1931," in *Screening the Past: The Sixth Australian History and Film Conference Papers*, ed. John Benson, Ken Berryman, and Wayne Levy (Melbourne: La Trobe University Press, 1995).

2. For an in-depth analysis of the attempt to regulate the recreational practices of the ethnic working class (especially the function of the saloon), see Roy Rosenzweig, *Eight Hours for What We Will: Workers and Leisure in an Industrial City, 1870–1920* (Cambridge: Cambridge University Press, 1983). For a study of the very different investments of Protestants and Catholics in the temperance movement, see Joseph R. Gusfield, *Symbolic Crusade: Status Politics and the American Temperance Movement* (Urbana: University of Illinois Press, 1963).

movie industry. At stake for censors was the definition of American-ness (determining both moral and national values). The gangster film presented a dual threat to both nativist-Protestant and Catholic moral interests. This crime cycle, as part of the institution of moviegoing, embodied the encroachment of consumer capitalism on republican idealist and orthodox Catholic conceptions of American life. These conceptions were rooted in a particular notion of the public sphere, a public sphere under pressure not only from industrial and con-sumer capitalism but from the pluralistic versions of American expe-rience that capitalist culture's leisure industry brought to the center of American life.

POLICING THE PUBLIC SPHERE: THE DEMISE OF THE OFFICIAL AMERICAN STORY

Any attempt to understand censorship of a mass cultural form like film has to be linked to the history of struggle over representation and collective memory. That is, censorship is symptomatic of a need to control the generation of meaning at a mass level, a policing of the "official" historical account that organizes the way a culture under-stands its relationship to the past. This we might recast as the control of collective memory, a memory that authorizes the continuity of a particular history and identity. In many ways such memory policing is actually about the reification of memory by securing static univer-sals that resist the corruption of time and transformation. Memory is turned into nostalgia the more the present seems to defy the idealized past. Memory loses its ability to transform the present and either be-comes a lament for something lost (a jeremiad) or motivates a desire to make the present a logical outcome of the past (by imposing a nar-rative of continuity over actual discontinuities).

According to historian David W. Noble, this is something that char-acterizes American intellectual historians' rationalizations of the rise of industrial capitalism.[3] In his examinations of the twists and turns Charles Beard made in working out the relation of republican idealism to capitalism, a conflict emerges between a desired public sphere of participatory parity peopled by yeoman farmers and artisans, and the

---

3. David W. Noble, *The End of American History: Democracy, Capitalism and the Metaphor of Two Worlds in Anglo-Saxon Historical Writing, 1880–1980* (Minneapolis: University of Min-nesota Press, 1985).

actualities of industrial capital organizing the society's infrastructure around cities and factories staffed by unskilled alienated labor. For Beard the preservation of an original "history" of a society of artisans and yeomen farmers becomes a guarantee of the continuation of a public sphere (at least as an imagined counterpoint to certain features and stages of capitalism). For nativists, America's identity depended on the fulfillment of the original promise that the country offered the first settlers.

By stark contrast, the movies (rooted as they were in the leisure practices of the urban ethnic lower class) were perceived to be symptomatic of the corrosive power of consumerism and modernization. As Lary May emphasizes, movies between 1910 and 1929 "dramatized the central theme of the age, the change from Victorian to modern life." [4] This break with the past was represented not only in the content of the movies but in the cultural practice of moviegoing itself. Films moved from the margins of American life (the ghetto theater) to its center (Main Street) as sanctioned entertainment for all classes. Censorship of Hollywood was an attempt, then, not simply at moral regulation. It was part of an effort to contain the larger threat of transformation such a practice posed to the sociocultural order and the nation's collective memory. If censors were interested in policing film, the film industry, to continue to reach the multiple and more ambivalent interests of its audiences, had to negotiate the impositions of a moral order. The problem that informs any discussion of censorship and film is rooted in this conflict, which is best embodied in one of the cycles that attracted most attention by moral agents: the gangster film. As Gregory Black has detailed in his intimate study of the Production Code Administration, *Hollywood Censored,* "more than any other genre, the gangster film created problems for [industry censors] in reconciling the code with drama." [5]

CENSORSHIP: AN EMBATTLED WASP HEGEMONY

In 1915 the Supreme Court handed down a major decision that excluded motion pictures from protection by the First Amendment right to free speech. In a landmark case the Mutual Film Corporation

---

4. Lary May, *Screening Out the Past: The Birth of Mass Culture and the Motion Picture Industry* (Chicago: University of Chicago Press, 1983).

5. Gregory D. Black, *Hollywood Censored: Morality Codes, Catholics, and the Movies* (Cambridge: Cambridge University Press, 1994). See especially "Beer, Blood, and Politics," pp. 107–48.

lost its appeal against the Ohio State Censorship Board, a board that had prohibited the exhibition of D. W. Griffith's *Birth of a Nation* in that state.

Mutual's motivation in fighting Ohio's censure of the film was rooted less in an altruistic interest in "freedom of speech" than in the more material interests of economic profit. State and local municipal censorship boards interfered with the film industry's distribution apparatus, demanding costly reworkings and alterations of films deemed censurable. This interference was costly in terms of time, delaying carefully planned release days and rupturing the industry's fundamental marketing strategies. As the Court described it, Mutual's grievance was grounded in interruptions of exhibition: "It is the custom of the business, observed by all manufacturers, that a subject shall be released or published in all theaters on the same day, which is known as release day, and the age or novelty of the film depends upon the proximity of the day of exhibition to such release day."[6] The Court took the position that "the exhibition of moving pictures is a business, pure and simple, originated and conducted for profit" and in this sense "not to be regarded . . . as part of the press of the country, or as organs of public opinion."[7] Movies were seen as commodities without an organizing moral purpose, which made them "capable of evil." In regarding movies as commodities rather than "organs of public opinion," film was removed from the guarantees of the First Amendment. Consequently, this decision mobilized a call for the moral administration of film products.

The National Board of Review, founded in 1908, came to the defense of the industry in the face of the Mutual decision.[8] An attempt was made to reach consensus on submission to moral standards within the film industry. The National Board was devised to aid the self-regulation of the industry; it circulated bulletins to collaborators and volunteers nationwide to persuade outside moral agencies to trust and believe in the movie manufacturers' intentions to produce "decent"

6. "Mutual Film Corp. v. Industrial Commission of Ohio" (United States Supreme Court, 1915) in *The Movies in Our Midst: Documents in the Cultural History of Film in America*, ed. Gerald Mast (Chicago: University of Chicago Press, 1982), p. 138.

7. Ibid., p. 142.

8. The National Board of Review was forged in 1908 out of a coalition of New York civic reform interests (the New York Board of Motion Picture Censorship) headed by John Collier and Charles Sprague Smith. It was renamed as the National Board of Censorship in 1909, and renamed once again in 1915 as the National Board of Review (to temper the stigma of being a censoring body).

and socially responsible products. The National Board had no legal powers, but it did have "contractual relations with the producers, distributors, or showmen of films."⁹ The National Board argued that no absolute standard on moral norms could be arrived at, given the heterogeneous makeup of the audience, and that setting up and enforcing a national standard would be highly impractical. Thus the Board articulated a position opposing the impositions of local censorship as well as some monolithic national standard. Moral standards were deemed negotiable, not given, and the Board set itself up as the negotiating agent. In this sense, the Board was still arguing for some form of standardization but one clearly in the interests of the film industry.

In 1915 the Board published a twenty-three-page booklet of formal standards designed primarily for filmmakers.¹⁰ In many ways this publication is the first version of the balancing act and rhetorical masquerade that would come to characterize the relations between outside moral agencies and the interests of the film industry for the next twenty years. The booklet was designed to show that the industry was aware of its influential position in society, and was prepared to police itself in the name of "responsible freedom," a catchall phrase that hid an economic imperative ("give the audience what it wants") behind a call for moral responsibility ("tell the audience what it should want"). Here were the seeds of the dilemma the Production Code Administration would have to face some twenty years later.

Without the guarantee of the First Amendment the industry became susceptible to a range of challenges for which it had to find increasingly sophisticated responses. Censors wanted to regulate the public mind top-down, and they saw the movies as a vehicle for this purpose. At the same time they were disturbed by the way the movies that were popular did not cohere with their moral agenda. In the interests of profit the industry had to find a way of satisfying both parties, to offset on one hand the impression that movies were a "moral holiday,"¹¹ and to satisfy on the other the audience demand precisely to be freed from dominant moral paradigms. This fear of the "lower" strata's emancipation from the moral code opened up a realm of new

9. John Collier, "Censorship and the National Board" (1915), in *The Movies in Our Midst,* p. 144.

10. Ibid., p. 147.

11. J. R. Rutland, "State Censorship of Motion Pictures" (1923), in *The Movies in Our Midst,* p. 187.

fears. Questions of moral purpose developed into raging debates over questions of Americanness that were laced with xenophobia. It is this combining of a moral agenda with defining an American identity that would come to expose the cultural stakes involved in policing the gangster film after the Wall Street Crash of 1929.

In 1923 the issue of state censorship was documented by J. R. Rutland as part of the *Reference Shelf Series*, a series devoted to collecting and gathering published debates on "timely topics." [12] The demand for a state censor was seen as an empowered corrective to "a strong public demand for salacious pictures" at a time when predominantly Progressive Protestant reform organizations such as the Women's Christian Temperance Union and the Daughters of the American Revolution (DAR) were desperately trying to protect a "traditionalist" notion of virtuous Americanism from disappearing before the corrupting forces of modernization.[13] The legalization of state censorship would be a means of fixing and preserving a uniform moral and cultural standard, a security against "insidious influences patent in unregulated exhibition of motion pictures." [14] Those campaigning for state censorship stated more specifically that such censure "would protect poorer sections against low, vulgar, or worthless films." [15]

This last comment was symptomatic of a pervasive view of moviegoing as a subaltern practice. The movies were born in the "poorer sections" of urban America as part of the working class's own entertainment practices, and as an essential means of expression in an environment where the underclass was otherwise culturally disenfranchised. The call for censorship in this sense was an attempt to protect the lower class from itself. The movies were clearly a vehicle

12. Ibid., p. 183.

13. Ibid., p. 186. Rutland's observations about the necessity for censorship in the 1920s coalesce with what Gary Gerstle has described as a fight to sustain "traditionalist Americanism" against competing and newer versions of Americanism. Traditionalist Americanism (what I have termed "old-stock nativism") is "rooted in nostalgia for the mythic, simpler, and more virtuous past when the essence of America was to be found on the farm and in the small town . . . and when all Americans were white, Anglo-Saxon, and Protestant." See Gary Gerstle, *Working Class Americanism: The Politics of Labor in a Textile City, 1914–1960* (Cambridge: Cambridge University Press, 1989), pp. 11–12. Gregory Black highlights how the case against the movies came to galvanize Protestant lobby groups in the 1920s, such as Reverend William H. Short's Motion Picture Research Council and Canon William Shaefe Chase's Federal Motion Picture Council. *Hollywood Censored*, p. 33.

14. Rutland, "State Censorship of Motion Pictures," p. 186.

15. Ibid.

to be feared by dominant interest groups inasmuch as they could disseminate new ideas of Americanness (or "un-American" versions of America) not simply in terms of class but in terms of ethnicity.

The same call for censorship also argued that state monitoring of the film industry "would eliminate from films suggestions that might give foreigners false ideas about our manners and morals." [16] An "us" versus "them" paradigm was set up whereby "hyphenated Americans" were understood to be in need of assimilation to "our manners and morals." As Rutland's report emphasizes, "many of our films shown abroad have given foreigners false ideas about our ideas and morals," and, more significantly, "immigrants get warped ideas of American social standards" as a result.[17] State censorship was deemed "in harmony with American ideas and ideals." [18] In this way, the ideological policing of morality betrays itself as predicated on the need to enforce a consensus on what is decent and compatible with some ruling definition of Americanness.

In a similar call for censorship in 1921, Dr. A. T. Poffenberger had this to say about the motion picture industry:

> As an agent of publicity, with its immense daily audience of young people, it has great possibilities for creating and developing in theme a true spirit of Americanism, a respect for law and social order which are recognized as the essentials for a democracy. Rightly used, the motion picture is indeed one of the most powerful educational forces of the twentieth century. Its possible influence in the Americanization of our foreign population, through a medium which shall be intelligible to all, regardless of race, is scarcely yet realized. But wrongly used and not carefully guarded, it might easily become a training ground for anti-Americanism, immorality and disregard for law. . . . We have therefore . . . to meet an emergency, to begin in time to make this truly public school the kind of educational force that it should be.[19]

If the demand for censorship can be read as a move to steward public consciousness, it also constituted cultural acknowledgment of the huge central place motion pictures occupied in American life. In this regard the Rutland pamphlet of 1923 points to other reasons for the Code's development, namely to wrest control of censorship from external stewards and to ensure that the movie industry conducted

16. Ibid.
17. Ibid.
18. Ibid., p. 187.
19. Dr. A. T. Poffenberger, "Motion Pictures and Crime" (1921), in *The Movies in Our Midst*, p. 202.

its own policing. The arguments against federal or state censorship included this statement: "No universal, absolute standard of morals and good taste can be formulated."[20] To support this claim, those against state censorship appealed to cultural differentiation—that is, acknowledged the diverse audiences for the film industry's products. Such an acknowledgment is significant to the extent that it recognizes no definitive American community, celebrating diversity instead:

> The conception of what is immoral, indecent, or not in good taste varies with the individual, social group, or in accordance with one's experience, education and environment.
>   a. Pictures of bathing girls, of dancing in short skirts, etc., would be received differently in different communities.
>   b. Although Schnitzler's "Anatol" on the stage or in the pictures would excite little adverse comment in Paris or in Vienna, it would be considered unfit in many an American community.[21]

This catalog of negative responses to censorship included such comments as "No state board can meet absolutely all community conditions," comments that led to an appeal to "local opinion" as "the best judge of the fitness of local amusements."[22] By leaving things up to "churches, clubs, parents and good citizens" to "enforce the standards of taste and morals,"[23] the industry sought to endorse the National Board of Review. Rather than issuing blanket terms for censorship, the Board could help "local opinion" ("churches and educational organizations") select from the industry's products the most "suitable" amusement for its community.

The censorship debate of 1923 reveals a growing cultural crisis over popular culture's ability to transgress the dominant moral and racial codification of American society. This debate anticipates the more virulent contest over the early 1930s gangster cycle wherein the film industry, much to the consternation of censorship agencies, addressed social themes deemed incompatible with "their" America. A combination of anxieties coalesced around film production in the 1920s: fear of foreigners (during a period of declared American isolationism), of immigrant cultures, and of the lower-class mob (all brought on by the staffing of America's industries with poor southern and eastern European labor); fear of working-class leisure practices, especially

20. Rutland, "State Censorship of Motion Pictures," p. 189.
21. Ibid., pp. 189–90.
22. Ibid., pp. 190–91.
23. Ibid., p. 191.

bars (these offered a space for ethnic working-class collective behaviors separate from the rationalizing power of the workplace), a fear that played no small part in fueling the move to Prohibition; and fear of the popular power of the visual to demonstrate something otherwise concealed in written or "official" discourse. All these fears were to come to a head around the early 1930s gangster film.

In the name of self-regulation, and in a move to legitimate "giving the public what it wanted" (a rhetorical masking of profit motive), the National Board of Review argued in 1921 against legal state censorship on the basis of the Constitution. Censorship would be "an invasion of constitutional rights" to the extent that it would exert "power over channels of public information" and impose some absolute standard of morals and good taste on the "conglomerate mixture of opinions and standards" that make up the public. Censorship could be "perverted for political reasons" and would refuse to acknowledge the heterogeneity of public opinion.[24] As such, the National Board concluded that the only basis for censorship rested with the public, not small interest groups.

However, these small interest groups had other ideas. Dr. Poffenberger argued:

> The old notion is outworn that it is necessary "to give the public what they want." It is the function of an educational medium and an entertainment medium also, to give the public what they should have, in order that they may learn to want it. The function of education is to create as well as satisfy wants.[25]

To help offset this image of a socially irresponsible movie industry, the National Association of the Motion Picture Industry (NAMPI) published in 1921 its "Thirteen Points," a series of guiding "codes." In the following year, NAMPI was dissolved and was then replaced by a more cohesive trade association, the Motion Picture Producers and Distributors of America (MPPDA). It was felt that the industry needed a more credible face, and this face came in the form of Will Hays, chair of the Republican National Committee and one time Postmaster General in President Harding's cabinet.

In an attempt to mediate moral demands in the industry's favor, Hays acknowledged the cultural significance of movies, stating that "even as we serve the leisure hours of the people with right diversion

24. National Board of Review, "State Censorship of Motion Pictures" (1921), in *The Movies in Our Midst*, pp. 191–94.

25. Poffenberger, "Motion Pictures and Crime," p. 204.

so do we rivet the girders of society."[26] To alleviate the worries of Poffenberger and other moralizers, Hays implored the film industry to build "an institution to exert an influence for good . . . upon our national life."[27] The epitome of republican "virtue," Hays leaned heavily on the notion of a responsible public in tandem with internal regulation within the industry to resolve the clash between moral stewards and motion picture makers. He was particularly attracted to the idea of an industry code "as a specific commercial antidote against agitation."[28] Taking the original "Thirteen Points" as "Moral Resolve I," Hays was to oversee the updating of this code on two occasions— Moral Resolve II came in 1927 as a list of "Don'ts and Be Carefuls,"[29] a list that in turn became the basis of the Production Code itself (Moral Resolve III) in 1930.

CATHOLIC INVOLVEMENT IN POLICING THE PUBLIC SPHERE: AN EMERGENT AMERICAN STORY

I have argued so far that demands for censorship were in part an attempt to secure the continuity of a residual Anglo-Saxon Protestant definition of Americanness in the face of sociocultural upheavals brought on by demographic and economic change. And certainly the industry's appointment of Will Hays, a conservative teetotaling Presbyterian mason from the American heartland (Indiana), was designed to ameliorate WASP fears. This "figurative Puritan in Babylon," as Gregory Black describes him, was, however, only a partial success in allaying the pressures of external moral interference on the film industry.[30] By 1929 the mainly Protestant antimovie lobby had seen through the various ruses of the studios and renewed its demand for federal censorship and legislation against block-booking. The latter was deemed an affront to fair business practice because it forced exhibitors wishing to select a particular feature film for their theaters to buy an additional block of films as a condition of purchase. Moreover, it forced exhibitors to take and exhibit material that they might otherwise have rejected on moral grounds.

26. Will H. Hays, "The Motion Picture Industry" (1923), in *The Movies in Our Midst,* p. 206.

27. Ibid.

28. Ibid., p. 213.

29. Motion Picture Producers and Distributors of America, "The Don'ts and Be Carefuls" (October 1927), in *The Movies in Our Midst,* pp. 213–14.

30. Black, *Hollywood Censored,* p. 31.

To counteract this pressure, two prominent Catholics ventured a solution. The first was Martin Quigley, a Catholic layman who published the movie industry's most powerful trade journal, *Motion Picture Herald;* the other was Father Daniel Lord, a professor of dramatics at St. Louis University, editor of a religious magazine entitled *The Queen's Work,* which devoted much of its space to ethical analysis of the movies, and a leading member of the Catholic Legion of Decency. What they proposed was a workable formula that would not attack the principle of block-booking, and whose stringency and endorsement by the Catholic Legion of Decency would offset the move for federal regulation.

The Catholic church had not been at the forefront of movie censorship demands until the late 1920s. Its emergent interest in the moral control of Hollywood by the end of the decade has to be understood in the context of a decline in Protestant moral hegemony. The Catholic leadership's role in drafting the Production Code represented an extension of a mandate to protect the faith. By comparison, Protestant involvement, while concerned with issues of faith, was also, and necessarily, focused on "Americanization." Privileging themselves as the "authentic" Americans, Protestants leaned on a traditionalist notion of "virtu" against which they had to fight off the corrosive features of capital. To be consistent with a truly "American" history it was essential to resist those elements of capitalist organization that pulled the culture away from the provincial small-town civic society ideal that nativists espoused. This idealized public sphere was built on the rejection of old-world feudalism, emphasizing a society of yeomen who operated and participated in society with parity. Some elements of this ideal were consonant with Catholicism, but not on the basis that they were exclusively American; rather, they were the conditions that guaranteed the domination of Christian moral standards.

Historian Richard M. Linkh has highlighted that the Catholic community of the Depression was rooted in two different traditions and reacted to socioeconomic disaster in two different ways.[31] Out of these traditions arose the primary agent of Catholic action, the Catholic Legion of Decency, to exert its influence on the movie industry. Catholic leaders were primarily concerned about what the experience of coming to America would do to their congregation. They feared what was called "leakage," whereby congregations would be

---

31. Richard M. Linkh, *American Catholicism and European Immigrants, 1900–1924* (New York: Center for Migration Studies, 1975).

lost to the secular attractions of capitalism (among which were the movies).

"Old" Catholics, those from northern Europe (with the notable and obvious exception of the Irish), had come across the Atlantic in pursuit of ideals generally commensurate with Protestant republican idealism. The nativist public sphere of civic virtue peopled by artisans and yeomen farmers was perceived as an extension of Catholic moral standards and community ideals. With the influx of southern and eastern European labor to staff an industrializing America, however, Catholics began to find their interests increasingly separated from and at odds with those of the nativists. This development lent sanction to the older resentments of the Irish-American Catholic constituency, which was the first to cluster in the cities and which had traditionally harbored a strong animosity toward Anglo-Protestantism in light of the terrible legacy of British colonialism.

The "new" immigrant was an unskilled laborer who came, not for reasons of idealism, but to make money. Many Italian and Slavic workers, for example, came not to settle but with the intention to return to the old country. Just as significantly, the "new" immigrant did not settle in the American wilderness but in the city. This new immigrant was neither an artisan nor a yeoman but was from the poor exploited European peasantry. Lured by the prospects of escaping economic destitution, this underprivileged group came to staff America's industries.

The ethnic urban lower class was perceived by Protestant culture to be a threat to Americanism to the extent that it was seen to be symptomatic of international capitalism's penetration of American exclusivity. The nativist attack on Catholics of the 1890s was fed by the cacophony of vernacular voices sharing Catholic orthodoxy, congregating in the nation's urban centers, and working in complicity with industrialization. As a consequence, in the years preceding World War I Catholic leadership was forced to deal both with the problem of its community's minority status and the demand to "Americanize" by anti-Catholic bigots. Catholic leadership had always seen its task as keeper of the faith, and Americanization was often understood as contradictory to this task. Americanization meant a lapse into irreligiosity, a rejection of clerical authority, and an emphasis on private rather than collective faith.

Linkh maintains that Italian Americans were the most symptomatic of this tendency. As a result, the Italian-American Catholic was attacked on several sides, both by nativist hatred and Catholic

"mission." In addition, of all the "new" immigrants Italians constituted the lowest rung on the socioeconomic ladder. Given the way
gangster melodramas were often centered on aspects of Italian-American experience, it is perhaps no wonder that Catholic moral agencies
would come to single out the gangster film for censorship.

The jingoism fueled by World War I only made matters worse as
Catholic immigrants were subjected to nativist calls for "accelerated"
Americanization. This demanded the dropping of hyphenated identities (e.g., the breakup of ethnic ghettos and their languages). Arguing that to be American was, by definition, to come from somewhere
else, Catholics responded with a notion of gradual Americanization.
Just as the "original" settlers had journeyed from another shore, so
too had the more recent Americans. The idea that America was a plural society had to be defended more rigorously in the light of wartime
patriotism.

To help ward off nativist attacks and offset Americanization, the
National Catholic Welfare Conference, under the auspices of the Social Action Department, set up a Civic Education Bureau designed to
teach the fundamentals of citizenship. This was done with specific
attention to the immigrant's heritage, highlighting the plural makeup
of American culture by pointing to the fact that America was made
up of multiple ethnic contributions. A theory of the melting pot was
advanced as a way to resist assimilation to a WASP order. According
to this theory, a new American identity would be forged out of the
mixture of contributions. This, of course, went against the static uni-
versals of Protestant nativism and posited instead a history subject
to constant alteration depending on who was added to the pot. For
Catholics this was fine since their primary goal remained one not of
defining a particular national identity but a universal monolithic
Catholic identity. The prerequisite to membership in the nation was
that one obeyed the Catholic moral paradigm. In essence, Catholics
felt that the nativist should also be subject to the melting pot.

The particular interest in policing Hollywood's products grew out
of this paradigm, one clearly different than that shaping WASP interests. A significant catalyst to Catholic involvement in drafting and
enforcing the Production Code sprang from Pope Pius XI's demand
for "Catholic Action" in May 1931. This was a way to turn socioeconomic institutions of American life into Christian channels.[32]

---

32. David J. O'Brien, *American Catholics and Social Reform: The New Deal Years* (New
York: Oxford University Press, 1968), p. 183.

Catholic Action demanded "the participation of the laity in the apostolate of the hierarchy." Where the society was "threatened by pagan forces," Catholic Action was "designed to return society to its Christian foundations." Most significantly, the Catholic Legion of Decency became the "foremost example of Catholic Action in America,"[33] and the primary force for movie censorship in the late 1920s and throughout the 1930s. From its ranks came Father Lord, who drafted the Production Code. Equally significant was the appointment in 1934 of Joseph Breen, a lay Catholic (very much a "No-Man in Yes-Land"[34]), as head of the newly formed Production Code Administration.

At the same time, and more overtly, the Roosevelt administration was actively courting Catholic sympathies. Emblematic of this were the appointment of Monsignor Ryan to head the Industrial Appeals Board in the National Recovery Administration and the dramatic increase in federal judiciary appointments for Catholics during the New Deal.[35] Aware of the crisis in the political establishment following the Wall Street Crash, Roosevelt acknowledged the importance of capturing the ethnic urban lower-class vote. Anglo-Saxon Protestant legitimacy had been predicated on the success of laissez-faire capital. With the widespread destitution the Depression brought, cultural resentment for Protestant elitism ran high. Roosevelt successfully courted Catholic leaders and repealed Prohibition, which embodied the discrimination of the Protestant nativist regime. Though Roosevelt risked alienating the traditional but provincial Democratic voting base in the South through these maneuvers, he never lost the powerful new urban ethnic vote. The latter was crucial to holding on to power, and the risk paid off because the "solid South" remained loyal to Roosevelt (albeit cautiously) throughout the next three Presidential elections.

Increased Catholic involvement in policing American morality, then, corresponded to the declining fortunes of nativism and Protestantism. Roosevelt's election strategy mirrored that of Will Hays, who saw that an alliance with Catholic moral leadership was necessary if one wished to establish and maintain authority in this time of crisis. Moreover, it served the industry's economic interests to employ Catholics to fend off external interventions in their business, especially threatened

33. Ibid., pp. 183–84.

34. The description is Gregory Black's, who also documents how Breen's obdurate attitude toward Hollywood authority was motivated by a virulent anti-Semitism in an industry controlled by Jewish moguls. See Black, *Hollywood Censored*, pp. 170–74.

35. Samuel Lubell, *The Future of American Politics* (New York: Harper & Row, 1952), p. 78

boycotts organized by the Catholic Legion of Decency. The Legion's involvement in censorship, however, cut both ways. While it is clear that the industry's courting of Catholics operated as a smoke screen to protect economic imperatives, Catholic leadership saw the invitation to become Hollywood's moral conscience as a major opportunity for group advancement.

Catholic concern about the deleterious influence of the movies was necessarily different than old-stock fears when it came to understanding the scope of the industry's threat to American virtues. Catholics stuck mainly to issues of moral lapse (especially lapsed sexuality), free of the Protestant-associated anxieties about the "un-American" nature of Hollywood. Such differences of opinion had probably helped militate against the formation of a Protestant-Catholic antimovie coalition.

This more limited concern about what the movies stood for seemed to make Catholic authorities more open to negotiation with the industry. As Richard Maltby highlights, Will Hays certainly found it easier to deal with the International Federation of Catholic Alumnae than with Protestant church organizations. Hays's recourse to Catholic leaders to draft the Production Code only confirmed some of the more xenophobic fears harbored by the Protestant antimovie lobby.[36]

For their part, Lord's and Quigley's contributions as Catholic leaders to the drafting of a moral code can be interpreted as a way to sanction the practices of the Catholic constituency as both respectable and "American." In the late 1920s the predominant part of the United States' 20 million Catholics were of ethnic working-class stock and lived in the large metropolitan areas. Not only did they constitute a major part of the moviegoing audience, but the movies themselves were turning increasingly to treatments of their lives.

In this sense, the Catholic impetus in drafting and supervising a motion picture code was part of a general move toward redefining the terms of assimilation. With the movies themselves drawing increasing inspiration and box-office revenue from Catholic audiences, Catholic leaders felt a growing obligation to monitor Hollywood. Moreover, the opportunity to become the chief arbiters of the film industry's moral conduct would put Catholic leadership (especially the Catholic Legion of Decency) into the national limelight precisely at a time when Protestant moral hegemony was most under duress. In the aftermath of the Crash, movie censorship became the visible exertion of

36. Maltby, "The Production Code and the Hays Office," in *Grand Design*, pp. 45–46.

Catholic clerical domination in a period of declining faith: "The Depression made clearer than ever the persistent conflict between Christian ideals and social practices and institutions, while the presence of the Catholic laity in a society that emphasized freedom and initiative was bound to lead to a clerical rejection."[37] And this was so in spite of the fact that of all the forms of clerical authority and moral policing in Depression America, it was Catholicism that had best maintained its cultural currency. Urgent measures were needed to counteract tendencies to "clerical rejection." Thus, when the chance to regulate the movies offered itself, Catholic stewards were quick to act.

Quigley and Lord brought the Production Code into existence in 1930. Faced with the problem of widespread and predominantly Protestant moral condemnation of the movies, Will Hays found in these two Catholics a possible solution to his problems. As an industry insider Quigley argued that what was needed was a coherent code that would govern Hollywood's self-regulation and that would be respected by an array of external ecumenical moral interests. Using the threat of universal Catholic boycott of Hollywood, Lord and Quigley coerced into being a moral code that was deemed enforceable.

In May 1933, the Code's original drafter, Father Lord, felt obliged to resign from the MPPDA out of deep dissatisfaction with the ability of Hollywood to "self-regulate." He joined a Catholic petition for the boycott of movies.[38] Ironically, Lord's resignation accelerated the development of a Production Code Administration (PCA) designed precisely to enforce moral stipulations. Key to this was the appointment in 1934 of Joseph Breen, a Catholic who had been working with the MPPDA since 1931, to the PCA as the Code's enforcer. It had taken four years of petitioning to bring this about, and one of the primary objects of controversy over these years in mobilizing an enforceable Code was the gangster film.

The conglomeration of antimovie interests that pressed the Code into being is testimony, if nothing else, to the significant cultural place the cinema had carved out for itself in American life. The movies presented a multiple threat to the order of things in their capacity to mass-mediate national identities and value systems; their competing narratives of American life; and their appeal to and propagation of consumerism (both in terms of the representations of American

37. O'Brien, *American Catholics and Social Reform*, p. 184.
38. See Black, *Hollywood Censored*, pp. 150–51.

culture displayed on screen and as a consumerist practice, "movie-going") and the concomitant need for moral leniency.

While the Catholic Legion of Decency tried to dictate what Hollywood could and couldn't make throughout the rest of the decade, even the most stringent of its supporters, Joseph Breen, eventually found himself at odds with the very constituency he thought he was representing. The antimovie lobbies continued their quest to suffocate cinematic expression, complaining that Breen's office had been compromised. The contradictory obligation of the Production Code to both conservative morality and the box office meant that censorship could never be a completed project. And no matter how much censors protested, Hollywood continued to produce controversial censurable material, key among which was the gangster film.

THE CODE AND THE EARLY GANGSTER FILM

It is significant that Poffenberger should have conflated anti-Americanism with criminality and disregard for "law and the social order."[39] In his mind moral lassitude was evidence of "alien," dissenting, or un-American behavior. It is precisely on this alien terrain, however, that gangsters form. The distinguishing features of the gangster formula are that it is set in the ethnic ghetto during the social order of Prohibition, holds a disregard for legitimate culture, and displays the criminal path to success (a path remarkably similar to that of the legitimate capitalist, built as it is on the principles of corporate organization, a preference for pinstripe suits, and so on). Not surprisingly, perhaps, as the evidence from the Production Code files will show, the early 1930s talking gangster films drew the particular ire of moral stewards.[40]

One of the first post-Crash talking gangster films to attract the attention of the Code administrators was Warner Brothers' 1930 production, *Doorway to Hell*. Directed by Archie Mayo (who would go on to make a more famous gangster film, *The Petrified Forest*, in 1936), the film starred Lew Ayres (Louie) as a gangster who goes straight, but through a love interest (Dorothy Matthews as Doris) and the invitation of his best friend (James Cagney as Mileaway) is lured back to crime where he meets a bloody end. Of all the elements in the

---

39. Poffenberger, "Motion Pictures and Crime," p. 202.

40. The Production Code Administration files are part of the Motion Picture Association of America's collection donated to the Margaret Herrick Library, Academy for Motion Picture Arts and Sciences (AMPAS), Los Angeles.

original script that the Production Code administrators found unacceptable, the ending was the cause of most concern.

The lead character, Louie Ricardo, avenges the death of his kid brother, an act that drags him back into a world of crime. After having carried out his vendetta, he is arrested but he escapes from prison. O'Grady, a cop, discovers Louie in hiding and informs him that his gangland rival, Rocco, is out to kill Louie. O'Grady wants to arrest Louie, but he has no case against him. Consequently, he announces he is happy to abandon Louie to Rocco's guns. Louie walks out of his hiding place to be gunned down.

The then chief supervisor of the Code (until Joseph Breen's appointment in 1934), Colonel Jason Joy, informed Darryl Zanuck that "the last instance of a cop, unable to secure a gangster's punishment by legal means and abandoning him to the mercy of other crooks" was "most objectionable."[41] The story, however, was accepted in principle as long as the image of law enforcement was rectified. The script was duly altered. O'Grady's visit to Louie after his jailbreak is made sympathetic. The cop now warns Louie that the jailbreak was a setup by Rocco's gang in order to get Louie beyond the protection of the law, and thus to kill him.

The Code administrators continued to raise objection about the film throughout 1930 (the film went into production May 19, 1930), a typical view holding that "the picture does not teach a moral, on the contrary it shows that the police haven't much chance against the machinations of gangsters."[42] This fear reflected a concern that the realm of gangsterdom signified the emergence of a world outside the control of the moral and political establishment. Prior to the establishment of the PCA in 1934, the body responsible for implementing the Code was the Studio Relations Committee (SRC). Its prime responsibility lay in guaranteeing that stories likely to be successful at the box office continued to be made. So, while the SRC imposed guidelines, it also sought rhetorically to defend the rectitude of even the most dubious and morally controversial products.

Accordingly, Carleton Simon (who became the crime consultant to the Hays Office) wrote on seeing *Doorway to Hell:* "This picture brings to mass consciousness the ruthlessness of organized crime, its great growth and the dangerous element that the police are continually combating. A picture such as this, presenting unadorned facts

41. Memo, May 29, 1930, PCA file *Doorway to Hell*, AMPAS.
42. Memo, October 8, 1930, PCA file *Doorway to Hell*, AMPAS.

performs a great public service." [43] This would remain the characteristic industry defense of gangster film production throughout the
Depression. The idea that such films would "bring home to every law-
abiding citizen the scope, the fearlessness and the indifference to
human life" [44] exhibited by the underworld was a rhetorical maneuver
to fight the objections of moral guardians. As Carleton Simon adds,
"As long as the public craves underworld pictures that demand must
be met." [45]

The justification of the gangster film as a product in demand always
left the rationale of the demand itself open to interpretation. External
moral guardians (such as the DAR, the Legion of Decency, and the
Protestant League) interpreted the gangster film as encouraging an
overturning of the moral order, and, as such, they demanded that the
industry's desire for profits be tempered by morally upright narratives
and images. But gangster pictures were pulling audiences at the box office in a period of economic calamity. In this context the industry was
bound to be reticent about dropping production. [46] In times of Depression the industry was particularly sensitive to audience demand. In circumstances when the industry no longer had control of public taste, it
was compelled to follow the public, not make the public follow it.

"Experts" such as Carleton Simon were employed by the SRC to
ennoble Hollywood's defense of the underworld feature. In arguing
that the industry was in no position to resist public demand, Simon
goes on to rationalize that demand as follows:

> To many minds this demand has always been unexplainable. Psycho-
> logically considered it is created by the inherent wish or yearning of
> one half of the world to know something of the other half. Whetted by
> newspaper accounts of similar occurrences, the public seeks vent for
> its curiosity to have a clearer understanding and a closer perspective
> as to the causes that lead to gang feuds. Frequently in the background
> is the wish to understand the problem so that a remedy can be found. [47]

43. Carleton Simon, "Review of *Doorway to Hell*," November 15, 1930, PCA file *Doorway
to Hell*, AMPAS.

44. Ibid.

45. Ibid.

46. For example, an examination by *Variety* of box-office successes between 1928 and 1932,
in terms of stars as well as films, reveals a remarkable change. Movies with criminal or social
problem themes increased in popularity, while the comedy of social manners so popular before
the Crash of 1929 recedes along with its stars. Cagney, Robinson, and Muni emerge, while
Mary Pickford, Douglas Fairbanks, Gloria Swanson, Clara Bow, and Norma Talmadge all but
disappear.

47. Simon "Review," PCA file *Doorway to Hell*, AMPAS.

If one edits out the attempt at moral rectitude in the above, we can see some awareness of the concerns at stake in the gangster film. The dialogue between one "half" of culture and the other is recognized as implicit to the gangster format as its essential appeal. This constitutes an acknowledgment that society is a seamed, not seamless, space—a space that contains the voices not only of the dominant culture but the socially subordinated trying to get heard. Nonetheless, the particular fear of moral stewards was directed more at the fact that these films attracted an audience disposed to listen.

The reactions and debates over *Doorway to Hell* came to a head over its more famous sequel, *Public Enemy*. To counteract the objections of morality groups and censors, Darryl Zanuck sought to claim that gangster films provided the lesson that moral codes would have no cultural currency as long as the social "environment" was inadequate. What was needed was less morality and more material improvements in the "living conditions in the lower regions," argued Zanuck.[48] Among the themes embodied in *Public Enemy*, he claimed, was "that PROHIBITION is not the cause of the present CRIME WAVE—mobs and gangs have existed for years and years BECAUSE of ENVIRONMENT, and the only thing that PROHIBITION has done, is to bring these unlawful organizations more noticeably to the eye of the public."[49]

While gangster films have to answer the censoring demands of moral guardians in "selling the idea that CRIME is not profitable,"[50] they have no obligation to pretend that criminality is simply a lapse in moral strength. Rather, the industry advocated the notion that gangster films were performing a public service in showing that "only by the betterment of ENVIRONMENT and EDUCATION for the masses can we overcome the widespread tendency toward LAW BREAKING."[51] Such rationalizations of gangster film production by Zanuck and Jason Joy were aimed ultimately at ensuring that crime (at least on screen) did indeed pay.

Gangster films were drawing at the box office because they addressed and brought into dominant discourse elements of formerly ostracized thinking. That is, the gangster film was a way of giving voice to such themes as social inequality within an albeit administered and regulated form, the Hollywood movie. The demand for the gangster film had to be answered, and no matter how much one tried to

48. Darryl Zanuck, Letter to Jason Joy, January 6, 1931, PCA file *Public Enemy*, AMPAS.
49. Ibid.
50. Ibid.
51. Ibid.

prevent sympathy being raised for criminality, industry and censors alike realized that this was almost impossible. As Zanuck's explanations show us, the point of the gangster film was that it spoke to social realities too obvious to ignore. If the only way to bring to the culture's attention the experience of oppression was through these controlled spaces (commercial culture/the movies), at least the gangster film maximized such a chance. As a result, the gangster film attracted the attention of many interest groups who felt threatened by its presence.

One of the more infamous cases in point was *Little Caesar*. This film became a rallying point around which the interests of movie producers and audiences conflated in battling guardians of the old order. In spite of being approved by the SRC, *Little Caesar* incited the wrath of many censor boards. Perhaps the SRC was not attentive to the full power of the gangster film to challenge dominant culture, or perhaps the local censor boards foresaw the demise of their powers (and their right to cultural dominance) if a film like *Little Caesar* could now get produced and sanctioned by a general censoring authority such as the Production Code.

It is in this framework of interests that Joy appealed to local censor boards to "catch the spirit of the Code" and to refrain from interfering by trusting the Code's integrity. The censors in British Columbia and in Ontario were singled out for their "return to their former small, narrow, picayunish, fault-finding attitude."[52] *Little Caesar* tested the extent of the Code's power. The Code had dire problems if it could not protect pictures from mutilations. Joy wrote to Hal Wallis at Warners, warning "this censor business is going to need some careful and strong methods if we are not to allow production to be taken entirely out of our hands and placed in those of the censors."[53] Joy's concern to maintain control of the industry's product and ward off moralist intervention conflated wittingly or unwittingly into a defense of subversive narratives. The Code constituted a level of protection at the national level (at least in the early 1930s) for the production of a new and critical social vision. This made available a space within mass cinema for the production of narratives that Depression culture demanded.

It should be stressed that such a space was not afforded through

52. Jason Joy, Letter to Hal Wallis at Warner Brothers, February 21, 1931, PCA file *Little Caesar*, AMPAS.
53. Ibid.

the altruistic benevolence of an industry suddenly sympathetic to the experiences and desires of working class and ethnic communities. Rather, it was created by an interest in profits in a time of scarcity and retrenchment. In effect, the industry was answering a demand generated from the bottom up. In this way we can see how the interests of commercialism and the popular classes were mutually reinforcing. In the case of the early 1930s talking gangster film the commercial apparatus stood to profit from serving the interests of under- or misrepresented groups in their quest for adequate representation.

Representations of ethnicity came with certain stigmas, however, and generated much contention. Fiorello La Guardia, the mayor of New York, announced after seeing *Little Caesar* that he was going to reverse his opposition toward censorship and sympathy for Mr. Hays because the lead gangster was an Italian. La Guardia maintained that "Mr. Hays would not dare to produce such a picture with a Jew as that character—he would lose his job if he did."[54] While La Guardia had probably hit on something true about Jewish control of the movie industry, MPPDA secretary Carl Milliken explained La Guardia's wrath as less a matter of ethnic pride than the fact that Edward G. Robinson bore a marked resemblance to the mayor.[55]

If anything, La Guardia's vehement objections demonstrate a contemporaneous awareness that gangster films were concerned with problems of ethnicity. The only way ethnic concerns could get a voice within a culture traditionally steeped in nativist symbols and definitions of Americanness was under the stigma of criminality. However, this contingency seemed to be overcome by the fact that criminality was no longer being rationalized as the product of immorality or innate evil. Gangster films put pressure on the ruling definitions of good and evil. What used to be "good" in the form of the law, capital, the state, and WASP identity became increasingly ambiguous to the extent that they relegated the ethnic and working-class experience to the "underworld." The possessor of a Lower East Side accent was inevitably cast as a criminal.

The injection of vernacular identities spawned in the city had to be constantly stigmatized as evil or criminal. Paradoxically, as I have demonstrated in the preceding chapters, this seemed to damage not

54. Will Hays's Secretary, internal office memo to Jason Joy, January 27, 1931, PCA file *Little Caesar*, AMPAS.

55. Carl Milliken, Memo to Joy, file *Little Caesar*, AMPAS.

the stigmatized (ethnics) but the "stigmatizer" (WASPs). Having always been cast as "un-American" by WASP nativism, ethnic identity had little to lose. As the Code's crime consultant Carleton Simon articulated to Hays in a letter dated January 26, 1931, regarding *Little Caesar:* "It is apparent that the public are interested in crime pictures by a packed audience. . . . Although no great moral lesson is taught by such pictures they nevertheless do perform a service by exposing the criminal strata that underlies society; similar in degree as that performed against slavery by the production of Uncle Tom's Cabin." [56] Although this does not herald the advent of ethnic consciousness, it does, all the same, point to a breakdown in the viability and popularity of the old moral narratives (all the more significant in the era of Prohibition, which was part of that old moral order).

Simon's rationalizations are designed to placate a range of concerns about the seditious propensity of the gangster film. Yet his admission that these films do not teach any "great moral lesson" signals the industry's shift away from an obligation to make "morally uplifting" narratives. In fact, there is an implicit acknowledgment of the redundancy and popular lack of faith in the old themes and social visions. As he had written of *Doorway to Hell,* Simon reiterates that the public fascination with criminality can be attributed less to a consensus on morality than curiosity about the realm of the cultural/social "other." He states, "with the old axiom in mind that 'one half of the world does not know the other half' it is quite natural to understand that such pictures faithfully portraying existing conditions startle and thrill by bringing into close proximity the things that audiences read about but barely if ever come into direct contact." [57]

Noticeably, Simon is unable to speculate that the gangster film's popularity might lie in its ability to resonate with the reality of its audience. It does not occur to him that the gangster film audience might actually belong to that world of things it brings "into close proximity." This was certainly true, as we have seen, for the new stars that came with the gangster film. James Cagney and Edward G. Robinson in their autobiographies describe themselves as ethnics and, furthermore, as ethnics who felt differentiated from "Americans" who were by definition "Anglo-Saxons." Cagney once described one of his childhood "loves" as a "pure American girl," clarifying this by saying, "I desig-

---

56. Carleton Simon, Letter to Hays, January 26, 1931, PCA file *Little Caesar,* AMPAS.
57. Simon, "Review," PCA file *Doorway to Hell,* AMPAS.

nate her nationality because our area [New York's Lower East Side] was almost exclusively first-generation German, Irish, Jewish, Italian, Hungarian, and Czech."[58]

As a Jew whose real name was Emanuel Goldenberg, Edward G. Robinson was always aware of his status as "non-Anglo-Saxon." His autobiography begins with how he changed his name while at the American Academy of Dramatic Arts: "it was suggested to me, ever so tactfully, that Emanuel Goldenberg was not a name for an actor. Too long, too foreign, and I suspect, though no hint was made of it, too Jewish." Additionally, the "few parts I would play [at the Academy] would not be Anglo-Saxon." His opinions of the power of such discrimination led him to see the oppressions of "assimilation," which he interpreted as an "effort to turn all aliens into one standard American image." This project "has met with dismal failure" because "people tend to be what their fathers and grandfathers were . . . they persist in remembering their ancestral language, if only through an occasional untranslatable phrase."[59]

Robinson's sentiments coincided very much with the vehicle that brought him to fame. The early 1930s talking gangster films had everything to do with an attack on the terms of assimilation and ruling definitions of America and Americanness. Objections to the gangster film were thus not limited to questions of morality but national self-image. *Little Caesar*, in fact, inspired condemnations from an officer of the Motion Picture Distributors and Exhibitors of Canada (MPDEC), which foreshadowed growing political concerns about the gangster cycle's negative representation of the American way of life:

> I am opposed to all these crime and gangster pictures. I recognise that there is a point of view from which one can argue that Canadians ought to be told about the wickedness of the United States. The Toronto Daily Star apparently takes this view and has just started a "gangster" story and advertised it as such. Nevertheless, I am not convinced that the U.S. is doing itself any favour, or paying itself a compliment when it sends gangster films abroad.[60]

Lest we feel that such a commentary would fall on deaf ears, it should be noted that following their eventual banning, *Public Enemy* and

58. James Cagney, *Cagney by Cagney* (New York: Doubleday, 1976), p. 14.

59. Edward G. Robinson with Leonard Spigelgass, *All My Yesterdays: An Autobiography* (New York: Hawthorn Books, 1973), p. 15.

60. Colonel John A. Cooper, Letter from MPDEC, February 11, 1931, PCA file *Little Caesar*, AMPAS.

Little Caesar were not re-released until 1953, and then only contingent on restrictions governing their worldwide distribution.[61]

Public Enemy and *Little Caesar* were prohibited from exhibition following the MPPDA's moratorium on gangster films in July 1935. Because they were films produced and released before 1934, they had never received the PCA's certificate (which came into operation in 1934). In August 1953, some twenty-one years later, Warner Brothers put in a request for the two films' re-release "with the hope that they might now qualify for a Code Certificate."[62] J. A. Vizzard, a Code administrator, wrote that the "theory behind this request was that the notoriety of these films had tapered off considerably and that they would be looked upon by audiences . . . as 'museum pieces.'" Although the films were passed as "period pieces," PCA representative Trilling stated that "in large parts of Europe and . . . the majority of Asia the twenty year time differential would not be appreciated." As such "[i]t seemed to us that we might be playing directly and blindly into the hands of Communists, offering them material which they could use to assault the American culture." The films were denied export release.[63]

The gangster's perceived attack on eternal American verities was understood by censors as emanating from a very specific sociocultural place, as another letter from a Canadian censorship officer confirms. Robert Pearson from the Alberta office of the chief censor bemoaned the nature of the pictures being released since the inception of the Production Code. The pictures were too "sophisticated" for a rural audience, bringing with them the experiences of "large American cities," which "people living in the smaller towns and remote from the great centres and more simple in their outlook, do not appreciate or enjoy."[64] The first gangster talkies constituted a challenge to traditional and idealized conceptions of the American way of life. Provincial and rural censoring authorities betrayed their fear and

61. Jack Warner, Letter to PCA, August 1953, PCA file *Little Caesar*, AMPAS. See also chapters 6 and 7 for a full discussion of why the gangster film was regarded as politically seditious in the postwar era.

62. J. A. Vizzard, Memo (regarding Warner's request for certification of *Little Caesar* and *Public Enemy*), August 1953, PCA file *Little Caesar*, AMPAS.

63. Trilling, Memo (regarding Warner's request for certification of *Little Caesar* and *Public Enemy*), August 1953, PCA file *Little Caesar*, AMPAS.

64. Robert Pearson, Letter from Alberta Film Censor Board, March 10, 1931, PCA file *Little Caesar*, AMPAS.

resentment of Hollywood's promotion in the gangster film of an alternative version of America rooted in the urban experience.

In the exchange between censors and the MPPDA over *Little Caesar*, the producers and the Code administrators rallied together to defend their right to control regulation. Under pressure from the New York State Education Department, specifically through its representative James Wingate, and Canadian censorship boards, the MPPDA extended an offer of assistance in defending *Little Caesar* to Hal Wallis at Warners, an offer that was duly accepted.[65] Joy wrote to Wingate in defense of *Little Caesar* (and therefore against the idea of centralized federal intervention in Hollywood): "The description of the lawless acts of the gangsters in *Little Caesar* is necessary in order that the audience may understand for what acts the characters are being punished." Joy argued that censoring details of "ruthlessness" and the "ghastly" in criminal behavior would "reduce and even destroy the moral value of the picture as a whole by leaving an impression in the mind of the audience that after all these men had not done enough to deserve their unhappy ending." In conclusion, Joy articulated on behalf of the MPPDA that "they [the producers] believe, and we think rightfully, that stories involving social moral problems have a place on the screen."[66]

In many ways the Production Code functioned as a prop to conservative Christian ideals, both Protestant and Catholic. Yet, in defending capitalist interests, the Code's representatives had to make compromises with popular voices. The conflicts and alliances formed over the gangster film between external censors, the Studio Relations Committee (in charge of the Code in the early Depression years), and the industry reveal the complex dimensions involved in trying to police historical transformation, especially during a period of extreme crisis. What is illuminated in these particular circumstances is the extent to which a capitalist commodity came to threaten agents of social control. Censorship was the product of the volatile relationship between mass culture and the status quo. The various prohibitions that afflicted the talking gangster film between 1931 and 1935 only confirm the extent to which the movies were far from being automatic agents

65. Hal Wallis, Letter from Warner Brothers Studio, February 4, 1931, PCA file *Little Caesar,* AMPAS.

66. Jason Joy, Letter from MPPDA to New York State Education Department, Representative Wingate, PCA file *Little Caesar,* AMPAS.

of moral and capitalist cultural stewardship. And just because the censors brought the boom down did not mean that the gangster cycle and the issues that it addressed went away.

THE GANGSTER'S LIFE AFTER DEATH:
CIRCUMNAVIGATING THE CODE

The significance of the 1935 moratorium lies less in any direct impact on the talking gangster film than in the fact that it was used rhetorically to demonstrate the Code's effectiveness. Most censorship activity by 1933–1934 centered on the representations of sex, not violence. Moreover, the moratorium was motivated primarily by the sensation of John Dillinger's death. The irony of this was that it masked the significant damage that had already been done to the first cycle of post-Crash talking gangster films. The industry's concerted defense of gangster products in the period of 1930–1931, which I have outlined above, proved to be a public relations nightmare. Concessions to increasingly hostile antimovie lobbies had been made as early as 1931, as the cases of *Little Caesar, Public Enemy,* and above all *Scarface* demonstrate.

Thus, by the time the Production Code Administration was formed in 1934, it could be argued that the gangster film was a tamed cultural vehicle. Yet, as the case of *Manhattan Melodrama* bears out, the talking gangster film even in adjusted form maintained the power to dissent. Studios had become well rehearsed in how to skirt Code prohibitions of gangster subject matter by the time of the 1935 declaration.

After the moratorium of 1935, producers found ways to circumvent Code strictures in order to continue to capitalize on the public fascination for gangsters. Most intriguingly, perhaps, was the attempt to convert Cagney, Robinson, and Muni to the side of law in *G-Men* (1935), *Bullets or Ballots* (1936), and *Bordertown* (1935), respectively. Cagney plays an FBI agent capable of passing for a gangster in *G-Men*, while Robinson also plays an undercover cop busting a racket in *Bullets or Ballots.*

For Paul Muni, there was the chance to play a redeemed hoodlum in *Bordertown* (1935). This film is a gangster film in everything but name. Muni plays a Chicano tough guy, Johnny Ramirez, in the barrios of Los Angeles who tries to go straight by going to night school to learn law. His efforts as a lawyer in representing the interests of working-class Mexican Americans, however, are compromised by a richer and more powerful WASP establishment. He "makes it" by running a gambling house in "bordertown" (a surrogate Tijuana), which draws the finer (whiter) clientele south of the border. In his confrontations with old-stock Americans (especially desiring women, who nickname him "savage"), Johnny learns that he belongs "to a different tribe." In a twist on the traditional gangster ending, he resolves to return to the barrio and fund a law school with his gambling fortune in order to advance the legal rights of Chicanos.

The familiar concern of the gangster film for the aspirations of lower-class ethnic "hyphenated" Americans fighting an old-stock establishment are once again given a full airing, but in a form that reflects the need to skirt censorship impositions. The film grants a token role to a Catholic priest who functions as Johnny's moral monitor (a device or tactic to appease the Legion of Decency that also crops up in 1938 in *Angels with Dirty Faces*). The "scene" of gangster activity is shifted from New York and Chicago to Los Angeles. The gangster's identity is transformed from its associations with European immigrants to Mexican Americans. These elements, combined with the story's constructive resolution, point to the innovative ways in which the gangster's provocative message about social and cultural inequity was sustained while appearing to cater to the censors' desires for an end to the gangster cycle.

Hollywood's sophisticated range of skirting strategies allowed it to keep the gangster cycle alive and to continue to make use of its gangster stars. For Edward G. Robinson there was (in addition to switching sides in *Bullets or Ballots*) an "autopsy" narrative, *The Last Gangster* (1937), which cast the gangster (Joe Drozak) as a man out of time. Joe is sent to prison and loses his wife and son to a law-abiding family man, Paul North (played by James Stewart). On release he experiences problems with his old gang, and abandons a vendetta against Paul when he sees what a positive future this man can guarantee his ex-wife and son. Joe dies in a shoot-out with a rival gangster, a redeemed but "retired" hero.

For James Cagney, there were similar redemption narratives following his transformation into an FBI agent in *G-Men*. Most notably, there was *Angels with Dirty Faces* (1938), where he shares the limelight with a fraternal priest (Pat O'Brien) and tries to self-consciously destroy the gangster myth in a powerful death row finale that centers on whether he fakes cowardice in facing the electric chair. He followed

Post-Code gangster mutations: Stranded in the desert, the gangster (Duke Mantee played by Humphrey Bogart) goes West, leaving his legitimating ethnic urban context behind in *The Petrified Forest* (1936).

this with an equally famous nostalgia piece, *The Roaring Twenties* (1939), which offset censorship objections by locating the classic gangster in an apparently bygone era.

There were also films that removed the gangster from his traditional class and ethnic affiliations by turning him into a cowboy (*The Oklahoma Kid*, 1939) and a Scottish aristocrat (*The Earl of Chicago*, 1940). Even more humorously, the gangster could be made the subject of rehabilitation and domestication, as in *A Slight Case of Murder* (1938) and *Johnny Eager* (1941). If he could not be made to go straight, then he could be made over into either a Runyonesque softie, as in *Tall, Dark, and Handsome* (1941) (which builds on a trend set by *Little Miss Marker* (1934), where gangsters befriend Shirley Temple!), or reduced to a one-dimensional picture of evil, as in *Public Enemy's Wife* (1936) and *Marked Woman* (1937).

Post-Code gangster mutations: The gangster as fugitive on the lam in *You Only Live Once* (1937). American "innocents," Eddie (Henry Fonda) and Jo (Sylvia Sydney), find refuge in the automobile while trying to escape from the fatally conspiring forces of civilization.

While many of these films attest to the defusing of the gangster's more contradictory and dissident features, they also signaled important shifts in what the gangster would come to signify in the wartime and postwar era. Films like *Public Enemy's Wife* and *Marked Woman*, for example, deal with the misogynist features of gangsterdom. The former deals with the insane jealousy of the gangster for his "moll," who becomes a friend of a G-Man. The latter features a prostitute's attempt to take her pimp and his syndicate (an ersatz Lucky Luciano) to court, prefiguring concerns that would mark the postwar crime cycle with its femmes fatales and images of a ruthless syndicate-controlled society.

Perhaps the most intriguing of the newer gangster treatments were probably *The Petrified Forest* (1936) and *You Only Live Once* (1937). Both centered on the notion of the gangster as fugitive. Based on

Robert Sherwood's hit Broadway play of the same name, *The Petrified Forest* was a "stagy" prestige Warner Brothers production that launched the career of Humphrey Bogart, an actor who would make his fullest mark on 1940s Hollywood. Bogart's screen portrayal of Duke Mantee (based on his performance of the role in the original Broadway production) foreshadows some aspects of the morally ambiguous characters he would personify after the war. This gangster owed little to the ethnic urban tradition. Duke Mantee is more of an updated frontier outlaw than city hoodlum (much more in the Dillinger mold than Al Capone's). While on the run to the Mexican border, Mantee holes up in a gas station in the Arizona desert where he meets an intellectual (Leslie Howard) who philosophizes about him as an American primitive representing the irrational and destructive forces of materialism.

You Only Live Once was directed by Fritz Lang, who would become synonymous with the 1940s and 1950s crime film, and expands on the problem of being on the run. In this case the story turns on the way fate conspires against a small-time offender trying to go straight. He is falsely accused of a bank robbery and murder, and sentenced to death. His fiancée helps him escape, unaware that he is about to be granted a pardon (the real crook having been caught). The couple take flight and are shot down on the verge of finding freedom across the border. Beyond Lang's film, the gangster could similarly be portrayed as an alienated fugitive even in his own neighborhood as in *Dead End* (1937) and *It All Came True* (1940).

Thus a major side effect of the attempt to circumvent the censors was that it encouraged filmmakers to operate beyond established gangster conventions. Not only was the containment of gangster representation never complete, but the gangster's transformations helped pave the way for the emergence of a new dissident crime cycle after the war. The shift toward the fugitive gangster type unanchored from ethnic moorings (as in *The Petrified Forest* and *You Only Live Once*), for example, prefigured the kind of existential crime dramas we now call film noir. This later cycle was clearly indebted to censorship-influenced mutations on the original gangster formula.

5 Crime, Inc.

Beyond the Ghetto/Beyond the Majors
in the Postwar Gangster Film

CAGNEY'S PSYCHOTIC TRANSFORMATION:
VICTORY OF THE CENSORS?

As Cagney's switching of sides in *G-Men* (1935) illustrated, there had long been concerted attempts to convert the gangster to the side of good. What was interesting about Cagney's 1940s transformations, however, was that they were of an entirely different order. The gangster narratives for which Cagney is best remembered after the war, *White Heat* (1949) and *Kiss Tomorrow Goodbye* (1950), mark the gangster as a psychologically crippled monster and a violent sadist, respectively. Cagney's famous performance as the deranged Cody Jarrett in *White Heat* depended both on the amplification of the gangster's psychological instabilities and on the muting of the type's ethnic street markings.

Traditionally, Cagney's personification of the gangster had the imprimatur of Irish-Catholic identity. Throughout the 1930s his most acclaimed gangster roles as Tommy Powers in *Public Enemy* (1931), Rocky Sullivan in *Angels with Dirty Faces* (1938), and Eddie Bartlett in *The Roaring Twenties* (1939) were enriched and troubled by questions of ethnicity and faith. The moral presence of that faith was variously encoded—in Tommy's doting mother, in Rocky's best friend, Father Connelly, and in Eddie's death on the church steps. While the incorporation of Catholic comment was part and parcel of the way gangster films could allay the intervention of censors, it helped anchor the rationale for the gangster's actions in a moral and socially real universe. The struggle between ethnic lower-class aspiration and moral obligation provided legitimating conditions that had made the 1930s film gangster such a powerful object of audience identification. Cagney's portrayal of the mentally sick Cody Jarrett in *White Heat*, however, changes the terms of audience identification with the criminal protagonist. Cody's madness places the gangster very much on the periphery of society. *Public Enemy*'s Tommy Powers might have been the boy next door and his criminal motivations stemmed from understandable desires to overcome the sociocultural barriers that condemned him to poverty. Cody's propensity to violence and crime, however, are rationalized as a matter of mental aberration. Moreover, dislocated from the determining factors of class aspiration and the ethnic desire for cultural acceptance, this gangster's activities take place not in the ghetto but in the countryside and prison.[1]

Such changes have been interpreted as evidence of the triumph of moral and political monitors. *White Heat* seems to defuse the gangster's socially critical power by replacing the circumstances that once lent sanction to the gangster's actions with psychological explanations of aberrant behavior. Tempting as this line of argument is, there are good reasons to resist it.[2]

The trend of relocating and redefining the gangster had been fostered by the emergence of a fugitive-gangster cycle in the pre-war years, including such films as *The Petrified Forest* (1936), *You Only Live Once* (1937), and *High Sierra* (1941). These, as I discussed earlier, were derived in part from the dual pressures of censors to prohibit the first cycle of talking gangster films and the public fascination

1. Equally, in *Kiss Tomorrow Goodbye*, the gangster-protagonist Ralph Cotter escapes from a prison farm and hides in a small town. While the film is an indictment of city-hall graft and police corruption, Cotter is not an agent of redemption. Instead he's the villain without compassion, a sadist who exploits existing corruption to his own ends. He bribes already corrupt cops, dates a local politician's daughter in order to sully her father's reputation—he even steals from the mob. In the end he dies not because the system (either city hall or the syndicate) is capable of breaking him, but because his mistress refuses to let him go. The film reveals the extent to which the public sphere is susceptible to (even designed for and run by) the likes of Ralph Cotter. Once again the ethnic and class component that informed the actions of Cagney's 1930s gangster is absent.

2. Interpreting the change in the gangster from the 1930s to the 1940s as a disempowering journey ("from slum-bred racketeer" to "inherent psychopath"), James J. Parker, for example, has argued that the psychologizing of the gangster in films like *White Heat* reflects the triumph of the censors. According to Parker, such degenerative mutations of the gangster were a product of wartime attempts by federal powers to gain control of the film industry, a codification of the world according to censor stipulations. James J. Parker, "The Organizational Environment of the Motion Picture Sector," in *Media, Audience, and Social Structure*, ed. Sandra J. Ball-Rokeach and Muriel G. Cantor (Beverly Hills: Sage, 1986).

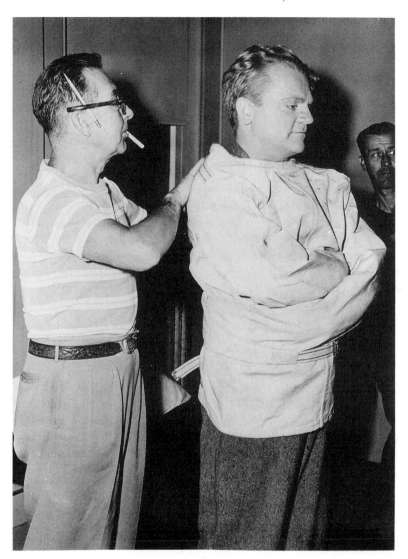

Restraining the "classic" gangster's return in the postwar era: James Cagney donning the straitjacket preparing to play the role of Cody Jarrett—the ethnic gangster as psychopath in *White Heat* (1949).

for Dillinger (and Bonnie and Clyde), gangsters who inherited the mantle of the frontier outlaw rather than that of Al Capone.

White Heat, then, reflects how innovatively the industry met the need to mutate its gangster formula in light of prohibitive censure and changing audience concerns. Cody Jarrett blends a "classical" ethnic intertext that came with Cagney along with the newer concern for the gangster as alienated social fugitive. Although informing socioeconomic and cultural contexts for Cody's behavior have disappeared, Cagney's dynamic performance grants this gangster much more character appeal and personality than his "good/sane"—but anonymous, impersonal, and plain—rival, Hank Fallon (played by Edmond O'Brien). The latter is a man who, as an undercover cop, necessarily must be capable of fitting in rather than standing out.

White Heat is in many ways an update of *G-Men,* featuring as it does the story of an undercover cop who gains the confidence of a crime ring's leader in order to bust it. Yet there's an obvious twist here. The undercover cop this time is not Cagney but someone out to get him. This reversal of fortune signified an important change in the way the gangster film mediated the line dividing legal from illegal America. In the 1930s, the G-man gained something from being able to pass for a gangster; he took on the positive attributes associated with the character type. The old gangster had feisty ethnic lower-class markings that defined him affirmatively and in contradistinction to the dominant culture and the forces that serviced it.

By comparison, the capacity of the new postwar G-man/T-man (Treasury agent) to go undercover and blend in had less to do with taking on a "personality" than with confirming one's lack of distinguishing features as a cipher. *White Heat*'s undercover cop (embodied in Edmond O'Brien's suitably stoic and mechanical performance) is successful because he is capable of being faceless and impersonal. This is a function of the film's overall attempt to sever the gangster's "color" and individuality from its sociocultural moorings and, instead, stigmatize the act of standing out from (as well as against) the establishment as something excessive and deranged. By comparison, fitting in and obedience to the law are conveyed as rational. This is consistent with the larger thematic patterns of the film, especially in its pitting of science (encoded in modern police detection devices) against the irrational forces of the mind.[3]

As a result, *White Heat* holds out two contradictory readings. On

---

3. *White Heat*'s battle between a clever psycho-killer and the forces of science (the ingenuity of police detection) builds on several predecessors. Most interesting among these are *This Gun for Hire* (1942), perhaps the earliest of its kind; *He Walked by Night* (1948) (where a cop-killer is featured as an alienated technical mastermind overcome in the end by the superior teamwork of the LA Police Department—the precursor to Jack Webb's *Dragnet* series); and *Follow Me Quietly* (1949) (an Anthony Mann story made by Richard Fleischer featuring a psycho-killer who believes he is performing a civic service in ridding the city of assorted criminal lowlife). Later entries include *Union Station* (1950) (featuring a brutal kidnapper of a blind girl, whom

one hand, it could be interpreted as a valorization of institutional power and its "organization man." Yet on the other hand, it is clear that the appeal of Cagney's performance rests in part on his rejection of the sinister aspects of a conforming culture embodied in Edmond O'Brien's faceless (and duplicitous) undercover FBI agent. While the plot deprives Cody Jarrett of the mitigating conditions that helped audiences understand the gangster's recourse to crime in the past, Cagney's deep association with this past (as a highly popular ethnic urban lower-class gangster-*star*) granted him more than a modicum of sympathy.

Furthermore, custodians of the nation's moral and political destiny in the 1940s would hardly have been pleased with a movie that, in the words of Warner Brothers, centered on "a homicidal paranoiac with a mother fixation."[4] Cody's defiant "Made it Ma! Top of the world!" and subsequently spectacular self-immolation in the flames of the gas explosion that marks *White Heat*'s ending only added to the gangster mystique. Box-office returns confirmed that audiences continued to find the gangster compulsive viewing.

During the war the Office of War Information (OWI) and its Bureau of Motion Pictures replaced religious agencies as Hollywood's major monitoring force. If in the 1930s religious authorities had felt that the gangster set a bad moral example to American audiences, and if Anglocentric groups had seen the gangster as the latest threat to nativist cultural dominance, the wartime administration saw in gangsters a threat to propagandistic efforts to manufacture positive images of the American way of life. This was especially true for the State Department, which, in the immediate aftermath of World War II in 1945, took on some of the OWI's brief, though with considerably less of its power, to intervene in Hollywood's production decisions. While the State Department's monitoring rights may have been smaller than OWI's, it too felt that it was incumbent on Hollywood to continue its patriotic agenda as an arm of Americanization abroad.

During the war Hollywood had provided audiences with films that posited national unity and maintained a climate of narrative certainty. Films such as *Air Force* (1943), *Destination Tokyo* (1943), and *Pride of the Marines* (1945) took formerly disparate and divided male members

he plans to kill even after he gets the ransom); *Gun Crazy* (1950) (which features two maladjusted thrill-kill fugitives); and *The Hitch-Hiker* (1953) (an Ida Lupino film about a hitchhiking psycho-killer who murders his rides).

4. Doug Warren with James Cagney, *Cagney: The Authorized Biography* (New York: St. Martin's Press, 1983), p. 171.

of American society (in all these cases they took John Garfield, an actor previously associated with social "misfit" roles), and put them in a confined space/surrogate community (such as a bomber or a submarine) where they were persuaded to overcome their differences (and injuries) in the interests of being good citizens and fighting the good fight. These and other war narratives fostered a sense of inevitable victory, telling stories with positive outcomes. Equally, films like *Mrs. Miniver* (1942) and *Since You Went Away* (1944) celebrated the stalwart and faithful mothers left alone to support and maintain family unity on the home front. In fashioning a sense of community spirit and obedience to a larger national interest, the war film affirmed not only a nationalist agenda but corporate goals as well. In this light, gangster films were perceived as counterproductive to the business of social rehabilitation.

The kinds of criminal images that received least attention were, accordingly, ones that disassociated the criminal from the mainstream of American society. Films that characterized criminal motivation as emanating from deviant or aberrant minds not only served the purpose of disengaging the gangster's traditional association with a larger group/social experience, but seemed to help naturalize mainstream society, by contrast, as a place of normative values.

A psychological gangster film like *White Heat* seems to have worked in this way to avoid censorship concern. In this sense, its mutations were part of a negotiated struggle between industry and censorship institutions (federal and religious) where the industry could continue to meet audience demand for gangster formulas, yet where the damaging features of the gangster could at the same time appear to be curtailed.

A case in point was the State Department review of the psychological crime film *The Two Mrs. Carrolls* (1947). This film met with approval because it "suggests nothing contrary to the Government's Overseas Information program," the villain (played by Humphrey Bogart) being "presented as a psychopathic individual, in no way representative of his nationality." This was consistent with the wartime fear reflected in a September 1944 OWI report, which stated that it wished to offset the Hollywood crime film's tendency to show "unsympathetic or unreal characters made typical of whole groups or nations." [5]

The climate of war and Cold War fostered a concern for the impact the gangster had on foreign impressions of the United States.

5. Parker, "The Organizational Environment of the Motion Picture Sector," p. 154.

These circumstances crucially affected the degree of attention monitors would commit to films made for domestic markets compared to those made for foreign markets, a difference that helps account for why the gangster film not only survived but thrived where it did in the industry in the postwar 1940s.

THE INDEPENDENTS, THE Bs, AND THE CRIME FILM

While the majors may have felt pressure to "internalize" censorship demands, the same could not be said of the small-budget companies. At first glance this might seem small recompense for the censor's incursions into "A" feature production. Yet, "B" feature and independent production was a highly significant and definitive part of the movie industry's changing organizational environment throughout the 1940s.[6]

The war constituted a boom time; box-office receipts jumped from highs of around $2.5 billion per year in the 1930s to $4.5 billion in 1946. Although fewer films were made during the war, they enjoyed longer runs. Restricted foreign distribution during the war and higher federal censorship control of exports after the war meant the studios were increasingly dependent on domestic revenues. Studios had to tread carefully in meeting censorship demands if they wanted a certificate for international release, something important when it came to expensive A features. In these cases the foreign market was an important consideration if studios wanted to cover costs.[7] B feature

6. Brian Taves's "The B Film: Hollywood's Other Half," in *The Grand Design: Hollywood as a Modern Business Enterprise,* ed. Tino Balio (Berkeley and Los Angeles: University of California Press, 1995), highlights succinctly the categorization and significance of the Bs primarily in the 1930s, and addresses the various changes that influenced the eventual demise of B production. He takes pains to illustrate how the low-budget "programmer" label associated with this kind of production disguised a whole host of maverick films and cycles, operating often as a place of thematic and aesthetic experimentation. Because the A / B distinction discouraged critical attention, B films were overlooked by reviewers in their time. See also Don Miller, *B Movies* (New York: Ballantine Books, 1973).

7. Ruth Vasey contends that Hollywood had always depended on meeting the needs of foreign markets. Marketing national identities that would not offend was not only a product of censorship, for it made commercial sense as well. *The World According to Hollywood, 1918–1939* (Exeter: University of Exeter Press, 1997). Vasey's study ends in 1939, and it seems that the traits she identifies up to that point were bound to be affected by wartime and Cold War nationalist animosities. The need to be even more vigilant about America's national self-image and the image of "others" in the context of fighting Germans and Japanese and then the Cold War against the Soviet Union seems to have polarized the agendas that affected films for export and films for domestic release.

production units, however, traditionally relied on domestic box-office returns anyway, and did not as a result have to kowtow to propagandistic federal ideas of wholesome film fare.

Dore Schary's tenure as head of MGM production (1948–1956) typified the way the majors tried to have it both ways after the war. MGM was a conservative studio traditionally associated with glitzy high production values and big-name stars. Even though this studio may have seemed to be the least likely to contradict State Department wishes, it could not ignore the public appetite for crime thrillers. MGM poached RKO for Schary, a producer prepared to put his name to such controversial portrayals of postwar society as *Crossfire* (1947) (a film about an anti-Semitic returning GI who murders a Jew), *Berlin Express* (1948) (a film about a residual Nazi underworld exerting control over the bombed-out ruins of Berlin), and *They Live by Night* (1948) (a dark prison-break caper film about doomed love on the lam).

Initially, MGM produced a series of "Crime Does Not Pay" shorts, which constituted a way to both address audience fascination with topical crime themes and to satisfy federal desires for a socially affirmative cinema. As it was, these no-name criminal shorts proved to be a precursor to the studio's association with and co-optation of B movie film talent, such as director Anthony Mann and his (Austrian exile) cameraman, John Alton, both champions of the low-budget crime film. Schary had noted the financial success of Mann and Alton's B features, *Raw Deal* (1948) and *T-Men* (1948), for Eagle-Lion. *Raw Deal* was a gangster narrative featuring an attempt by imprisoned gangster Joe Sullivan (Dennis O'Keefe) to exact revenge on his partners who had framed him. This violent film features a macabre love affair in which Pat (Claire Trevor), to consummate her love for Joe, commits murder. The narrative's determinism is enhanced by John Alton's camera work, which features classic uses of chiaroscuro lighting and oblique angles. *T-Men*, while it ostensibly featured the heroism of Treasury agents, had as its central dramatic interest the duplicitous life of an undercover agent. The film's juxtaposition of a stentorian voice-over with John Alton's highly mannered and subjective camera style (deep focus, extreme and oblique angles, coupled with dark mise-en-scène) typifies the contradictory impulse of trying to have it both ways. Behind the veneer of accord with moral and political stewards, such films communicated far more complicated and pessimistic messages about life in postwar America.

The B crime features produced by MGM during Dore Schary's regime included *Border Incident* (1949), *Scene of the Crime* (1949),

Mystery Street (1950), *The Strip* (1951), *Cause for Alarm* (1951), and *Rogue Cop* (1954). Collectively, they present a disturbing picture of a psychologically crippled culture at the mercy of prejudice and graft. They illustrate how at least at the level of B production the majors acted in concord with smaller studios in being prepared to risk the wrath of censors in continuing to make gangster and other kinds of crime films. In fact, the largest group (one-third) of products denied export licenses by the State Department's Office of Censorship were crime features made by smaller producers.[8]

The reactivation of the antitrust suit (Paramount suit) in 1944, and the Supreme Court's decision in 1948 that indeed the film industry was in breach of antitrust laws, underpinned this shift toward independent production after the war.[9] In sum, these conditions created an environment where small-budget films and independent studios would become most responsible for the continued manufacture of crime features, and thus the most likely to have a run-in with the State Department. Add to this the fact that independent studio production increased because of wartime tax breaks from 1939 to 1945 (the number of independent production companies increasing from ten to forty),[10] and we get a disconcerting scenario for censors after the war:

8. The OWI monitored 86 percent of Hollywood film production (May 1942–August 1945), of which 32 percent had to be doctored before it met with OWI approval. Another 30 percent needed no attention having been made to suit OWI needs. While studios were under no legal obligation in the home market to kowtow to OWI demands, they knew that federal regulators would exert authority in prohibiting films they disapproved of from export. Most significant in this regard was the fact that one-third of the films (50 out of the 150 total) denied export during the war were gangster or JD films. Parker, "The Organizational Environment of the Motion Picture Sector," p. 153. Not only were such films viewed as detrimental to the image of America abroad, they were seen as cutting into the revenues of the major studios. While new foreign countries started to place restrictions on American imports, B crime features continued to make it overseas. While a foreign nation may have accepted these features because such low production-value films presented the least threat to local film industries, the State Department saw in these films an accompanying destruction of America's image abroad. As a result it forged an illegal collusion with the major studios' foreign trade association, the Motion Picture Export Association (MPEA), to sponsor major studios over independents in promoting products for foreign markets.

9. In 1938 the Justice Department launched an antitrust suit against the eight major studios, arguing that their monopolistic control of all aspects of film exhibition (i.e., theater ownership), distribution, and production constituted a breach of antitrust law. The suit sought to liberate theater exhibitors from the stranglehold studios had over what could and couldn't be shown. Exhibitors were forced to buy blocks of movies from the studios, denying them freedom to select individual films. Although the suit was temporarily allayed in 1940, its revival in 1944 signaled to many the impending breakup of the studio monopoly system, and gave impetus to those who wished to work independently.

10. Parker, "The Organizational Environment of the Motion Picture Sector," p. 151.

not only were crime features still being made, but that part of the industry most responsible for their production (autonomous and independent) was increasing. The volatile conditions had been established where maverick and politically unpredictable movie talent could move beyond both the confines of the majors and the purview of the censors to contribute to the production of what federal regulators considered detrimental images of the American way of life.

The collusion between independent companies and the illicit crime film was encouraged because on one hand this film form posed a low financial risk, and on the other it provided a way of representing American life that satisfied the artistic and political integrity of many independent filmmakers. The crime film was both topical and low-budget. It was amenable to cost-saving devices, such as location shooting, use of everyday fashion, low-key high-contrast lighting (which saved on expensive set design and costumes), and long takes (which saved on film stock). Not surprisingly, at war's end, the crime film emerged as a prized venue for newly independent studios and for quasi-independent offshoots of the majors, which included Enterprise Studios (a production company offering actors and directors a share of the profits; it attracted prominent left-liberal film talent such as Abraham Polonsky, Robert Rossen, and John Garfield), Cagney Productions, John Huston's Horizon Production Company, Hal Wallis Productions, and Mark Hellinger's International Pictures (the most profitable of the "indies" and later subsumed as a wing of Universal). Significantly, all of the latter were composed of film talent once associated with Warner Brothers' crime and social problem films. On finding the studio increasingly unwilling to maintain its concern for films of "socially significant" content after the war, they sought the necessary autonomy to keep this tradition alive.[11]

While at Warner Brothers, Hal Wallis had been at the forefront of producing classics of the social problem film (*I Am a Fugitive from a Chain Gang*, 1932), the gangster film (*High Sierra*, 1941), and the detective film (*The Maltese Falcon*, 1941). Following his departure from Warner Brothers, he set up his own production company, Hal Wallis Productions, which produced a range of classic postwar crime thrillers, such as *I Walk Alone* (1948), *Sorry, Wrong Number* (1948), *The*

---

11. See Brian Neve, *Film and Politics in America: A Social Tradition* (London: Routledge, 1992), p. 108. It is significant that during the period before Hal Wallis's and Mark Hellinger's departures from Warner Brothers (pre-1944–1945), gangster films constituted nearly 10 percent of the studio's production. Afterward (1944–1950), this level fell to only 3 percent. See Parker, p. 155.

File on Thelma Jordan (1950), and *Dark City* (1950). Mark Hellinger was associated with the production of some notable pre-war gangster films, *The Roaring Twenties* (1939) and *High Sierra*. After the war he specialized in producing pessimistic and aesthetically innovative crime films and in hiring European exile film talent to make them. Before his untimely death he produced *The Killers* (1946), *Brute Force* (1947), and *Naked City* (1948). Two other crime films planned by Hellinger, *Criss Cross* (1949) and *Knock On Any Door* (1949), were made posthumously. In many ways, Hellinger's International Pictures proved to be Universal's financial savior after the war. Much like MGM's engagement of Dore Schary, the Universal-International arrangement highlighted the degree to which the majors, in spite of federal and moral objection, could not afford to ignore the postwar audience's continued appetite for hard-boiled social realism and dramatically heightened treatments of crime.

As the Warner Brothers' exodus of film talent associated with this kind of filmmaking illustrates, major studios may have been initially willing to go along first with OWI and later State Department desires. On observing the increase in crime film production among the smaller independent studios, however, the majors were quick to realize the degree to which such compliance might cut into their profit margins. In fact, while Warner Brothers' gangster film production dropped drastically after the war, low-budget independent crime film production rose from forty films in 1945 to one hundred by 1947.[12]

That 1947 was also the year the House Committee on Un-American Activities (HUAC) launched its inquisition into Hollywood's seditious propensity suggests some connection between the industry's readjustments and political fears. The changing terms of gangster film production signify not so much the successful outlawing of the cycle, but its rebirth in the less policed and less conservative areas of the industry. If federal monitoring agencies felt Hollywood to be an essential part of sociocultural regulation, it was apparent that significant sections of Hollywood were ill suited to this task. The gangster film

---

12. James J. Parker, against the grain of his own argument, makes the point that such low production values only exacerbated the impression that the independents were responsible for promoting "poor representations of America." He adds that after the war, once the OWI and Office of Censorship were terminated and the monitoring of film exports was taken over by the State Department, the latter institution "became increasingly disturbed about the uncontrolled flood of U.S. films in the foreign market that portrayed America unfavorably. Many of these were low-budget crime films from indies, whose number had swelled from 40 in 1945 to 100 in 1947." Parker, p. 157.

was particularly problematic as it constituted an avenue for "indies," promising the best financial returns in their quest for autonomy from various kinds of authority (moral and political censorship, as well as the studio system and its monopoly on aesthetic and financial resources).

Unable to spread financial risk across a wide array of products, the independents proved more vulnerable to box-office fluctuations than the majors, and became a short-lived late 1940s phenomenon. The general demise of the socially critical gangster film is linked not only to the fate of the indies, but to the downfall of B picture production units in the majors (following the infrastructural rearrangements that followed from the antitrust suit).[13] The fate of the gangster film, however, cannot be considered independently of the powerful mitigating factors of federal intrusion in Hollywood, which discouraged the majors from associating themselves with this kind of filmmaking immediately after the war (a subject detailed in the last two chapters).

Before the demise of the organizational frameworks that could host the gangster film, filmmakers made the most of the opportunity to develop the cycle's capacity for telling social commentary. Independent movie talent and mavericks within the majors were also not shy to exploit the rich range of issues the gangster film could encode.

Two of the more repeated gangster variations in the postwar 1940s were the gangster-syndicate film and the gangster-caper film. In examining the appeal and significance of these variations, especially to the more "independent" filmmakers, I have isolated two rich examples: first, of the gangster-syndicate film, *Force of Evil* (1948), and then of the gangster-caper film, *The Asphalt Jungle* (1950).

FORCE OF EVIL: THE CORPORATION AS RACKET

The list of 1940s and 1950s gangster-syndicate films is long, and it is not my goal to be exhaustive. Suffice it to say from the outset that most syndicate films concern the plight of an individual (normally a syndicate foot soldier) working against an impersonal and brutal system. Most obviously, such films constitute ways to dramatize people's

---

13. While the antitrust suit may have provided initial impetus for the move to independent production, it somewhat ironically undermined the financial security that had previously underpinned B movie production. In the days of monopoly control the studios could guarantee that B movies would be sold to exhibitors as part of the block purchase agreements they enforced (where exhibitors had no choice but to buy a package of preselected A and B features from the studios). See note 6.

general concerns about the relations of power between themselves and the organizations they serve. Compared to the 1930s gangster narrative, the syndicate film switches its focus from people who lead or stand out in organizations to the anonymous followers, telling stories not of "making it" but "making do."

A film such as *Force of Evil*, for example, takes to its limit the gangster-syndicate film's propensity for a damaging political critique of corporate power and the advent of the "organization man." The film starred John Garfield, an actor of left-wing political beliefs and long associated with sympathetic social "misfit" roles.[14] And of all the films made by the Enterprise team of Roberts/Polonsky/Garfield, *Force of Evil* most clearly displayed a leftist political line.[15]

Force of Evil starts with an establishing shot of New York's financial district where skyscrapers dwarf and frame Trinity Church. This visual motif is obviously meant to underpin a thematic concern about the corrupting force of money. With the words "This is Wall Street," the voice-over of Joe Morse (John Garfield) accompanies the camera's movement downward to the street and into the foyer of a financial building. Describing himself as a lawyer for the numbers racket, Joe then articulates how the numbers racket works by relying on 20 million "sucker" bets to generate more than $100 million a year.[16] The

14. In the pre-war period Garfield had played the role of a boxer on the lam in *They Made Me a Criminal* (1939) and a drifter who ends up subjected to institutionalized brutality as a prison inmate in *Dust Be My Destiny* (1939). During the war he was featured as a disgruntled aviator who learns how to become a team player in *Air Force* (1943). In the postwar period he reprised his boxer role (this time he's in trouble with the mob) in *Body and Soul* (1947).

Focusing on the politically corrupting power of an organized underworld, *Force of Evil* was reminiscent not only of *Body and Soul,* but other earlier Garfield vehicles, such as *Out of the Fog* (1941), which featured the clash between waterfront racketeers and fishermen trying to make an honest living, and *Fallen Sparrow* (1943), an anti-Fascist film in which a Spanish Civil War veteran finds himself hunted down by the Nazi underworld on his return to New York City.

15. As a screenwriter, Abraham Polonsky's political leanings could be discerned from his choice of subject matter and themes. Garfield's attraction to certain misfit roles and socially critical narratives meant that his left-liberal sentiments were apparent. By comparison Bob Roberts's political outlook was more open to conjecture. Roberts was Garfield's business representative. Together they formed Roberts Productions and entered into a business relationship with Enterprise Studios in 1946 in order to facilitate making independent films. Responsible for the production of such politically contentious films as *Body and Soul* (1947) and *Force of Evil* (1948), Roberts was eventually to fall victim to the inquisition mentality of the early 1950s. The actor Martin Berkeley was to accuse Roberts of being a Communist during HUAC's Hollywood witchhunts. See Robert Sklar, *City Boys: Cagney, Bogart, Garfield* (Princeton: Princeton University Press, 1992), for a fuller exposition.

16. Based on Ira Wolfert's novel, *Tucker's People,* Bob Roberts and Abraham Polonsky had wanted to call the film "The Numbers Racket." The Production Code Administration, however, raised objection to the word "racket," and Enterprise changed the title to *Force of Evil.*

Force of Evil (1948). Crime goes corporate as the syndicate's officers meet to discuss the tallies of the adding machine. John Garfield (as the appropriately named Joe Morse) plays the modern gangster as a glorified accountant calculating profit margins.

equation between this massive daily swindle and the operations of Wall Street is the film's main issue. The message: scratch the surface of Wall Street and you will find the corruption that buttresses it.

The line separating authorized "business" from the racket is revealed to be extremely thin. As Joe states laconically, "temporarily our enterprise was illegal." His job as a "corporate lawyer" is to get legislation passed to change the numbers racket into a legal lottery. Before this takes place, however, the syndicate plans to fix the numbers such that 776 (the old "liberty number") will turn up on July 4th—when most suckers let patriotism dictate their bet. In this way the smaller collection houses will "go to the wall" trying to pay off their clients, and the syndicate will move in to take over their territory.

Force of Evil is saturated in business rhetoric, concerning as it does the corporate takeover of smaller numbers "banks" by "the organization" or "combine." Amidst the language of mergers and percentages, Joe is faced with the resistance of his brother, Leo (Thomas Gomez), who refuses to go along with his brother's scheme to merge his bank into the combine. "I do my business honest," declares Leo as he denounces Joe's affiliation with "gangsters." Joe points out that Leo is part of the very system of graft he is denouncing, stealing nickels and dimes from the "little people." It is clear, however, that the differences are real, that Leo is a caring employer, and that his employees like working for someone who treats them with dignity and respect. Once the combine does take over, Leo's employees object to "higher management's" ruthless leadership style. Joe's affection for his brother and romantic attachment to Leo's secretary, Doris (Beatrice Pearson), operate as voices of conscience. And when Leo's quest to remain a human being in a world of graft eventually gets him killed, Joe makes a decision to change his ways.

While clearly intended to offset the emerging corporate order, Leo's old-style ideals of provincial small-scale business are not left unscathed either. In one exchange, his wife, Sylvia, urges that he have nothing to do with his brother:

> *Sylvia:* Don't have anything to do with him Leo—you're a businessman.
> *Leo:* Yes! I've been a businessman all my life and, honest, I don't know what a business is.
> *Sylvia:* Well, you had a garage. You had a real estate business.
> *Leo:* A lot you know! Real estate business: living from mortgage to mortage, stealing credit like a thief. And the garage! That was a business! Three cents overcharge on every gallon of gas. Two for the chauffeur and a penny for me. Penny for one thief, two cents for the other. Well Joe's here now. I won't have to steal pennies anymore. I'll have big crooks to steal dollars for me.

That hallowed American space of individual private enterprise is revealed to be just another form of graft. An ethical business community remains something more imagined than real. This feature is indicative of the way the postwar gangster film no longer saddled the ethnic with capitalism's problems. This was probably a consequence both of censorship (which, ironically, continued to censure emulations of the older urban-ethnic style of gangster) and of a culture that had changed quite radically since the early 1930s. In this postwar film the allegorical power of gangsterdom (the syndicate world) points no longer to the margins and "the other half" but to the very heart of the enterprise culture as the source of sociocultural breakdown.

Although made by a politically motivated group within an independent company, *Force of Evil* should not be viewed as exceptional in its critique of corporate capitalism and its organization men. It is clear that across the political spectrum filmmakers and studios were taking advantage of the gangster film's constitutive engagement with capitalist mythology. While *Force of Evil*'s political message may have been more overt than that of other gangster films, the fact remains that it made its point within the conventional parameters of the gangster formula.

Force of Evil shares concerns common to much of the postwar gangster-syndicate cycle. Its Cain and Abel clash between Joe and Leo mediates shared postwar concerns about the disappearance of one order and the rise of something sinister to take its place. *Force of Evil* typifies a shift in the gangster narrative's attention from leaders to grunt soldiers; from Algerism to corporatism; from sociological problems of ethnic environment to the more bourgeois concern for an inner world of psychological (in)stability or (mal)adjustment to the new order of things. In sum, the film embodies a turn toward examining the criminal terms of "making do" as opposed to "making it."

A common thread that links gangster-syndicate films of the late 1940s is the dramatization of maladjustment to a changed world. Leo's perception of himself in *Force of Evil* as hopelessly anachronistic in the face of new forms of "organization" is shared by a whole host of protagonists in the postwar gangster-syndicate film. The old ways of doing things are outmoded, as are older notions of what constitutes the gangster's community—the gang becomes a syndicate.[17]

Some notable entries in the late 1940s gangster-syndicate cycle, such as *Nobody Lives Forever* (1946), *Somewhere in the Night* (1946), and *Ride the Pink Horse* (1947), feature the double problem of GIs returning to criminal organizations that have been radically transformed. In *Nobody Lives Forever* Nick Blake (John Garfield) returns from the war to find his gambling operation and his girl have been taken over. In *Somewhere in the Night* George Taylor (John Hodiak)

---

17. The concern about the loss of the old-fashioned gangster "community" (gang) is part of such films as *Nobody Lives Forever* (1946), *Somewhere in the Night* (1946), *Ride the Pink Horse* (1947), *The Gangster* (1947), *I Walk Alone* (1948), and *Race Street* (1948). All feature the problems of old-styled "ethical" gangsters failing to adjust to the new order. All tell tales of alienated individuals up against the faceless organization that has usurped the "faced" gangster of the prewar era.

is an ex-marine and amnesiac who embarks on a quest to recover his pre-war identity. He turns out to be an ex-mobster called Larry Cravat who stole two million dollars in a caper and withheld their share of the take from his gang. The money is deemed to be war contraband from Germany.

This complicated interweaving of war, larceny, loss of memory, and identity is also key to *Ride the Pink Horse.* Gagin (Robert Montgomery) is a cynical ex-GI and a lower-echelon foot soldier in the syndicate. He journeys to a small New Mexico town, San Pablo, during fiesta to blackmail a big-time mobster, Frank Hugo. Gagin is motivated out of revenge, Hugo having killed Gagin's partner following a double cross. Displaced from his Chicago roots, Gagin is left to wander alone through a strange landscape made stranger by the adornments of carnival. The ritualistic encoding of Gagin's attempt to right the past is tied in with his admonition that he's up against war profiteers, and is trying to exorcise the demons that have irrevocably changed the America to which GIs returned.[18]

This sense of returning to a changed-for-the-worse world, however, is key to a series of non-vet crime films, such as *The Dark Corner* (1946) and *I Walk Alone* (1948). *Dark Corner* is a surrogate returning vet film. The protagonist has been released/discharged from prison (an obvious metaphor for return and domestic rehabilitation in 1946) after serving time for a crime he did not commit. Resuming his job as a private investigator, he finds himself once again the object of a frame-up. Unable to extract himself from a situation in which he has been stripped of all autonomy, he cries out "I feel all dead inside. I'm backed up in a dark corner and I don't know who's hitting me."[19]

Such feelings of impotence are the core to *I Walk Alone.* As in *Dark*

18. The metaphor of return that informs these films is clearly connected to the collective experience of Americans trying to adjust to peacetime domesticity. This is most obvious in crime films that feature returning GIs, such as *Cornered* (1945), *Nobody Lives Forever* (1946), *Somewhere in the Night* (1946), *Till the End of Time* (1946), *The Blue Dahlia* (1946), *Ride the Pink Horse* (1947), *Act of Violence* (1947), *High Wall* (1947), *Crossfire* (1947), and *Dead Reckoning* (1947).

19. This sense of malaise and alienation pervades *The Gangster* (1947), which focuses on a small-time hood, Shubunka (Barry Sullivan), who is facing a syndicate takeover. This highly mannered film, which is about inaction rather than action, goes against the grain of the classic gangster formula. Shubunka is too concerned about whether his lover loves him, and too preoccupied by petty vanities and jealousies, to pay adequate heed to his partner's warnings that a rival is moving in on his territory. *Race Street* (1948) features similar problems. George Raft plays an honorable small-time bookie fending off the encroachments of an extortion racket. This old time gangster-protagonist is portrayed as an ethical dinosaur, the residue of a less complicated era.

Corner, the protagonist is an ex-convict. Frankie Madison (Burt Lancaster) returns from a long prison term, having taken the rap for his gangster partner, Noll Turner (Kirk Douglas). In the Prohibition days Frankie and Noll had run a nightclub. One night their truck full of bootleg is intercepted by the police; the partners decide to split up to divert them. If either one is caught, the other promises to continue to run the nightclub, saving half of the profits for him on release. Frankie goes to prison, and on his return finds that Noll has transformed the organization into a complex corporate enterprise. Noll is not prepared to split the profits generated by this streamlined operation, only those made on the old nightclub before it was sold. Frankie, unable to comprehend the new corporation anyway, feels doubly betrayed and alienated. When Noll kills Frankie's brother (the syndicate bookkeeper), Frankie executes a revenge killing that leaves the path free for him to try his hand at a legitimate business.

Less romantic in its understanding of the "simpler" past is *Key Largo* (1948), which features an aborted comeback of the 1930s gangster. Johnny Rocco (an aging Little Caesar), played by Edward G. Robinson, attempts to return from deportation to make it in postwar America, only to be thwarted by a cynical GI (Humphrey Bogart). Like other gangster films concerned with returning undesirable aliens, such as *Gambling House* (1950), *Deported* (1950), and *His Kind of Woman* (1951), *Key Largo* delivers an ambivalent message. Although these films reveal that the days of the ethnic hoodlum are over (he is either deported or fails to make it back to America), they are uncertain about the benevolence of what has taken its place.

While the gangster-syndicate formula was one likely to attract audiences and guarantee box-office returns, it served, concomitantly, as a forum for assorted concerns about the postwar social order. Collectively, gangster-syndicate films played on contemporaneous anxieties about the loss of individual (predominantly male) agency in the name of serving the organization. GIs had already "sacrificed" autonomy in order to serve the war machine. The context of war had enforced a principle of governmentality for the duration of the conflict. The disciplining features of wartime organization, not only at the front but in the munitions factories, had not only helped fashion a homogeneous notion of American identity in the name of nationalist teamwork, but had set in motion the corporate invigoration of the American workplace. Returning from the war, GIs, like their female partners, were insecure about the order they had defended, uncertain about the rewards for such self-sacrifice.

Symptomatic of the confusions of the postwar period were the rash of strikes that resulted in the Taft-Hartley Act of 1947, American organized labor's historic compromise with management.[20] The insecurity about what others were doing in one's interest led to internal strife between union representatives and significant sections of the rank and file. The gangster-syndicate films of the period played on doubts and fears about the totalizing nature of loyalty to a whole range of "organizations."

These films were also forerunners of a spate of 1950s syndicate "exposé" features made following Senator Estes Kefauver's televised investigation of organized crime in 1950–1951.[21] While some of these use the syndicate milieu as an opportunity to valorize institutions such as the FBI and to demonize unions, most of them take as their central dramatic interest not so much the fight between "good" and "bad" institutions, but the fact that nothing (including the judicial system, politics, real estate, the union, and trade) is immune to graft and mob control. These films focused on the decline of individual agency before the power of organizations, collectively reflecting the inquisitional climate of the Red Scare that had only exacerbated the general paranoia about institutional power.[22]

20. See George Lipsitz, *A Rainbow at Midnight: Labor and Culture in the 1940s* (Urbana-Champaign: University of Illinois Press, 1994), for a full exposition on the battle for and against this compromise. The agreement certainly secured an era of relative stability in capital-labor relations, but it also left significant sections of the rank and file with the feeling of having been sold out.

21. Key examples of post-Kefauver syndicate exposés include *Appointment with Danger* (1951), *The Enforcer* (1951), *The Racket* (1951), *The Mob* (1951), *Captive City* (1951), *The Strip* (1951), *Hoodlum Empire* (1952), *The Narrow Margin* (1952), *The Turning Point* (1952), *The Big Heat* (1953), *The Miami Story* (1954), *On the Waterfront* (1954), *Suddenly* (1954), *New York Confidential* (1955), *The Big Combo* (1955), *When Gangland Strikes* (1955), *Chicago Confidential* (1958), and *Underworld U.S.A.* (1961).

22. Images and stories about a syndicate-controlled society overlapped Cold War concerns about Communist conspiracy. Anti-Communist films like *Red Menace* (1949) (Communism takes advantage of disenchanted war vet), *The Woman on Pier 13* (1949) (also released as *I Married a Communist*—Commies return out of the past to blackmail a shipping executive), and *The Trial* (1955) (Commies infiltrate the justice system) dramatized the Communist spectre as another form of underworld mob organization whose tentacles extended even into the heart of the all-American family (as in *My Son John*, 1952). On the foreign front, *The Third Man* (1949) and *Berlin Express* (1948) extended into the postwar era those conventions of the spy thriller that once focused on Nazi syndicates. Fear of the fascist threat was now transferred onto Communism. These Red Scare portrayals of illicit corporate and even global organizations capable of unrestricted power abuse found their apotheosis in films such as *World for Ransom* (1954) and *Kiss Me Deadly* (1955), which synthesized fear of the syndicate with fear of the atom bomb.

THE GANGSTER-CAPER FILM: *GEMEINSCHAFT* VERSUS *GESELLSCHAFT* IN *THE ASPHALT JUNGLE*

The gangster-syndicate film revealed that Prohibition and Depression-era gangsters had no chance in postwar America. As the Bogart character, Frank McCloud, stated in *Key Largo,* fighting a war against a common enemy had helped exorcise many "ancient ills." In bringing Americans together to fight the common foe, older ethnic and class divisions had to be overcome. As the film illustrates, however, the irony of this transformation was that one was left with a lack of identity, a potentially faceless and displaced life in an increasingly impersonal world. Syndicate films testified to a cynicism and confusion about the terms of corporate existence and *embourgeoisement.* While the gangster-syndicate films told tragic stories of alienated action against the corrupting power of large unethical criminal machines, the gangster-caper film dealt with a more organized attempt to defy the system. The execution of the caper or heist involved putting together a team against the system. In many ways, the caper film replayed the dynamics of the independent/major studio conflict, drawing attention even more poignantly than the syndicate film to the lost possibility of *Gemeinschaft* (civic community) before the totalizing power of *Gesellschaft* (society/corporation).

The Asphalt Jungle, made in 1949 and released in 1950, was an independent John Huston production venture, distributed through MGM.[23] In 1948 Huston had, in conjunction with his old studio, Warner Brothers, made *Key Largo,* a film that met with considerable censorship problems.[24] Given this experience, it is interesting that Huston, in an independent capacity, would have chosen to return to a film form that he knew would guarantee a hostile reception from moral and political stewards. While Huston's political affiliations were not as radically marked as Polonsky, Roberts, Rossen, and Garfield at Enterprise, he was associated with a vast array of left-liberal causes. Not only this, he was one of the most prominent anti-HUAC protestors. A founding member of the Committee for the First Amendment (CFA), which tried to defend the rights of Hollywood workers against the political inquisition, Huston was one of only two members

---

23. Huston's contract with Warner Brothers expired in 1947. In a quasi-independent capacity, he continued to make films with Warner Brothers as a releasing company and used some Warners production staff, such as (on *Key Largo*) Jerry Wald. In 1948 he set up an independent production company, Horizon, with Sam Spiegel.

24. See my discussion in chapter 6 of *Key Largo*'s censorship reception.

at an emergency meeting of the Screen Directors' Guild to object to Leo McCarey's insistence that everyone take the Oath of Allegiance following the first HUAC hearings in October 1947. McCarey was a prominent director who went from making relatively "innocent" Oscar-winning fare like *Going My Way* in 1944 to making a polemical anti-Communist feature, *My Son John*, in 1952. To Huston, McCarey was a "Machiavellian figure" who embodied everything he detested about Hollywood's political transformation after the war.[25]

In many ways, *Asphalt Jungle* is a product of these mitigating influences, reflecting Huston's postwar dispondency and disenchantment. As Carl Macek points out, this was to be Huston's swansong to the American crime film; he was thereafter to devote his independent efforts to other kinds of film material, especially film versions of literary classics.[26] Thus his choice in this independent framework to make a film like *Asphalt Jungle* was a product of several factors, not the least being that the crime cycle was a proven box-office commodity and a lower financial risk for an independent venture. More significant, however, much like *Force of Evil*, *Asphalt Jungle* can be read as a response to a climate of shrinking political possibilities, a film that reflects on a lost virtuous and ethical American (populist and pre-lapsarian) landscape that has been corroded by city filth and political graft. *Asphalt Jungle* can be interpreted as Huston's lament on the disappearance of New Deal liberalism and the death of civic culture. This political disenchantment, however, is not something unique to the director. In fact, it's something dramatized in other gangster films released in the same year as *Asphalt Jungle*, such as *Kiss Tomorrow Goodbye* and *Underworld Story*, both of which portray small-town USA as an environment infested by graft and subject to mob manipulation. *Asphalt Jungle*, then, was just one example (albeit one of the most powerful) of how the gangster formula could be exploited to air concerns about the corruption of civic virtue.

Asphalt Jungle extends author W. R. Burnett's jeremiad vision of a culture in declension, which was first realized on screen in *High Sierra*

25. Billy Wilder confirms John Huston's story that when Leo McCarey insisted that all the directors take an open Oath of Allegiance to communicate their collective support for the investigation, only Wilder and Huston (out of over 150 directors present) raised objection to this demand. Hellmuth Karasek, *Billy Wilder: Eine Nahaufnahme* (Munich: Wilhelm Heyne Verlag, 1994), pp. 366–67.

26. See Carl Macek's entry on *The Asphalt Jungle* in Alain Silver and Elizabeth Ward, eds., *Film Noir: An Encyclopedic Reference to the American Style*, 3d ed. (Woodstock, N.Y.: Overlook Press, 1992), p. 15.

(for which Huston had written the screenplay). In the latter film, Roy Earle (Humphrey Bogart), a Dillinger-styled gangster, is released from prison to lead one last job. He finds, however, that he is an anachronistic vestige of the outlaw era, and is driven to the outer fringe of society where he meets his death in the mountains. Where Earle was clearly a "leader," *Asphalt Jungle*'s most sympathetic character, Dix (Sterling Hayden) is (typically for the era) just a foot soldier. As a displaced country hick Dix yearns to escape the city and return to the Kentucky of his youth. This journey, however, is no longer a possibility because his father died and the banks foreclosed on the farm and stable. Dix lives off the dream of winning enough on the horses to buy back the farm in what amounts to a tragic metaphor for the end of pastoral idealism before the forces of consumerism and urbanization. Dix's fate encodes even more bitterly the certitude that the world he embodies is indeed just a dream (an imagined community, nothing more).[27] The nature/city conflict he embodies is reconstituted as a battle between dreams and reality. The city is here to stay. It sucks the farm population into the city where they too must succumb to its corruption. This vision is, of course, different than that in *Force of Evil*, which doesn't pit country against city but small business against big. While *Force of Evil* delivers an indictment of urban corruption, it doesn't propose an alternative landscape of possibilities. As a pragmatic acknowledgment of the urban character of modern American life, it is involved in the business of trying to redeem the city.

Asphalt Jungle, by comparison, contains the residue of frontier mythology in its appeal to some more authentic American landscape. Yet the film's critique of the present is enforced by the fact that this other American space is wholly illusory—a thing of childhood not maturity, a thing of the past not the present. Dix, an American primitive (a mix of farm boy and hoodlum), occupies the lowest echelon in the modern crime organization. Unlike *High Sierra*'s Roy Earle or *Petrified Forest*'s Duke Mantee, pre-war gangsters who encoded country-styled outlawry, Dix is not a leader type whose career traces a heroic rise and

27. Dix's desire to run away to another landscape is shared by other characters, such as Emmerich (or at least his girl) who looks at advertisements for Cuba, and Riedenschneider who warns a fellow German expatriate (a cab driver) that he had once tried returning home and it wasn't worth it. The ideals of another place are for him diversions from the truth of having to survive in the present. This oscillating play between here and there, present America and somewhere else (either its imagined purer past or Europe or Cuba), feeds an atmosphere of disenchantment and dashed hopes.

fall. Dix is a loser. He's an average guy, entertaining simple (albeit Oedipal) aspirations (he just wants to go home). He has a virtuous code. He is honest, which is of course his biggest flaw in a world where dishonesty and the double cross are the keys to success (a fact embodied in Emmerich, the shyster lawyer, played by Louis Calhern).

At the film's outset, the camera follows police patrol cars as they prowl into the warehouse district of an anonymous midwest city. They follow a shadowy figure (Dix) to a sleazy cafe. After a silent exchange in which the cafe proprietor (Gus, played by James Whitmore) hides Dix's gun, the police arrive and arrest Dix for vagrancy. From the outset, light/dark relations are defined in terms of the relationship of criminal to police. Police drive into the dark part of the city. Dix is arrested and taken to a lineup where low-key high-contrast lighting becomes a device associated with the practices of police interrogation and criminal identification (a light is shone directly onto the lineup, while police and witnesses remain in darkness). This is carried over as a consistent part of the mise-en-scène, many shots echoing each other in their structure and content. Throughout the film, characters must negotiate long dark corridors before finding lit spaces, which, paradoxically, offer no source of relief, becoming instead harshly lit spaces of confinement rather than freedom. There is the long corridor in the bookie's joint that leads to a spartan backroom, which echoes the sewer that connects the gang to the jewelry vault, which echoes the jail corridor that leads to the prison cells. All these spaces are filmed via deterministic linear tracking shots.

The anonymity of the city and its claustrophobic dwelling places are what are underscored, not the features that distinguish one city from another. To this extent, the choice of locale is vital. *Asphalt Jungle*'s action takes place in a nameless urban environment, without the distracting meanings associated with pre-war gangster cities, such as New York and Chicago. Once again, in the postwar gangster film, the traditional associations of the cycle with ethnic types and the urban working–class neighborhood are stripped away. This shift is perhaps best embodied in the replacement of New York and Chicago tenements with the suburban sprawl of Los Angeles as the preferred postwar criminal cityscape. The ethnic ghetto is replaced by the amorphous no-man's land found in "anycity" USA. And, while *Asphalt Jungle* relocates the gangster not in Los Angeles, but in an unnamed midwest city, it is symptomatic of this change.

Key to this transformation is the fact that the caper draws on various community members across ethnic and class lines. Put together by a German criminal genius, Riedenschneider (Sam Jaffe), the gang is composed of various social misfits with different forms of griev-ance, financial, psychological, and physical. The gang's members are a bankrupt lawyer, Emmerich, who once had city hall in his pocket and is cheating on his bedridden wife; Ciavelli (Anthony Caruso), the safe-cracking Italian American with a sick kid and a wife to look after in a cramped tenement; Cobby (Marc Lawrence), the nervous bookie who defines success in the modest terms of "making book" (covering costs); Gus, the hunchbacked cafe owner, whose physical deformity has cursed him; and Dix, the displaced country boy who wishes to buy back his family's farm, lost during the Depression, and return to the clean water of Kentucky where he can wash off the city filth.

Even Riedenschneider is not free of problems. Not only is he some-one who has misdirected his technical and theoretical aptitude to con-jure up ways to rob banks and jewelry stores, but he has an unhealthy sexual appetite for teenage girls, which eventually proves his down-fall. To this extent the caper gang only emphasizes alienation rather than community. The gang constitutes a false community, or a false melting pot, brought together in the common interest of committing a crime. The film's plot only reinforces this sense of an ephemeral or pseudo-collectivity. And like other postwar caper films, *Asphalt Jungle* is oriented not so much around the gang's construction as its inevi-table disintegration.[28]

On the other side of the tracks, the police are perceived to be in the service of graft and the system that has crippled the gang's members. Lt. Ditrich (Barry Kelly) is being paid to look the other way. The commissioner (John Ireland), the one voice of moral certitude in the film, seems to function as a moral distraction designed to appease the censors. In the end he delivers a speech that tries to rectify the film's general indictment of police corruption. This constitutes a for-lorn attempt to reestablish the dissolving borders between criminals and police (and sustain a morally compensating narrative).

He claims before assembled members of the press that Lt. Ditrich is an exception to the rule; nearly all police, he asserts, are above re-proach in their honesty and commitment to duty. He then goes on to

---

28. The caper films that underscore this idea of group destruction include *Criss Cross* (1949), *Armored Car Robbery* (1950), *Kansas City Confidential* (1952), *Violent Saturday* (1955), *I Died a Thousand Times* (1955), and *The Killing* (1956). There are other forms of caper film that are less gang-oriented, such as *They Live by Night* (1948) and *Gun Crazy* (1949), which feature fugitive dysfunctional nuclear couples, and *The Big Steal* (1949), a chase-caper film that tells its story from the pursuer's point of view, not the heister's.

The Asphalt Jungle (1950). The values of *Gemeinschaft* under duress—the caper-gang of social misfits as dark metaphor for outmoded and fatally flawed American community.

describe Dix as a cold-hearted murderer. His attempt to control the reception of Dix (who is the prime object of audience identification) is, of course, laughable and entirely at odds with the way the narrative has presented Dix as a man of principle, an average guy with highly understandable desires.

Far from being the social deviant that censors and moral authority may wish him to be, Dix is not a megalomaniac or psychopath, but a man whose present actions are informed logically by the past. He is haunted by the loss of Depression-era hopes. As a result, the irony of the commissioner's comment is that it is so clearly "pat" and misses the mark. The commissioner's moral voice is aurally dissonant, helping register itself as an illogical intrusion on the narrative. Much like earlier concessions to moral censorship that marked "classic" 1930s gangster films like *Scarface* (see chapter 2), this only serves to distance the moral voice and increase the bond between audience and gangster.

Ultimately, the police are portrayed as just another system subject to graft. This is nothing new, for it is consistent with both the prewar gangster film and contemporary postwar gangster-syndicate films like *Scene of the Crime* (1949) (in which police front for the mob). Rather than setting the bad against the good, these films reveal the falsity of the opposition itself, the gangster film's primary function being to reveal the dark side of the apparently "good" society.

Thus, *Asphalt Jungle*'s gathering of social and cultural detritus is presented as an ad hoc mix of Americans. No one social group is singled out for derision. Instead, gang members are drawn from the entire social spectrum (through the device of the caper) and lumped awkwardly together. Collectively, they provide a disturbing picture of a culture without redemption. Their shared aspiration to escape the misery of the present represents an unholy matrimony of dissatisfactions and disenchantments beyond the ghetto. The action places this assemblage of misfits "underground" in sewers and vaults. The camera peers from behind windows to survey the legitimate world no longer from the specific site of the ethnic working class, but from the abstract place of cross-class ennui and frustration. To this extent, the feeling of entrapment is even more intense here than in the prewar "classic" gangster narratives I have discussed, which locate crime in a particular social space. At least in those narratives there was a sense that one could make it out of certain confines to a more emancipatory space. In *Asphalt Jungle* there is no social echelon or space within the American present that is free of frustration and corruption. Even the baroque confines of the lawyer's mansion are not immune. They prove to be just a facade that masks the mansion's function as a glorified asylum for a bankrupt shyster lawyer who is cheating on his psychologically sick wife. There's simply no way out. As Emmerich points out when his wife objects to his association with criminals:

> There's no difference between us and them. After all, crime is only a left-handed form of human endeavor.

This is, ultimately, *Asphalt Jungle*'s most critical point: that crime is not to be ghettoized as a condition exclusive to the dispossessed (traditionally, the ethnic working class in 1930s gangster films). It's endemic to all human behavior. Within the horizons of the gangster-caper film, crime is dramatized as something that infests every aspect of postwar American society, robbing one of any standard by which to make law effective. In order to succeed, the caper involves the collusion of an array of representative social types. It needs financial backing, protection, fences, bribable cops. And everyone can be bought because everyone has a reason to be dissatisfied. In terms of integrity, all that's left is an alienating personal code of honesty, a code that is hard to maintain when one receives nothing in return, and when the only way to "make do" (let alone "make it") is through crime. In the end, these postwar gangster films reveal that what was once a condition describing the ethnic working class is now a universal problem.[29]

The disappearance of the gangster myth's ethnic context did not rob the postwar cycle of its enduring ability to dramatize and critique the terms of urban living, "business" ethics, and capitalism's destructive effects on human relations. Freed from the ghetto, the gangster moved into the center of American life as a way to represent the corruption of the social contract. The benefits of America's *embourgeoisement* were not easy to discern, and the crime film was at the forefront of popular culture in addressing this. To liken corporate and political power to the operation of crime syndicates was to draw attention, at the very least, to the inequitous relations of power between subject and authority. The gangster films revealed how everyone was now living in a kind of gangland. Everyone was working for the boss. The metaphor of the syndicate-run society upset traditional generic limitations and typology. There was no longer an inside/outside social split (the ethnic lower-class ghetto opposed to "legitimate" society). Instead, postwar gangster films told stories of how the average guy was trapped within large determining and corrupting systems. These totalizing systems deprived him of his agency, and thus of his ability to change things.

Thus, far from visions of social "chaos," we are provided pictures of merciless social machines: *Asphalt Jungle* is about how dehumanizing laws apply to the urban environment; *Force of Evil* reveals how

---

29. While *Asphalt Jungle* conveys a sense that crime is endemic to American life, it also suggests that crime is a craft sponsored by the sociocultural elite (something encoded in Emmerich). This is also key to films like *Destination Murder* (1950) (where crime is just a form of aesthetic escapade for the bored upper class) and *Crack-Up* (1946) (where crime is portrayed as a modernist disease associated with the machinations of those who trade in decadent "high" art). Equally in *Laura* (1944), murder is the art of the criminal aesthete (this time the host of a highbrow radio show). This antimodernist fear that a decadent class has corrupted American pragmatism is one more way in which the loss of American innocence is conveyed in the postwar crime cycle. Intriguingly, this thematization of modernist indulgence becomes part and parcel of even HUAC's attempt to exorcise "un-Americanism" from Hollywood. As chapter 7's discussion of Weimar exile filmmakers in Hollywood will reveal, HUAC's political interventions had dire aesthetic consequences for Hollywood.

class aspiration and desire for self-advancement can be subjected to mathematical exploitation for profit. To this extent, these postwar crime films are not so much about lawlessness as they are about the immoral and unethical character of certain power regimes that organize the terms of existence (work and play). Ironically, in the postwar gangster film we actually see a surplus of law. We see the subjection of individuals to the tyranny of deterministic logic, a logic at odds with American myths of individualism and entrepreneurship. To stand out is to resist and thus to be condemned. To assert an individual code is to become, much like Depression gangsters, an outlaw/vigilante. And this is the shared contradiction that links pre- and postwar gangsters.

In an abstract sense, gangsters are relics of an American idealism oriented around individualism and freedom of expression. While there is nothing in this myth that makes it intrinsically politically "progressive" (i.e., conducive to political orders arguing for commitment to social responsibility), there is much in the myth that makes it a threat to the legitimation tactics of organizations, and much in it that draws attention to the abuses of power.

BEYOND GHETTOIZATION BY CATEGORY: THE RUBRIC OF FILM NOIR AS IT APPLIES TO POSTWAR GANGSTER FILMS

It is clear then that the postwar gangster feature was significantly different from its forebears. The significance of this difference can be understood only if we remember the past from which it deviates—the aspects of its forerunners that are dropped (ghetto/working-class context) and those that are intensified (psychopathology/crime as an endemic national condition). Such changes led to conventional category disintegration. Gangster films could be subsumed under additional labels such as "psychological melodrama" and "detective drama." The mixture of contemporaneous terms for the crime film testified to the transformation of established generic distinctions in the 1940s.

Partly in response to this, French critics of the postwar period came up with an alternative term to describe the collectively dark and pessimistic characteristics shared across film forms of the period: namely, film noir. In many ways this term's vagueness has been entirely appropriate to the facets of these crime melodramas it seeks to describe. That is, film noir is a non-genre-specific "second order" textual category. While it attempts to do justice to those aspects of film form that traverse traditional category boundaries, the term can assume the guise of what Joan Copjek calls a "positivist fiction."[30] In trying to master the unmasterable, to grant an existence and coherence to a group of films that precisely threaten such conventional paradigms of containment, the term goes against the grain of the very body of films it attempts to name. Moreover, the term's axiomatic status in film scholarship has tended to obfuscate the prehistory of the films that constitute film noir.

Marc Vernet complains, for example, that the characteristics (visual and thematic) that are regarded as exclusive to 1940s films noirs can be found in an array of pre-war films.[31] My own argument is that the term has aided an ahistorical vision of crime film forms. More particularly, it has aided a "forgetting" of the continuities that link 1930s and 1940s Hollywood. This is no small thing because the political and ideological status of the films we discuss under the rubric of film noir can only be fully understood in terms of how their relationship to the past dictated their contemporaneous reception. As this introduction hopes to demonstate, the 1940s gangster film constituted a mutation of 1930s prototypes; the films that have been labeled as films noirs did not appear out of a vacuum.

While such films certainly addressed the realities of 1940s America, their "sedition," in the eyes of censors, lay in their perceived reinvigoration of a repressed American film tradition. As I wish to pursue in the ensuing chapters in more detail, it was the perceived continuity rather than the difference between 1940s and 1930s crime films that was the main source of concern for those interested in monitoring Hollywood in the postwar era. The postwar crime cycle signaled the comeback of the gangster film, a socially critical film form that had been subject to much censure, and whose return to popularity had been delayed by Hollywood's commitment to supporting the war effort.

---

30. Joan Copjek, introduction to *Shades of Noir: A Reader*, ed. Joan Copjek (London: Verso, 1993), pp. vii–xii.

31. Marc Vernet, "Film Noir on the Edge of Doom," in *Shades of Noir*, pp. 1–32.

6
Screening Crime the Liberal Consensus Way
Postwar Transformations in the Production Code

The Production Code Administration (PCA) was formed during the 1930s to act as Hollywood's moral enforcer. While ostensibly an agent of Christian values designed to monitor and control what could pass for entertainment on screen, the Code had also been the product of compromise with an array of moral interest groups. As I argued in chapter 4, a key part of the PCA's raison d'être was to protect the film industry from damaging outside intervention in its business, a function that at times tempered and even contravened its moral mandate. I have stressed how Protestant and Catholic "leagues" and "legions" only had surface similarities in their hostility toward Hollywood, and that the promotion of Catholic moral leadership via the PCA in the 1930s can only be fully understood when located in the context of a major cultural battle over reigning definitions of "true" American identity and values.

The Catholic stake in becoming prime arbiters of the Code tells us much about the significance the movies held for groups competing for power in Depression America. While Catholic stewardship (especially the Legion of Decency) had a vested interest in the maintenance of the nation's moral order, its view of nationhood was not concomitant with that of the Anglo-Protestant nativist. To the latter, Hollywood symbolized the forces of consumerism and the new Americanism (immigrant and predominantly Catholic), twin threats to the traditional American order. As the talking gangster film bore out, the movies

144

were becoming one of the key arenas where ethnically subordinate constituencies with Catholic allegiancies could exert an influence on the national culture. As I have argued, such gains for groups traditionally designated as American "others" were not easily given up, and the prospect of kowtowing to Anglo-Saxon Protestant demands had to be negotiated. Thus, while clearly invested with a moral mandate, the Code became a place where the "new" Americans could consolidate their newfound power by forging an alliance with the industry's economic interests. The appointment of Joseph Breen, a lay Catholic, as the Code's enforcer provided a way for the industry to protect its affairs behind the mask of moral integrity.

This is not to say that the Code was morally lax. In fact the PCA (or Breen office) performed its duties with zeal. The PCA still had an essentially "prohibitive" character. It remained committed, at least in principle, to an agenda it shared with external WASP moral interests. Its task was to enforce a system of "Don'ts and Be Carefuls," to carry through a negative mandate by censoring violations of Code stipulations. The Code delimited how Hollywood could represent morally contentious issues, especially of criminality and sex. Yet, consequent to the Code's enforcement, such socially significant issues did not vanish from the screen. Instead the film industry found increasingly sophisticated ways to circumnavigate censorship strictures and meet audience demand for an adequate representation of American life. As a result, by the mid- to late 1940s the Code seemed to be in a state of crisis, applying a set of dated principles to an industry now well attuned to "skirting" strategies.

In 1947 director Irving Pichel observed:

> The unity of the war years has vanished. The abstract principles of right and wrong, of justice, of humanitarian feeling to which we subscribed during the war, under which we condemned the practices of a hideous enemy, have become blurred and inapplicable to domestic situations and strains concerning which not so long ago we were perfectly clear.[1]

By the end of World War II the moral order that the Code was purportedly designed to defend was itself anachronistic. That is, it was not simply the case that the Code apparatus was in need of a facelift, but that the order it was meant to defend found itself increasingly

---

1. Irving Pichel, "Areas of Silence," *Hollywood Quarterly* 3 (fall 1947), p. 53.

irrelevant. Censorship scholarship has noted that the Code appeared to have relaxed after the war, citing, in particular, as evidence of this the lack of PCA activity regarding 1940s crime films (those we now call films noirs). Such observations tend to isolate the Code's activities from other forms of censure in the 1940s, overlooking that (1) the Office of War Information (OWI) and its Bureau of Motion Pictures' Office of Censorship assumed a prominent role as the arbiter of Hollywood products (especially for export) throughout the war in the interests of propaganda (see chapter 5); and (2) following the war, the State Department's reinvigoration of the Office of Censorship and the inquisitions by the House Committee on Un-American Activities (HUAC) from 1947 to 1953 more than made up for the PCA's apparent lassitude. The OWI, the State Department, and HUAC in large part augmented the PCA's role as the film industry's "prohibitor," begging questions about the relevance of the Code after the war.

Symptomatically, perhaps, the history of the 1940s PCA seems a catalog of failures and increasing redundancy, its limelight stolen by HUAC and its meaningful life ending with its failure to win its case against *The Moon Is Blue* in 1953 (something I shall return to later), the last year of HUAC's inquisition. What gets forgotten in this story is the extent to which the PCA remained a crucial sorting house for ideas about Hollywood's postwar responsibilities. That is, in the changing contours of the political landscape after the war, the PCA found itself adjusting to new prerogatives, not simply left to defend outmoded ones.

What I shall first attend to here is the period of confusion after the war (preceding HUAC's interventions in 1947), in which the debate over Hollywood's responsibilities (and the PCA's role as the regulator of such responsibilities) found itself crystalized, yet again, around the production and release of a gangster film—namely, *Dillinger* (1945). Second, I shall attend to the actual changes to the PCA film analysis form subsequent to the 1947 HUAC inquisition as symptomatic of a new way to understand the political value of Hollywood's products, one more appropriate to the style and character of the new political order: the ideology of liberal consensus.

The differences between New Deal and postwar ideas of political economy were subtle. Loosely characterized as a shift from "social Keynesianism" to "commercial Keynesianism," postwar ideas about liberalism turned away from the social democratic tenets that had informed the expansion of central government responsibilities during

the Depression.[2] In the climate of emergency, the Roosevelt administration established strong federal powers over the management of the
national economy. In the context of the Depression the word "liberal"
was associated with the federal government's guarantees of social security and employment.

The war had breathed new life into American corporations. With
the cessation of hostilities the government moved away from regulatory programs toward more conservative fiscal policies designed to
support a high consumption economy. Business brokered more autonomy to run its own affairs, while government policy was increasingly directed toward helping sustain the growth of the average standard of living. There was a consensus that American capitalism could
bring about prosperity for all, and that this fiscal goal was not incompatible with the desire that the government maintain (even expand)
certain social and economic safety nets for the citizenry.[3]

2. See Steve Fraser and Gary Gerstle, eds., *The Rise and Fall of the New Deal Order, 1930 –
1980* (Princeton: Princeton University Press, 1989), pp. ix-xxv.

3. For definitive evaluations of postwar liberal consensus ideology, see Charles S. Maier,
"The Politics of Productivity: Foundations of American International Economic Policy After
World War II," *International Organization* 31, no. 4 (1977); Godfrey Hodgson, *America in Our
Time: America from World War II to Nixon* (New York: Doubleday, 1976); Alan Brinkley, "The
New Deal and the Idea of the State," in *Rise and Fall of the New Deal Order*, pp. 85 –121; Nelson
Lichtenstein, "From Corporatism to Collective Bargaining: Organized Labor and the Eclipse of
Social Democracy in the Postwar Era," in *Rise and Fall of the New Deal Order*, pp. 122 – 52; and
Alonzo Hamby, *Liberalism and Its Challengers* (New York: Oxford University Press, 1985). According to Maier, the ideology of consensus was the cement that would bind postwar society
and culture to the economic agenda of a so-called politics of productivity. Hodgson outlines the
main assumptions, ideas, and beliefs that underscored a liberal consensus culture, adumbrating
the rise of notions such as unlimited economic growth and productivity. Brinkley and Lichtenstein outline how the postwar remobilization of business powers, combined with the demand for
the demobilization of centralized federal responsibilities, compromised the project of social democracy. This was replaced by a "social market consensus," as Iwan Morgan puts it, in his
Beyond the Liberal Consensus: A Political History of the United States since 1965 (London: Hurst
and Company, 1994). Hamby describes Eisenhower's administration as one that consolidated
this shift. This Republican president agreed to retain important elements of the New Deal legacy; they had become prerequisites to electability. Eisenhower viewed his mission as "holding
the line" in terms of containing the growth of federal responsibilities. Significantly, he differed
from the old guard of Republicanism (embodied in Robert Taft and Joseph McCarthy), who
wanted to reverse the New Deal. Eisenhower believed that such a stance would spell the end of
the GOP's credibility with the electorate. All these scholars are concerned to show how this
dominant ideology invested capital with a democratic mandate, believing that productivity
would solve all socially divisive problems and cripple the possibilities of any other alternative to
capitalism in the organization of American society after World War II. This too was the guiding
principle behind Eric Johnston's political philosophy as head of the MPAA.

The movies became embroiled in a dispute over the implementation of this new political creed. Eric Johnston, taking over from Will Hays as head of the industry's trade association, believed that Hollywood should be an advocate of the liberal consensus. Members of HUAC desired that Hollywood be purged of its New Deal (more social democratic) leanings. While Johnston's political beliefs should not be confused with HUAC's, both parties wished to shift Hollywood away from Depression-era sociopolitical associations.

As Senator Joseph McCarthy saw it, the mission of the committee was to expunge Communism and all constituencies associated with the leftward margins of the New Deal coalition from all walks of American life in the name of right-wing Republicanism. HUAC's fanatical cause provided an umbrella for more moderate anti-Communists who did not necessarily share in the senator's 100 percent Americanism. Hollywood was understood as a branch of New Deal liberalism, infested if not with Communists then at least with Popular Front advocates. HUAC posited itself as a foil to the attempted leftist indoctrination of the American public via the movies.[4]

While HUAC's interest in Hollywood can be rationalized as part of a general quest for publicity and vindication, the industry's vulnerability to attack rested, ironically, on a perception of Hollywood's lack of ideological commitment. Hollywood's apparent neutrality (and scepticism) in the face of postwar political changes made it open to accusations of treason by groups inside and outside the industry. Within Hollywood, the Motion Picture Alliance for the Preservation of American Ideals asserted that "anyone who is not FIGHTING Communism is HELPING Communism," and welcomed HUAC's 1947 investigation as a chance to correct politically lapse behavior.[5]

As I shall suggest, changes in the role of censorship (from direct intrusion to the development of more sophisticated means of audience and film content analysis derived from social science methodology) seem to be indicative of crucial postwar transformations in attitudes toward Hollywood's cultural and political responsibilities. No longer were the movies to be viewed as agents of immorality and cultural contamination but as forces central to hegemonic regulation.

---

4. See Michael Heale, *American Anti-Communism* (Baltimore: Johns Hopkins University Press, 1990).

5. See Stephen J. Whitfield, *The Culture of the Cold War* (Baltimore: Johns Hopkins University Press, 1991), p. 127.

SCREENING THE GANGSTER'S RETURN

On June 20, 1945, Hollywood director Frank Borzage wrote a letter of complaint to the film industry's trade association, the MPAA (Motion Picture Association of America), in reference to the recent release of the gangster film *Dillinger*:

> I have viewed with growing alarm the trend towards another cycle of gangster and racketeer films. Nothing can do this country and the motion picture industry more harm at this particular time than films designed to glamorize gangsters and their way of life.
>
> At present our entire nation is working desperately on a plan which will bring peace and prosperity and good will to all the world. Foreign nations are looking to the U.S. for guidance. Much of the guidance and influence we will wield on the outside world will be transmitted through the medium of the motion picture.
>
> This is certainly an inopportune time for us to convey the impression that America is made up largely of gangsters, black market operators, petty racketeers and murderers.[6]

Borzage frames not only the gangster film but the entirety of Hollywood's production in the light of America's postwar rise to global superpower. This newfound role dictated that the PCA attend to larger issues than moral uplift in Hollywood's products. The inward-looking America of the Depression and early New Deal years was a thing of the past. In this context, as Borzage emphasizes, Hollywood had a special responsibility in the generation of affirmative images of American life and society.

In many ways, Borzage's concerns about the return of the gangster to popularity engaged the contemporaneous uncertainties about the postwar political landscape. The "return of the gangster" signified very specifically the return to public attention of negative Depression-associated issues. The 1930s gangster's quest to overcome economic and social discrimination (especially in the guise of John Dillinger) reminded audiences of a time whose problems demanded radical New Deal solutions. Postwar attempts to outlaw this kind of gangster's comeback were tied to certain groups' fears about the counterproductive power of New Deal memories. The stated goal of HUAC's inquisitions in the late 1940s as articulated by J. Parnell Thomas, the chair of the committee, was to "expose the New Deal as a Communist

---

6. MPAA/PCA file *Dillinger*, Margaret Herrick Library, Academy for Motion Picture Arts and Sciences (AMPAS), Los Angeles.

project and New Dealers as subversive per se."[7] Representations of America that remained tied to the New Deal era unsettled more than just the fanatical right. Paradoxically, HUAC's function was to do the dirty work for the emerging political order of liberal consensus, which actually had much to gain from the vilification of certain more centralized aspects of the New Deal legacy, those that militated against the belief that capitalism could service a democratic mandate.

Borzage's concern for the detrimental impact of the gangster film on global opinion of the United States was symptomatic, then, of a general awareness about how Hollywood's mediating powers needed regulation. The film industry did not lend itself naturally to positive mediations of "Americanism." Rather it would need to be coerced into producing the kinds of narrative representation appropriate to such a task. While it would be a mistake to conflate Borzage's desires for a socially constructive Hollywood with HUAC's goals, the point remains that many parties in the immediate postwar years held a shared fear that the film industry's propensity for feeding the climate of crisis was stronger than its propensity for resolving it.

Thus, the significance of Frank Borzage's letter lies less in its ostensible demand that Hollywood toe the liberal consensus (or even HUAC) line than in its converse recognition that the commercial film industry was not an automatic agent for an affirmative ideological agenda. Borzage's letter constituted a warning to the industry that it had significant responsibilities to fulfill in a turbulent period of peacetime readjustment. While he does not warn of anything on the scale of a HUAC intervention, Borzage was clearly sensitive to an impending crisis if Hollywood did not act carefully in the war's aftermath. He could see just how vital a political force Hollywood would become for postwar power interests.

The degree to which Borzage influenced changes in the PCA is not the issue here. Rather, what is significant is that it was the gangster film in particular that galvanized his worries. What Borzage proposed was essentially a recipe that Hollywood should follow if it wanted to avoid fiery demands for external intervention in its activities. As we shall see in the following discussion of the *Dillinger* case, Borzage advocated a revitalization of internal and voluntary self-censorship goals. Key to this would be steering clear of material that would be bound to offend, particularly the gangster film. This film form could

---

7. Brian Neve, *Film and Politics in America: A Social Tradition* (London: Routledge, 1992), p. 93. See also my discussion of HUAC's motivations in chapter 7.

Dillinger (1945). "Unwanted"—the unwelcome return of the Depression-era gangster type in the postwar 1940s (Lawrence Tierney in the title role).

only stir up antagonistic memories of Hollywood's last battle with
the advocates of federal regulation. Moreover, the gangster invoked
troubling memories of the New Deal and Depression that could only
interfere with the project of cultural reprogramming in postwar
America.

MEMORIES OF DEPRESSION: *DILLINGER*

In 1945 the King Brothers produced the film *Dillinger*. The choice of
bringing out, at the close of the war, a film so clearly rooted in a pre-
war culture is an obvious point of interest to us here. How would the
Code interpret the reemergence of the gangster film, especially one,
like *Dillinger*, so deeply associated with the Depression, and so directly associated with the outlaw figure who provoked the 1935
moratorium?

Surprisingly, the PCA files show that the Breen office passed the
film with very little problem. The general premise the producers used

to "sell" the film to the Code Administration to gain its Seal of Approval for general release was to argue that *Dillinger* gave its audience a classic example of how "crime doesn't pay." Yet, as the PCA file reveals, once the film was exhibited, it generated strongly adverse criticism from all kinds of interest groups. The various objections to *Dillinger* expose different motivating reasons for exorcising the gangster and demonstrate the extent to which Hollywood was viewed as crucial territory to be won or lost in postwar power struggles. To fully understand what was at stake, the figure of Dillinger himself needs to be framed in terms of the history of the Code's problems with the gangster film.

The popularization of Dillinger during the Depression as a champion of the dispossessed was perceived as a distinct threat by moral and civic guardians, corporate capitalists, and the state. In the early 1930s Will Hays, the head of the MPPDA (Motion Picture Producers and Distributors of America, the pre-1945 incarnation of the MPAA), was under pressure from all moral and civic interest groups to minimize, if not erase, any screen representations of criminality. The volatility of popular representations of Dillinger had threatened to bring direct interventions from the state in the regulation of Hollywood's products. In the context of the Depression, as a real-life oppositional figure bringing the institutions of state and law enforcement into disrepute, Dillinger had fed an already antagonistic popular disposition toward political and cultural leadership.

Given my previous discussion of the 1930s gangster film's antagonistic relationship to moral and civic interest groups, it hardly needs stressing just how sensitive an issue Dillinger would have been for the PCA. On March 20, 1934, Hays sent a telegram to Joseph Breen, warning that:

> No picture based on the life or exploits of John Dillinger will be produced, distributed or exhibited by any member company of the [MPPDA]. This decision is based on the belief that the production . . . of such a picture would be detrimental to the best public interest.[8]

This warning was a precursor to the moratorium on all gangster film production declared on July 15, 1935.

It is in the context of this kind of censorship history that *Dillinger* was released in 1945. On June 28, 1944, Breen wrote to Franklin King regarding Monogram's proposed production of a film based on

---

8. Will Hays, Telegram to Joseph Breen, PCA file *Dillinger*, AMPAS.

Dillinger's life. King was not deterred by warnings of the sensitive nature of Dillinger as a topic for screen entertainment, nor the fact that, owing to the March 20, 1934, order (see the telegram above), any script would have to negotiate itself around not only the PCA but Hays himself. The original (June 26, 1944) proposal had maintained that the film would be a "partly factual and partly fictitious story of the outlaw, John Dillinger, told with the idea of developing the theme 'crime does not pay.'"

At the time there was little that the PCA found controversial in the script, primarily because the screenwriter, Phil Yordan, provided an acceptably diluted version of the Depression hero. As the *Variety* reviewer of the film suggested, "In obtaining that Production Code Seal, so important to a general release, the brothers King were forced to make more or less a sissie of the Hoosier lad." The review goes on to state that Lawrence Tierney in the title role "stood out in spite of a Hays-office-weakened-script." Furthermore, "Max Nosseck's direction was as good as Philip Yordan's script. Not that it was Yordan's fault that Joe Breen's boys clamped down."[9] By contrast, another review saw the film as evidence "of the new thoughtfulness of Hollywood's production men. Here is no glorification of a social menace, but a cold, hard factual report of a killer's life."[10] In both reviews there is a recognition of the PCA's role in controlling representation, even if one sees this as debilitating and the other as beneficial.

While reviewers acknowledged or lamented that *Dillinger* betrayed the morally structuring force that the PCA continued to exact on Hollywood's gangster products, others were not so impressed. For a range of differing reasons, a diverse group of interests found a common enemy in the return of the gangster film and chastised the PCA for not doing its job. For both Borzage and traditional civic pressure groups alike, the problem was not that *Dillinger* was an immoral story per se. Rather, *Dillinger*'s problem was that it resembled a traditional gangster film, and as such connoted something more dangerous than simply moral violation.

A clue to what kind of danger *Dillinger* constituted can be found in the *Hollywood Reporter*'s comments that the film "recalls the vigor and excitement of the gangster film cycle."[11] This "cycle" is, of course, that of the early 1930s. The point was that *Dillinger*, in spite of being

9. *Variety*, March 12, 1945, in PCA file *Dillinger*, AMPAS.
10. Ibid.
11. *Hollywood Reporter*, March 12, 1945, in PCA file *Dillinger*.

a heavily censored gangster product, could still engender provocative memories through its clear links to the particular group of early 1930s films, including *Little Caesar* (1930), *Public Enemy* (1931), and *Scarface* (1932), that had brought about the first enforcements of the Code against the gangster film.

The correspondence that flooded the PCA on the release of *Dillinger* exposes a wealth of cultural anxieties that even the most censored and seemingly defused objects (as *Dillinger* no doubt would appear to us today) could set off in the postwar 1940s. In 1945 tensions were particularly high in Dillinger's home state of Indiana. The PCA was sent letters and articles printed in the July 22 *South Bend Tribune*. Commenting on the increase in teenage crime in South Bend, one article expounded that "too many parents are rearing their children to have criminal instincts instead of a desire to become decent worthwhile citizens capable of being a benefit to humanity." The model of social worth and citizenry that this writer was defending was clearly devoid of an understanding of environment and social milieu in the nurturance of criminality. Criminality was rationalized as "instinctual," the product of loose morality. Following this logic, the article went on to point to the corrupting influence of movies, blaming them for creating youth's criminal disposition. Boys had "learned increased cleverness in committing crime by closely observing . . . a motion picture shown in South Bend depicting the life of the notorious criminal John Dillinger." The article concluded that

> proof of the bad influence of crime pictures of the *Dillinger* type . . . will prompt not only local but all theaters to refuse to show such pictures and producers to stop making them. Here is a great chance for the Catholic Legion of Decency to show its great power.

In the postwar era, if the film industry could return to producing gangster pictures under PCA auspices, then the old moral guardianship would feel it had truly lost its central position in legislating cultural practice. This anxiety was corroborated in another newspaper column sent to the PCA about *Dillinger*. A woman in Cranford, New Jersey, wrote to her local paper, stating:

> Now that we've had the life of Dillinger on the screen—with what Hollywood considers good box-office results—I suppose we'll have a cycle of gangster pictures inflicted on us once more. . . . Hollywood will justify itself by concluding each picture on a "crime does not pay" note. But the kids will puff their reefers and swagger defiantly that "it was fun while it lasted."

The editors forwarded this letter to the MPAA, urging all readers who felt similarly to write to the studios and the PCA directly.

For these writers, then, the appellation "gangster" was enough to link any film to a "cycle" that by definition was antagonistic to their vision of moral stability and civic responsibility. In many ways these reactions betray the residues of the old contest that the early 1930s gangster film had engendered. That is, the cycle continued to offend moral and civic interest groups after the war for much the same reasons that it had in the 1930s. For others, however, the resurrection of the gangster film and the collective memory of the Depression had profoundly different ramifications, ones that reflected the shifting status of Hollywood for the new postwar political order.

Frank Borzage's letter to the MPAA was also a response to the release of *Dillinger,* but it is profoundly different in orientation to the correspondence from South Bend. His letter is less concerned about an internal domestic cultural battle, and reframes the effect of gangster movies in an international arena. He argues:

> Only too well do we in Hollywood remember that once before we gave this impression to the world. Now it is conceded that the large proportion of crime films which flooded the foreign picture markets during the 30s did more than any other single factor to distort the minds of our neighbors toward the American way of life.

Borzage interprets the early 1930s gangster as a threatening "distortion" of American verities. In the context of the postwar era it was important to wipe the slate clean and construct and endorse an affirmative version of American life appropriate to the new realms of American influence post–World War II. Equally, Borzage was maintaining that America's chances of controlling the international realm would be greatly enhanced if certain representations of Americanness were suppressed:

> With the reopening of foreign markets it is of supreme import that the film industry immediately set up a system of voluntary censorship so that motion pictures in the future give the outside world a true impression of the people who make up this great country.

In this context, the film products to be most feared were gangster films:

> A cycle of crime pictures at this time for domestic and foreign markets would be a grave injustice to those who have fought and died in this war. I have no doubt that crime pictures could prove as damaging here

in America as in foreign countries. As we know, our Justice Department has announced that a great increase in crime may be expected in
this country after the war. Here the motion picture industry has the
opportunity to help stamp out this crime wave before it begins. The
first step is the total elimination of the glamorized gangster movies.

The PCA file on *Dillinger* further illuminates the new significance
and stakes of producing a crime film in the postwar environment,
framing the possibilities and limits of the gangster film in the 1940s.
The critical reaction to the film reveals a complex mix of ongoing
residual struggles left over from the Depression, and the emerging
new demands of presenting a vision of liberal consensus to the world.
The postwar battle over *Dillinger* was part of a larger conflict within
the industry that had its roots in the 1930s. At the same time, the
concerns articulated by Borzage provide clues as to how the task and
aims of the PCA in managing Hollywood's social vision would come
to change after the war.

KEY LARGO: "SYMBOL OF EVERYTHING THAT WE ARE TRYING TO AVOID GOING BACK TO."

One of the most noticeable features about the mid-1940s PCA files on
gangster films is the lack of censorship activity surrounding their production. In the case of *Dillinger,* the first postwar "gangster bio-pic,"
the Breen office may have presumed that an old-style gangster film
would be of comparatively little significance to postwar audiences.
Nowhere in their correspondence before the film's release do they pre-
dict the barrage of complaints they would receive.

Subsequent to *Dillinger,* however, it is clear that the PCA was re-
awakened to the controversy gangster films provoked, as is evidenced
in the problems producer Jerry Wald and director John Huston had
in getting *Key Largo* past the censors in late 1947. Stephen Jackson of
the PCA sent a letter to Jack Warner stating that the film's material
was "still very much objectionable under the provisions of the Production Code." The prime reason was that "the Murillo character is
definitely a gangster surrounded by his henchmen and his kept
woman." He went on to assert: "As you must well be aware, the public
reaction to gangster stories, particularly where the gangster can be
identified as some past or present gangster, is extremely violent and
vociferous." [12] Jerry Wald's internal correspondence over the PCA's

---

12. Letter to Jack Warner from Jackson, November 28, 1947, in Rudy Behlmer, *Inside Warner Bros., 1935–1951* (New York: Viking Penguin, 1985), p. 292.

response reveals some key points about the problem the PCA was having with its censoring categories. His main contention was that the Breen office somehow had not "seen" a whole host of contemporary gangster films (all of which he lists), such as *Brute Force, Kiss of Death, Desert Fury, The Strange Love of Martha Ivers, The Gangster, The Killers,* and *Ride the Pink Horse,* adding that *Body and Soul* was "cluttered with gangsters and henchmen."[13]

Wald's confusion, however, lies precisely in the fact that all the films he cited were not gangster films in the traditional sense (symptomatically, they have nearly all been reclassified in postwar film scholarship as films noirs rather than gangster films). Although some of them had problems getting past the Code, the key difference between them and *Key Largo* lay in the latter's quite clearly connecting itself to an "identifiable" gangster (real and fictional). As Richard Brooks, the screenwriter, pointed out, Rocco (Edward G. Robinson) was based on Lucky Luciano. Add to this Robinson's direct associations with the "classical" 1930s gangster cycle, and it was clear that *Key Largo* was indeed an "identifiable" gangster product.

Wald's anger was directed at the anachronous nature of the Code that led to its completely missing the point of his film:

> The Breen office goes by a production code that was written in 1930. Many important events have taken place since the code was written. Is it possible that the code is dated? Certainly a re-examination is due. . . . The story we are trying to tell in *Key Largo* is a moral one and certainly there is no better way to point a moral than to use a gangster as a symbol of everything that we are trying to avoid going back to.[14]

The stakes for the PCA, however, had everything to do with the intertextual ability of *Key Largo* (like *Dillinger*) to drag up the first talking gangster cycle and its war with civic and moral interest groups. But this attention to only the identifiable attributes of 1940s gangster films betrayed precisely the shortcomings of the Code as well. Wald's naming of other gangster films that seemed to escape censure highlighted a group of crime features that I wish to call *ersatz gangster* films. These films found a way to circumnavigate the Code stipulations by covering up the features that would most directly betray them as gangster products.

13. Ibid., pp. 292–93.
14. Ibid., p. 292.

The continuing battle between the old moral order and the gangster film distracted from the cycle's far more significant engagement with power after the war. While Wald, film reviewers, and no doubt a substantial proportion of the audience might have objected to the compromises postwar Hollywood still had to make with an anachronous Code, the fact was that the Code's very datedness made it ill suited to identify and regulate how the crime film could pose problems for the new American order.

ERSATZ GANGSTERS: NEGOTIATING THE CODE WITH *BRUTE FORCE* AND *BODY AND SOUL*

There are many reasons why the gangster film changed over time, and I have done my best to cover the most significant causes. Not least of these is the Code itself. As I have argued, although the Code still insisted even during the postwar era on enforcing stipulations laid down in 1934, this did not mean that the issues that defined the gangster film simply disappeared. Rather, the film form mutated. Its transformation was determined by a combination of interrelated and changing aesthetic, infrastructural, and historical concerns. The Code, in clinging to its original postulates, found itself sadly out of step with both the realm of sociocultural developments and changes in Hollywood's system of representation. While it could exert an influence on certain features of cinematic representation, it was unable to keep pace with both fundamental sociohistorical changes and the mutable forms that especially Hollywood's crime features adopted in order to continue to address the contemporaneous social realm. Although an anachronistic Code may have served the economic interests of studios in continuing to feed audience desire for hard-boiled crime dramas, it is clear that this contravened the ideological declarations of external moral and federal forces, as well as the goals Eric Johnston (the former head of the U.S. Chamber of Commerce) held out in 1945 for the industry as the new head of the MPAA.

What is now termed film noir in particular took on significance as the new covert space of otherwise outlawed gangster discourse in Hollywood. It is no coincidence that this dark and pessimistic postwar crime film cycle, above all other forms, was the site most affected by HUAC's interventions. While HUAC knew what its target was, the PCA either did not or had changed its goals. The PCA seemingly having relaxed its enforcement, one could argue that HUAC arose in 1947 to do the job that the PCA was neglecting. At the same time, it

Negotiating the censors in the postwar era: the boxer (John Garfield as Charlie Davis) as ersatz gangster trying not to take a fall for the syndicate in *Body and Soul* (1947).

is clear that the rise of the ersatz gangster film was not simply a question of reproducing the same old problems that characterized its outlawed forebears. Rather, the new gangster film addressed new issues in new ways.

Whether we argue that after the war the PCA's vigilance relaxed, or that its lack of enforcement is testament to the success of filmmakers in finding ways to circumnavigate Code strictures, the point remains that the changes the gangster film underwent in no way debilitated its socially antagonistic function. If anything, such transformations may have helped refine the form's social critique.[15] Two of

15. I have already documented some classic examples of this in dealing with both the rise of the "Crime, Inc." or syndicate film in chapter 5, and shall pursue this further in explaining the attraction of the German exile and independent production companies to the Hollywood crime film in chapter 7.

the most powerful examples of this development, *Brute Force* and *Body and Soul,* were released in June and August of 1947, respectively, just prior to HUAC's first hearings in October of that year. Both films featured film talent who were soon to be blacklisted, and provide evidence of the kind of Hollywood of which HUAC was most fearful and which the PCA was least capable of policing.

The most graphic example of this is *Body and Soul,* produced by Enterprise studios in 1947. Here was a film that was identified by contemporaneous critics as being an ersatz gangster film, yet had slipped by the censors (something pointed out by Jerry Wald in his complaint about PCA objections to *Key Largo*). Here was a film conceived and executed by future high-profile blacklist victims: written by Abraham Polonsky, directed by Robert Rossen, starring John Garfield. Not only this, but here was also a film made by a film collective trying to establish relative autonomy from the monopoly structures of the major studios. In all, a truly heady mix of politically motivated personnel were harnessed to the film form that would best serve their social critique. While these filmmakers worked institutionally in a space outside the control of the majors, aesthetically they worked within a well-known formula that would guarantee a large audience.

In *Body and Soul* John Garfield is not a gangster but a boxer named Charlie Davis, who becomes involved with the mob on becoming champion. Charlie is initially intoxicated by the attention and money that comes with his success. However, gradually he becomes aware of the more sinister side to the world he has entered when he witnesses the exploitation and death of Ben, a fellow pugilist, trainer, and friend. He has trouble with his gold-digging girlfriend, and finds solace in a woman who wants him to remain honest. The mob orders him to take a fall. Understanding that the business he is in is fixed, Charlie decides to defy the order. He wins the fight (and loses the fix money) and gains back his self-respect. This drama of the honest fighter up against a controlling mob clearly parallels the gangster-syndicate films of the same period.

It could be argued that in the post-Code era the boxing ring assumed the space once occupied by the gangster's speakeasy as a privileged site for the dramatization of social oppression. After July 1935 (and arguably since the first prohibition in 1931), the exigencies of censorship meant that alternative metaphorical realms to gangster-dom had to be found. Boxing was one way to recast the gangster film without doing it undue damage. The "ironic" avenue to success through boxing resembled (and had deep connections with) the gangster's parodies of Algerism. Not only this, but the boxing milieu often coincided with that of the gangster's, the ethnic urban inner-city ghetto. This system of resemblances enabled the boxing film to engage a range of collective memories about the 1930s similar to the gangster film.[16]

Contemporaneous reviews described *Body and Soul* in terms that could just as well describe a classic gangster scenario. Although the film is ostensibly about a boxer, one review remarks that the "yarn flashes back to his beginnings in the racket. . . . It all starts when he sees his hard-working dad . . . accidentally shot in a bootlegging vendetta during the prohibition era."[17] Another review emphasizes that this deliberate invoking of the 1930s was doubly exploited through the film's use of Johnny Green's "well plugged song hit of the '30s, 'Body and Soul.'" More than this, *Body and Soul* was the story of "a wiry little scrapper from New York's lower East Side who claws his way to the top of the fight heap," a man "of innate decency even though he's tied up with a bunch of cut-throats."[18]

The Lower East Side was the traditional "ghetto" gangster locus in the American imagination, and any film situating itself in this milieu could not fail to associate itself with this tradition. The very rhetoric of the review—"clawing" one's way to the top—replays the gangster narrative trajectory in its parody of the Alger myth. This overlap was only exacerbated in the figure of Garfield himself. Like the gangster stars of the early 1930s, James Cagney, Edward G. Robinson, and Paul Muni, John Garfield was born and brought up in New York's Lower East Side. Not only this, but like Robinson and Muni, Garfield was also a Jew who had anglicized his original name, Jacob Julius Garfinkle.

Through such a complicated system of simulation and intertextual reference, an ersatz gangster film like *Body and Soul* invoked memories of the Depression that were perhaps even more volatile than those

16. It should be noted that this strategy was one Garfield had used before in the 1939 Warner's feature *They Made Me a Criminal*. There are many other examples of the gangster/boxer combination, including *The Killers* (1945), *The Set-Up* (1949), *Second Chance* (1953), *The Killer's Kiss* (1955), *The Harder They Fall* (1956), and *Somebody Up There Likes Me* (1956), all of which, like *Body and Soul*, invoke the concerns of early 1930s social problem and gangster dramas.

17. *Hollywood Reporter*, August 1947, PCA file *Body and Soul*, AMPAS.

18. PCA file *Body and Soul*. This quotation is taken from a review on file that is without citation. It is dated August 13, 1947, and is probably taken from *Variety*.

engendered more directly by *Dillinger.* For, unlike *Dillinger,* whose story is framed by the Depression, *Body and Soul* was not limited to being a "period" piece. Rather it was a film about 1940s America that utilized the 1930s gangster intertext to anchor its indictment of the tenets of American society in an established popular aesthetics of social consciousness. That is, this kind of reference to the 1930s depended for its effectiveness on regenerating certain generic Hollywood traditions, such as the ethnic urban lower-class gangster film and the social problem film. While most gangster films had moved on to address more abstract psychosocial problems of postwar maladjustment, a film like *Body and Soul* posed questions about class and ethnic background more characteristic of the early 1930s, reminding audiences of issues that might have been repressed in the prosecution of the war.

The gangster film's postwar metaphorical resuscitation was not limited to the boxing film but extended into areas such as the prison melodrama, a film form that had often overlapped with the gangster film. A key example of this is *Brute Force,* which, like *Body and Soul,* involved a future blacklist victim (and exile) associated with socially critical filmmaking, Jules Dassin, the film's director. *Brute Force* was similarly a product of an independent studio syndicate, Mark Hellinger Productions. The latter was inextricably tied to the gangster film and was committed to sponsoring candid hard-boiled social realist treatments of modern American life.[19] The film's screenplay was written by Richard Brooks, who had composed the first postwar critique of American anti-Semitism in his screenplay for *Crossfire* (based on his own novel *The Brick Foxhole*) and who would go on to screenwrite a gangster classic, *Key Largo.* This mix of talents with an investment in developing the traditions of the gangster and social problem films in the postwar context was augmented by the film's lead actor, Burt Lancaster, who had recently starred in another Hellinger crime film success, *The Killers,* as a boxer-gangster antihero.

Fresh from this success, Lancaster was cast as the leader of a group of convicts who carry out an elaborate prison break. We learn through

19. While at Warner Brothers, Mark Hellinger helped produce two classic gangster films, *Roaring Twenties* (1939) and *High Sierra* (1941). Almost all his subsequent ventures, *The Killers* (1946), *Brute Force* (1947), and *The Naked City* (1948), were refinements on the gangster and social problem film, offering directors with a penchant for the crime film and the aesthetic of social realism (like Robert Siodmak and Jules Dassin) a chance to employ their talents free of the major studios' restrictions.

flashbacks that each of the prisoners' criminal motivations is born not of paranoiac or sociopathic behavior but intensely human needs. One prisoner is there because he stole to pay for his wife's battle against cancer, another stole a bag and a coat to give to his wife to save his marriage, and another is taking a rap for a woman who shot her own father to keep military police off the prisoner's trail. These ordinary men are subject to the ruthless and sadistic brutality of the head of the prison guards. The film ends with a suicidal and extremely violent riot against the prison authorities.

Consistent with the shift in the metaphor of gangsterdom—from something tied to the ethnic ghetto in the early 1930s to a way to dramatize or recast some universal social condition in the 1940s—the prisoners are cast as common men whose "normal" bourgeois desires lead them to crime. The psychologically unstable paranoiacs in this film are not the incarcerated criminals but the prison guards and warden. This prison world features a population of inmates in a position of absolute subservience to the sadistic dictates of a jailer.

For some, this metaphorical indictment of the propensity of contemporary American society to tolerate fascist-like abuse of power went too far. The fact that the "convicts are the much abused heroes and the villain is a cold, sadistic jailer" was something critic Bosley Crowther found particularly objectionable. He complained that this would only encourage juvenile delinquency. Moreover, "we wouldn't give you two cents for the impression this film will make upon any and all the spectators to whom it may be shown in a foreign land. What a sweet piece of propaganda for the American way of life." [20] On one hand, Crowther's words reflect an awareness that Hollywood was indeed a potential weapon of mass persuasion. On the other, his fear of the crime film tells us more about how Hollywood was ill suited to the task of promoting the vision of American society as a harmonious, classless, and ideologically "free" space. The crime film's social realist visions of urban realities constantly interfered with the desires of both liberal consensus advocates and the fanatical right to turn Hollywood into an agent of political affirmation.

While films like *Brute Force* and *Body and Soul* were not typical of all Hollywood production, they did represent a propensity too significant to simply ignore. In fact, as members of the cycle of crime and social problem films we now call film noir, they were part of a dark

20. Bosley Crowther, *New York Times*, July 20, 1947, PCA file *Brute Force*, AMPAS.

vision of American society that came to constitute almost a quarter of Hollywood production by 1947.[21] In this context, *Brute Force* was clearly received as an unambiguous indictment of the status quo. The *Hollywood Reporter* emphasized how Dassin's "direction . . . concentrates on establishing the mood of the inmates' futility and their hatred of the social system that is punishing them with confinement."[22] *Variety* informed audiences that the film was "about the toughest bit of hard-boiled realism to hit the screen to date . . . the atmosphere created is that of almost documentary realism." The review went on to stress: "a close-up on prison life and prison methods, *Brute Force* is a showmanly mixture of gangster melodramatics, sociological exposition and sex."[23]

This identification of the film's intertextual realm reveals the way in which it transcends its apparent "prison melodrama" limits. Beyond its metaphorical recasting of the relationship of the state to citizen into that of the jailer brutalizing the prisoner, the film generates its dramatic power by alluding to the conventions of gangsterdom. The evocation of gangster melodramatics is part of a surreptitious play with code and memory that reflects the changed nature of the gangster film and the sociological issues it dramatized. Characteristically for a postwar crime melodrama, part of *Brute Force*'s power lies in its refusal to be contained by established generic categories, categories that tend to exert single meanings over the multiple and contradictory nature of the problems and desires Hollywood's films address. Thus, a simple and clearly "identifiable" return to the gangster film like *Dillinger* (which the PCA was capable of policing) was in many ways less a cause for consternation than the more mutable forms to which the gangster film gave way following its heavy censure.

Brute Force is not a gangster film in the orthodox sense. Its power rests, however, on its associations with this crime cycle, and in its transformation of old signs into new ones capable of engaging the world of 1940s American urban lower- and middle-class society. The

21. The main source of statistics on this is Dorothy B. Jones, "Communism in the Movies," in John Cogley, *Report on Blacklisting I—Movies* (New York: Fund for the Republic, 1956). Her report attempts to quantify the number of Hollywood films that seriously "documented" contemporary social, economic, and political problems. Her own figures reflect a drastic decline in the "social problem" film subsequent to HUAC's investigations in 1947, which testifies to the negative effect of the inquisition on sponsorship of socially critical filmmaking.

22. *Hollywood Reporter,* July 1947, PCA file *Brute Force,* AMPAS.

23. *Variety,* July 20, 1947, PCA file *Brute Force,* AMPAS.

resistance to categorization that characterizes films like *Body and Soul* and *Brute Force* is in significant part a by-product of gangster discourse having to find a new home because of censorship. Paradoxically, it is precisely this mutability that makes these films emblematic of what I have argued to be a politically "dysfunctional" Hollywood, useless to those seeking to shape Hollywood after their own ideological agendas. Not only could the ersatz gangster film slip through the censorship net, but its metamorphosis enabled it to remain in touch with the contemporaneous concerns of the audience and prevent it from reifying itself as belonging to a bygone era. Rather, New Deal liberalism and the demand for social reform were kept alive as residual possibilities for the shaping of the postwar order. Certainly, as the *Dillinger* and *Key Largo* cases bear out, the PCA was aware of the linkages of these 1940s products with the early 1930s cycle of gangster films, and sought to delimit and control these allusions. However, the PCA's grounds and goals for intervention missed the point and left unscathed the more significant aspects of the crime film that were dramatically pertinent to 1940s culture. Even if reviewers and audiences were able to see these films' connections to a 1930s tradition as a metaphorical resuscitation of the gangster film, *Brute Force* and *Body and Soul* provided the PCA itself with little that was "identifiable" as gangster material in the orthodox sense, and the MPAA/PCA files on these movies are conspicuously devoid of objections to the screenplay. In short, the Code's censuring activities (at least until 1949) were performed on behalf of an outdated set of principles no longer applicable to a transformed social sphere and film industry. Thus, in what was tantamount to a misapplication of its censuring duties, the PCA let the crime film's truly critical capacities pass through undetected.

The PCA's failure to accord any significance to the ersatz gangster films' clear references to 1930s gangsterdom was perhaps because they could only be indirectly deduced. Yet, as contemporaneous reviews stress, the connotative power of these films to instantly situate themselves in a particular (taboo) tradition of Hollywood filmmaking was an essential part of *Brute Force* and *Body and Soul*'s appeal. By contrast, the PCA censorship procedure in 1947, still rooted in a Code forged in 1930, must have appeared to be a rather crude instrument of control.

Yet, while it is clear that the capacity of the Code to be an ideological and moral enforcer was perceived to have weakened in the postwar 1940s, this is only half the story. The Code, in spite of Jerry Wald and other filmmakers' claims, did not remain still and static. While the PCA's direct objections to certain kinds of filmmaking may have remained mired in outdated moral rhetoric, the changes that the PCA film analysis forms underwent after HUAC's intervention testify to an attempt to shift censorship sensibilities. This shift cannot be explained away as simply a matter of censorship relaxation.

BAROMETERS OF CHANGE: THE PCA FILM ANALYSIS FORM

The symbiotic nature of the crime film and the censoring agency meant that the crime film was always in a position to test the limits of censorship or was forced to negotiate censorship as a primary condition of its existence. While all Hollywood production had to be screened by the PCA, the gangster film was one form singled out for particular attention. At the same time, the PCA itself had to adjust to the changing ways Hollywood represented society, especially to those representations most likely to prove problematic for moral or political guardianship. In turning to the PCA film analysis forms themselves, my interest focuses both on the fact that the forms changed and on the nature of these changes (see appendix for examples of the forms themselves).

The PCA's negotiations with producers over a script's potentially controversial subject matter were carried out at the early stages of any given production. Interventions at this stage, however, did not mean that the end product would be free of problems. The PCA analysis forms were for use at final screenings to record potentially problematic topics that might incur the wrath of state censor boards or civic and moral interest groups. While these forms did not influence the production stage of a film, they could be used to recommend alterations of the finished product prior to receiving a Seal of Approval, or to warn studios about exhibition problems in spite of having been granted the Seal.

What is interesting is that this final vetting form underwent very little change until after HUAC's first investigations. Between 1934 and 1949 the Code form underwent only one minor revision (in 1941), which lends substance to arguments that the Code was a hopelessly anachronistic institution. Indeed, HUAC's interventions in 1947 testify in many ways to the PCA's seeming redundancy and its failure to execute OWI and State Department directives on the domestic front.

In light of extreme and embarrassing interventions by a House committee, it is perhaps not surprising that the PCA exhibited a desire to rethink its priorities.

The PCA film analysis form exploded in size from a one-sided document defending the Code's tenets (the Ten Commandments) to a comprehensive seven-part, multipage itinerary of all the possible "sociological factors" Hollywood mediated. Such a change can probably be construed as an index not only of the industry's fears but of the general social paranoia fostered by the Red Scare, and symptomatic of the panoptical desire to examine every aspect of postwar society in order to uncover and then purge it of its "un-American" features.

The post-HUAC PCA form, while it exploded in size, remained largely unenforced. Perhaps the Code's relative passivity reflected the degree to which HUAC had triumphed in its task. There is, however, much that speaks against the Code simply becoming a backup to an order already established by HUAC. First, the authority of Eric Johnston, guru of modern corporate capitalism and the Code's ultimate overseer, reflected a different set of ideological prerogatives to those espoused by HUAC; second, the nature of the changes to the PCA film analysis form reflects a more nuanced and sophisticated understanding of Hollywood's communicative powers than HUAC would have granted.

In the context of late 1949, alterations to the Code's film analysis form occurred in the fallout of HUAC's first and most devastating investigations of alleged Communist infiltration of Hollywood. The climate of the Red Scare had infected all walks of life. Mistrust had been fostered of everything once held inviolable. The Reds had apparently contaminated everything from government leadership, to one's neighbors, and perhaps even one's spouse or children. In this climate of inquisition and confession there was a call for a blanket political cleansing of the whole of social life.

While this demand was motivated by paranoia and couched in heated and violent terms, it provided the preconditions for the expansion and development of more sophisticated and "scientific" kinds of social screening. In this sense, not only was it important that Hollywood be identified as a crucial area of social mediation, but that ways of measuring and regulating its effects and uses be developed as well. It was clear from the way Hollywood's products were being policed for export that the film industry was regarded as a vital force for American propaganda abroad. At home, however, such policing could not be so easily sanctioned or enforced. It is in this context that I shall situate the expansion and transformation of the Code's film analysis form.

POLICING THE POSTWAR HOME FRONT: QUANTIFYING THE FIELD OF TRANSGRESSION

In 1935, as a supplement to the formulation of the PCA's film analysis form, chief administrator Joseph Breen had provided a three-scale system—classified as Class I, II, and III—to regulate films currently in production and exhibition. Class I was a category determining that "the release of the picture be halted now and that no additional contracts be taken on." Into this category fell most gangster films, which meant that a film like *Blondie Johnson* was immediately removed from cinemas, unable to complete its run, and others such as *Little Caesar, Public Enemy, Doorway to Hell,* and *Scarface* were prohibited from re-release. Class II was assigned to films "permitted to finish out present contracts, but that no new contracts will be taken." A film such as *Manhattan Melodrama* fell under this category, thereby allowing it to finish its run but not to be shown again until its classification was relaxed. Class III was decreed "acceptable screen entertainment . . . permitted to continue along without difficulty."[24]

These "class" stipulations lent the PCA teeth as an enforceable entity with an essentially prohibitory character. The first film analysis forms were one-page surveys that minimized and drew very roughly the areas designated as censorable. This relative lack of detail contrasts starkly with the expansive and more carefully broken-down form introduced in late 1949. This change in detail seems to coincide with the shifting terms of hegemony. The sophisticated 1949 form coincides with the aftermath of HUAC, but at the same time reflects the final capitulation of the PCA/Breen office to the terms of the new MPPDA after its change of leadership in 1945 from Hays to Johnston.

The character of the PCA had been bound up with its supremo, Joseph Breen, who was a legacy of the old guard, a residue of 1930s concerns, and a man of distinctly moral priorities. His vision of the edifying function of motion picture entertainment did not substantially contradict that of Will Hays, his former boss. Eric Johnston, however, was the sign of an emergent order. As the author of *America*

---

24. Joseph Breen, Memo to Will Hays, February 20, 1935, PCA file *Manhattan Melodrama,* AMPAS.

Unlimited in 1944, Johnston came to the MPPDA espousing the ideals of liberal corporate consensus. He argued that a culture of abundance had to be built upon the principles of full production, and that this necessitated the eradication of the Depression-associated "nightmare of class rhetoric."[25] This order would take time to establish its hold over Hollywood, waiting for HUAC, somewhat conveniently, to clear the path of New Deal ideological detritus.

My analysis of the PCA's relation to the mid-1940s gangster products revealed where the PCA was inadequate in its policing of gangster films. Capable of identifying more traditional film forms, it allowed potentially subversive gangster mutations to slip through its censorship net. The reasons for this probably lay in the PCA's own uncertainty about whose interests it was defending or negotiating in the confusions of postwar America. These confusions also characterized postwar politics, for political leaders were divided over whether to commit themselves to a return to the idealism of the New Deal and social reform or to advance the new affiliations of capital and liberalism instead. In this divisive political climate, themes of social reconstruction were volatile screen material, and the Code had problems detecting and managing them.

The late 1949 PCA film analysis/censorship form constitutes a watershed moment for censorship and the goals of institutionalized textual interrogation. In its initial form the Code employs a strategy that identifies subversive themes by an inventory of "Don'ts and Be Carefuls." Until 1949 the film analysis form limits its attention to the characterization of professions; the "angle" the film demonstrates (e.g., is it of a political, religious, or military nature?); the treatment of state institutions (courts and public officials); whether any "Don'ts" surface (e.g., adultery, illicit sex, suicide, and divorce); and the presence of crime and liquor. These are questions rooted in the surface of the text that do not attempt to analyze the deeper and less surface elements, for example, of character motivation. The censors' interest in crime is limited to its "type," and, if killing occurs, they want to know the number of deaths (see appendix).

While all this points to an attempt to quantify a field of transgression, it reveals a very "denotative" way of thinking about how meaning is generated on screen. That is, the PCA could identify and locate transgression only where it was overtly displayed or signified. As we

---

25. Eric Johnston, "Utopia Is Production," *Screen Actor* 14 (April 1946), p. 7. See also Johnston's *America Unlimited* (Garden City, N.J.: Doubleday, 1944).

have seen, this proved to be inadequate in policing texts that generated a critique of society through more covert methods. "Denotatively," *Body and Soul* was not identifiable as a gangster feature, unlike *Dillinger* and *Key Largo,* which were. Rather, *Body and Soul* was a gangster film by intertextual association, through its playing on cultural memories of the Depression and the 1930s city. In short, the pre-HUAC PCA found itself unable to effectively police films that used the "connotative" capacities of generic allusion and memory.

In 1949 the PCA film analysis form expanded from one page to a seven-part, multipage format. More significantly, the kinds of questions asked attend to the "connotative" aspects of film texts. For example, questions oriented around crime and alcohol expand to motivation and class. It is no longer enough to identify drinking; one must look carefully at its "social acceptability" and whether it occurs in "common man" or "well-to-do" settings. It is no longer enough to know whether a crime is committed; we must evaluate it according to the film's "classification" (genre/cycle). It matters whether the crime occurs in a "Western," "a story involving political wrong-doing," or a "social problem" drama. And what justice do our criminals meet? Are they "killed by law" or "by criminal"? Are they "punished"? Do they "reform"? All these questions are oriented around the less quantifiable features of how films "enlist the sympathy of the audience." As such they indicate a more connotative awareness of the capacities of movies.

While such post-HUAC changes indicate an increased awareness of the socially manipulative capacities of mass cinema, they do not betray a specific political allegiance to the goals of HUAC. Rather, the nature of the questions and the areas of Hollywood's representations of life they address betray concerns far more appropriate to the functioning of corporate capitalism and liberal consensus ideology. In what follows I shall establish more concretely how the PCA film analysis form was transformed into an expression of a positivistic sociopsychological discourse. This transformation, I wish to argue, reveals a shift in the definition of censorship designed to serve the prerogatives not of HUAC, but of liberal consensus ideologues like Eric Johnston.

SOCIAL SCIENCE AS THE LEISURE POLICE

It is noticeable that most scholarship concerned with Hollywood censorship tells a story of an increasingly redundant Code. The Code is seen after its inception to have a degree of efficacy in defending a set of moral dictates and in protecting the industry from interference by external censorship. However, as time goes on it is emphasized how the Code became both inadequate and a hindrance to the very institution it was in essence designed to protect. The supreme insult to its capabilities was probably its inability to offset the 1947 inquisition. In the age of HUAC, the PCA could only have been perceived as out of step with the realities of the movies' modern context and as the anachronistic residue of some older Judeo-Christian morality sorely out of place.[26] As an enforceable entity the Code had always been perceived as something negotiable. It could even be argued that the so-called noir style was a result of sophisticated ways of negotiating Code restrictions about representations of America's seamier side. Others,

---

26. See Stephen Vaughn, "Morality and Entertainment: The Origins of the Motion Picture Production Code," *Journal of American History* (June 1990), for an example of this. The heavy concentration by scholars on the Code's inception (e.g., Arthur F. McClure, "Censor the Movies! Early Attempts to Regulate the Content of Motion Pictures in America, 1907–1936," in *The Movies: an American Idiom* [Rutherford, N.J.: Fairleigh Dickinson University Press, 1971]) has led to an historical account of the Code's declension in prohibition capabilities, its significance limited to its establishment rather than its ultimate enforcement. Another example of this decline narrative is Hortense Powdermaker's *Hollywood, the Dream Factory: An Anthropologist Looks at the Movie-Makers* (Boston: Little, Brown, 1950). Even Gregory Black's *Hollywood Censored: Morality Codes, Catholics, and the Movies* (Cambridge: Cambridge University Press, 1994), which actually emphasizes the degree to which the Catholic Legion of Decency successfully "sterilized" Hollywood, sees the Code as static and anachronistic. Because such accounts associate the Code exclusively with the figure and authority of Joseph Breen, they tend to overlook the significance of changes in the PCA. These changes illuminate not something anachronous but something new.

More recent censorship studies argue that the Code's significance has, to some extent, been overvalued, given that Hollywood movies had always been the product of negotiation with moral monitors and had always exhibited a tendency to avoid controversial subject matters. See Lea Jacobs, *The Wages of Sin: Censorship and the Fallen Woman Film, 1928–1942* (Berkeley and Los Angeles: University of California Press, 1997); Richard Maltby, "The Production Code and the Hays Office," in *The Grand Design: Hollywood as a Modern Business Enterprise*, ed. Tino Balio (Berkeley and Los Angeles: University of California Press, 1995), pp. 37–72; Ruth Vasey, *The World According to Hollywood, 1918–1939* (Exeter: University of Exeter Press, 1997). Although the scope of these studies is limited to the pre–World War II era, they all suggest that Hollywood's relationship to external and internal regulators was dynamic and sophisticated. My work follows this logic through to the wartime and postwar era in suggesting that Hollywood remained one step ahead of the attempts to police it morally and politically. This maneuvering was driven by commercial rather than ideological imperatives (profit depending on the need to address popular audience desires, even if this contravened the wishes of moral and political watchdogs). We should not conclude ipso facto, however, that the films that emerged out of this circumnavigation of Code strictures in the name of profit were aesthetically or ideologically lame.

such as Leff and Simmons, have argued further that film noir's existence is testament to the relaxation of the Breen office's monitoring of Hollywood.[27]

This having been said, some curious facts remain unexplained. While Breen office regulations may appear to have been relaxed, and the signs were that filmmakers had found effective ways to negotiate the Code, the alterations to the Production Code analysis form itself reflect a shift in censorship concerns over this same period. Likewise, independent polling organizations such as Gallup concentrated for the first time on quantitative wholesale measurements of Hollywood's products and their reception in the period from 1940 to 1950. What are we to make of this intensification of "positivistic" inquiry into Hollywood?[28]

One answer is that the apparent relaxing of one kind of vigilance belied the rise of a different kind of policing with different goals. This shift coincides with the 1945 arrival of Eric Johnston to take over from Will Hays as head of the MPPDA. This arrival signified not only a changing of the name of the trade association (from the wordy MPPDA to the slicker MPAA), but a changing of the guard in terms of the political prerogatives to which Hollywood was meant to kowtow after World War II. If Hays had been the institutional overseer of a Judeo-Christian moral paradigm (a hangover from a Victorian order), Johnston declared himself to be a missionary of different cloth: namely, the herald of the postwar liberal consensus, the angel of "democratic capitalism" come to make Hollywood an instrument of a new and positive American idealism. As he declared to the industry in March 1947, the negative ghosts of the Depression had to be exorcised:

> We'll have no more *Grapes of Wrath*, we'll have no more *Tobacco Road*s. We'll have no more films that show the seamy side of American life.[29]

The degree to which Johnston's declamations percolated downward into influencing movie content is debatable, but his arrival as

27. Leonard Leff and Jerold L. Simmons, *The Dame in the Kimono: Hollywood Censorship and the Production Code, from the 1920s to the 1960s* (New York: Grove Weidenfeld, 1990).

28. Even a mass circulation magazine like *Life* took part in promoting the climate of sociological inquiry. In June 1949 it staged a "Round Table" on the movies and their social responsibilities, where an open critique by film scholars, "progressive" filmmakers, businessmen, and actors and actresses of issues such as censorship was aired. *Life*, June 27, 1949, pp. 90–110.

29. Murray Schumach, *The Face on the Cutting Room Floor: The Story of Movie and Television Censorship* (New York: William Morrow and Company, 1964), p. 129.

Hollywood's main public relations man has to be framed within a larger postwar debate in which Hollywood came to figure as a key player.

The goal of postwar liberal consensus advocates was the reconstruction of a political order conducive to corporate and consumer economic interests. This new order would depend for its success on a particular kind of social/power management built around the winning of consent to its right to dominance. Consensus politics had to be enforced differently than had previous orders, for its claim to legitimacy would depend on its appearance/self-representation as a natural democratic order—ideology-free and positively rather than negatively reinforced. This order's new policemen would not behave like preachers telling people what they should not do. Rather, they would act as experts and technicians who could empirically and "scientifically" prove to the citizenry that the new order was the best of all possibilities.

In other words, this new order could not afford to lose its legitimacy by being seen to be "ideologically" imposed or policed. Rather, its route to power would lie precisely on concealing its contingency. To this extent, censorship or regulation of value attitudes would have to take on new forms and be less visible, less demagogic. This censorship must be disposed toward enabling an affirmative representation of the new order (a positively defined function) rather than enforcing prohibitions (a negatively defined function). In keeping with the consumer and corporate capitalist economic principles it was meant to endorse, the ideology of consensus had to be "sold" to the population, and the movies would become a key arena for its effective advertising.

Two key elements needed to be marshaled to achieve these ends. First, instead of making mass culture a political enemy, it had to be converted into servicing the new order.[30] Second, a system of cultural surveillance had to come into effect to ensure that mass mediation performed its hegemonic obligations. McCarthy made Hollywood his enemy, a profound political mistake that had also haunted earlier conservatives. Johnston's attitude toward the mass media was profoundly

---

30. Johnston felt that Hollywood needed to be harnessed to an agenda that exorcized the ghosts of New Deal political rhetoric and promoted the goals of consensus and abundance instead. The crime film was a primary example of the kind of socially dysfunctional Hollywood both McCarthyites and consensus liberals wanted to eradicate. The crime film was a problem not because it could be tied to any specific ideological agenda (e.g., Communism) but precisely because it could not. Its most effective use was in the undermining of authority, not its endorsement.

different. Instead of concentrating on how movies were harmful, he focused on the positive propensities of cinema to endorse "democratic capitalism." This difference in focus also helps explain in part the shift in censorship tactics that the Code underwent when Johnston took over from Hays.

Johnston was someone who could wield persuasive force within the film industry on the part of those trying to turn the industry into an agent for the positive representation of the American way of life. In many ways his desires matched those of authorities outside the industry, such as the Office of War Information and the State Department (see chapter 5), who saw Hollywood as a means to promote and sanction America's rise to globalism, but whose power only extended to the prohibition of products for export.

The transformation of the Code's film analysis format during Johnston's tenure, especially its expansion into quantifying the "sociological issues" Hollywood films mediated, parallels the rise of a specific kind of positivistic social science to political prominence over the same postwar period. As Terence Ball has illuminated, the institutionalization, legitimation, and remarkable growth of the social sciences during and after the Second World War had everything to do with "the growth of American power abroad and of the central government at home." In the context of war and Cold War, in the battle of ideas, ideologies, psychology, and propaganda, "the social scientist had, or purported to have, something special to contribute." [31] The war had employed social scientists as practitioners, technicians, and engineers, expanding their self-conception as the architects of "social engineering" beyond the realm of industry (specifically, the factory/shop floor) where they had traditionally found a "practical" calling. After the war, as Ball emphasizes, social scientists found a market for their nomological knowledge skills in the interests of corporate power, civilian intelligence, internal security, and the administration of the welfare state.

The Depression had afforded the social scientist a new public role in helping shape government policy. For postwar advocates of liberal consensus the use of a purportedly "disinterested" and "rational-scientific" search for knowledge held a singular appeal as a major instrument not simply for the measurement of social phenomena but

---

31. Terence Ball, "The Politics of Social Science in Postwar America," in *Recasting America: Culture and Politics in the Age of Cold War*, ed. Lary May (Chicago: University of Chicago Press, 1989), p. 82.

their prediction and control. This seemingly ideologically neutral "science" could be employed to sanction a particular and partial political order. Put another way, the apparently objective and impartial interests of social science constituted not only the best form of camouflage for an ideological agenda, but a system of social regulation entirely appropriate to strategies of legitimizing liberal consensus.[32]

Ball rightly points out that such an arrangement was less a product of deliberate conspiracy (as C. Wright Mills maintained) than the convenience of economic forces. Social scientists went looking for funding, and the groups with most at their disposal, not surprisingly, were the Rockefeller, Carnegie, and Ford foundations. Unlikely to sponsor research in directions critical of the forces that underpinned corporate power, these foundations have had a profound effect on the direction most quantitative research has taken—mostly devoted to improving the existing system, not demanding its dismantlement. In the turbulence of the postwar period, social science departments of all political persuasions saw an opportunity to capitalize on the situation and engaged in a program of extensive self-advertising, which expanded the territory in which they argued they had a stake. Not the least of these territories was the movies.

Here another economic coincidence occurred that advanced the expansion of positivistic social science into the leisure sphere. Social scientists could find their legitimacy in the eyes of the movie industry as providers of new and improved ways to measure audience response. This vital area for studio marketing interests became a site where the social scientist could gain sponsorship. One of the first wholesale attempts to guage the appeal and influence of the movies occurred in this era—namely, "Gallup Looks at the Movies," which systematically covered the period from 1940 to 1950 through yearly audience research reports. For my purposes here, it suffices to highlight that this is the context of the Production Code's changing format, and might help explain the change in the character of the PCA's vigilance once Eric Johnston took over the MPPDA / MPAA.

A comparison of the early Code format with its 1949 manifestation reveals shifts that clearly parallel developments in positivistic social science methodology. In this context, the Code's transformations

---

32. As an agent of the new corporate order of "repressive tolerance" this kind of social science did come in for criticism—from C. Wright Mills in particular—but too many factors militated against such a critique being taken on by the social science community. There was too much to lose in biting the hand that fed you.

might best be understood as symptomatic of hegemonic change, revealing the new status accorded commercial cinema as an essential ingredient for the sanctioning of the new order. The Code film analysis form was turned into an instrument of quantitative data collation designed to measure not only what social phenomena the movies mediated but how they did so. Before the war the movie industry was perceived by civic and moral interest groups to have a degenerative effect on society, and the Code was designed in part to offset this propensity. After the war (and because of the war), not only did perceptions change, but the range of vested interests in the movies expanded. While residual civic and moral pressure groups still maintained their old attitudes, state and corporate interests found they could not afford to take the same stance. The movies had vast potential as agents of social planning and the making of a new postwar political order.

As Eric Johnston declared, the task then was not to restrict Hollywood but to expand its efficacy as the arbitrator of "democratic capitalism." The expansion of the censorship form was symptomatic of this shift in focus. The range of issues and social phenomena the new forms attended to reflected the influence of positivistic social scientific procedure on the PCA. This influence in turn reflected the changing goals of "screening" Hollywood's products. We need look only at Parts 6 and 7 of the 1949 Code film analysis forms to see just how precise and nomological the Code's examination of film's mediation of society had become (see appendix). Far from looking for moral violations of the tenets of the Ten Commandments, the new form is invested in breaking down just what movies do communicate (not what they don't). That is, the emphasis was no longer negative (focused on prohibition), but positively disposed toward discovering how movies shape the entire realm of audience value attitudes.

The 1949 film analysis form expands on elements already present in its earlier mainfestation. There is a continuation of interest in the overall "angle" (political, racial, scientific, etc.); the predominant "settings"; the major and minor characters' "professions" and how they are portrayed (sympathetically or unsympathetically, etc.); race and nationality; liquor (both where the drinking takes place and how much is drunk); crime (its type, the fate of criminals, number of killings); the treatment of law and religion; and whether "adultery," "illicit sex," "divorce," "marriage," "suicide," or "gambling" takes place.

While the early Code form was interested in how official and sanctified professions and institutions were portrayed (bankers, doctors,

lawyers, journalists, public officials, judges, justices of the peace, police, D.A.s, sheriffs, religious workers), the level of "sociological" inquiry into the private realm was limited simply to whether things like
"adultery" or "divorce" took place.

Turning to the 1949 form we can see how an issue, such as
"Crime," once granted only one line, and whose significance was limited to the fact of its occurrence and nothing more, now becomes an
entire section of questions (Part 5). Just as spectacular is the increase
in space devoted to the elements once clustered together on the bottom line of the old form. Issues of "marriage," "divorce," "adultery,"
and so on are given expanded treatment in two new sections (Parts 6
and 7) devoted to "sociological factors." Part 1 of the new form attends in greater detail to "setting," breaking this nebulous category
down to nameable "locales," such as "City," "Suburban," "Small
Town," and "Rural." There is also a new interest in class as the form
tries to document the economic status of the "setting." The question
of the story's "angle" is expanded to include new categories that center on the way Hollywood mediates the domestic realm, such as "Juvenile," "Educational," "Psychological," and "Family Life."

What is new then is not simply that the 1949 form tries to itemize
more things, but that it increases its attention to how Hollywood mediates more than just "public" institutions. The direction of the questions is toward a documentation of the film industry's dramatization
of the inner life of the nation: family, youth, upbringing, and psychological stability. For example, while an older category such as "portrayal of professions" remains, the newer rubric of "sociological factors" gives the issue of character portrayal an added examination, this
time in terms of "motivations."

Thus it is no longer enough to know what a given character's job
is, and whether it is portrayed "sympathetically" or "unsympathetically." What the new form tries to document is whether characters are
consumed by a desire for "social prestige," "acquisition of wealth,"
"obedience to duty or job," "marital happiness," or "power for its
own sake." Furthermore, these motivations are sociologically quali-
fied by the noting of each character's "economic status," "marital
status," and "social age." All these elements deal for the first time
with how Hollywood addresses the divided nature of American
society.

These evaluative categories acknowledge and attempt to name a
realm of fundamental value attitudes, both divisive and unifying,
which had a pronounced control over the lives of everyday Americans.

Beyond this, the PCA had an investment in looking at how Hollywood communicated these values/motivations, for it was also interested in whether these motivations were realized ("Yes," "No," "Not Clear") and how they were portrayed ("Sympathetically," "Unsympathetically," or "Both"). That is, behind a disinterested attempt to quantify the realm of common desires and drives that informed the content and plot of many Hollywood films, there lay a continued investment in controlling outcomes.[33]

This added a new dimension to the ways in which the crime film, in particular, could be judged as "criminal." While the section on crime betrays some residues of the older evaluative system (e.g., attending to the "fate" of the criminal), its focus falls on new ways to define the criminal, the realm of crime, and how criminals "enlist the sympathy of the audience." The censors are interested in what kinds of genre crime takes place in. The classifications run the gamut of possibilities from traditional genres like the Western, Mystery, and Musical to more nebulous areas such as the "Psychological" and "Social Problem" film. This interest in the cross-genre and even extra-generic presence of crime is partly indicative of the PCA's attempt to improve its screening techniques of Hollywood's most slippery and controversial entity, that crime cycle we now call film noir, but for which precisely no category existed at the time.

More significant, the expanded censoring treatment of crime's generic realms testifies to a greater awareness of the full range of social and psychological elements that could be "criminally" encoded. That is, the crime section of the PCA form is concerned not only with improving the measurement of what made a crime film "criminal." Rather, the interest is in the way crime pervades not just films "involving professional criminals" but other kinds of stories and other realms of life. Hence the crime section itself points to other ways of evaluating crime's impact on Hollywood representation and toward its impact in mediating that realm of "sociological" issues dealt with in the form's last two sections. It risks overstatement to claim that the PCA was finally coming to terms with how and why the crime film constituted a privileged site for the representation of certain kinds of sociopsychological problems. It is clear, however, that the attempt to find out where crime emerges, and the uses to which it is put, cannot

33. It is notable that on Part 1 of the new form a concern for the "ending" is first articulated ("Happy," "Unhappy," "Moral").

be disengaged from other attempts in the form to measure Hollywood's sociopsychological worth.[34]

The emergence of a sociopsychological discourse within the PCA indicates an important shift in the definition of censorship and its goals. The 1949 film analysis form signifies an awareness that the real influence of the movies on the lives and minds of the citizenry lay not in its dramatizations of spectacular conflicts between law and crime, but in its representations of the private and banal concerns that characterized America's interior domestic spaces. Hollywood's mediations of national "well-being" had to be measured by new standards. Evaluating the damage inflicted on the national self-image by Hollywood depended less on determining the degree to which public institutions were brought into disrepute (in conflicts between gangsters and police, for example), but on analyzing the way films portrayed the stability of home life and private desires.

This was significant in particular for the terms of postwar sociopolitical regulation. The new concentration on elements that might damage or endorse the standing of corporate loyalty, capital, and its organization of life ("acquisition of wealth," "obedience to duty or job"), and the new concentration on the private realms of nuclear family relations and propensities to psychosis ("psychological adjustment/peace of mind," "marital happiness," and "establishment and maintenance of a happy home"), were obviously key to a culture adjusting to peacetime prerogatives. But they also rose to be key components of the liberal consensus order.

At one level, this signifies a considerable expansion of interest, on the part of the new ideologues, in coupling Hollywood to an agenda rather than stopping it from carrying out one. At another, less ideologically motivated, level, the form's expansion is a symptom of the confusion and uncertainty that characterized this postwar period of adjustment. The form's more comprehensive "gridding" of Hollywood's products testifies to a search for new ways to account for

34. To this extent, the PCA was finally catching up with transformations in the gangster film itself, which had long shifted the site of its dramatic interest away from simple law/outlaw conflicts to the interior realm of criminal motivation (to the psychology of criminal behavior) and to issues of delinquency. As I argued in the previous chapter, a 1940s gangster film like *White Heat* became a way to metaphorically render the disturbed psychic condition of the nation as a whole. "Crime, Inc." films like *Force of Evil* and *Asphalt Jungle* connected psychological distortions to the realm of determining and corrupting social values. These films' impact lay in their dramatization of the sociopsychological disintegration of everyday life, not in their portrayals of law/criminal confrontation.

Hollywood's audience appeal and for new ideas about its realms of influence and use. The crucial difference between this concept of censorship and what had reigned previously was that it constituted not so much a search for new ways to police Hollywood but a way to turn Hollywood itself into an effective sociocultural policeman.

The symptoms of this change are to be found in the discussions among social scientists themselves. The summer 1947 volume of the *Journal of Social Issues* concentrated precisely on the integration of social science method into mass-media analysis. The journal's editor, Franklin Fearing, stresses the significance of film and radio for the postwar era:

> Altogether a very large number of persons—social scientists, educators, members of various creative crafts, writers, directors, musicians, animationists, and (some) producers—are conscious that these media have meaning for a democratic culture which is at least as important as their significance as a business or industry.[35]

Fearing was a professor of psychology at UCLA, a psychological consultant for radio programs and movies, and a founder and editor of *Hollywood Quarterly* (now called *Film Quarterly*), one of the first critical journals devoted to a serious scholastic examination of Hollywood's social, psychological, and political significance. For Fearing the movies had been misunderstood as "pure entertainment" or "escapist fare." He maintained, instead, that Hollywood's function should be compared to a "teller of tales" who has "interpreted, explained, and psychologically structured the world of his audience." At the same time, Fearing railed against inadequate concepts of the audience "as made up of featureless robots with blank minds and low intelligences." The challenge for social science was to start taking the mass media seriously by abandoning the previous restricted notions of entertainment and audience that had helped to "rationalise a policy which confines motion picture 'entertainment' to a restricted type of content on the grounds that the 'mass audience' doesn't 'want' or can't understand anything else."[36]

Fearing's remarks about social science "misapprehension" of mass media parallel a similar shift in PCA censoring goals, away from a restricted notion of movie content and audience makeup that underpinned a prohibitive mandate toward a more nuanced understanding of the "affirmative" propensities of mass media in social regulation.

35. Franklin Fearing, *Journal of Social Issues* 3, no. 3 (summer 1947), p. 2.
36. Ibid., pp. 3–4.

Fearing attacked existing forms and uses of institutionalized censorship expressed in "formal codes." Instead, he proposed that social science be called in to find an alternative way to regulate mass media's social responsibility. New standards and techniques of evaluation had to be developed for films:

> There is a need for a large amount of clarifying research, particularly on the crucial problem of the relation between content and meaning as apprehended by the mass audience. It is startlingly true that if a group of socially minded makers of film together with an equally socially minded group of social scientists, operating with an unlimited budget with unrestricted facilities, wished to make a film alleviate, say, interracial tensions, they would not know precisely what to put in it. . . . This is a sad state of affairs.[37]

Fearing's argument was that if the mass media were to operate as a force for social good, it was incumbent on social science to catch up with or get ahead of its object of knowledge. He recognized how powerful the movies were as a mediating sociocultural force, acknowledging at the same time that the task of quantifying this force lagged behind the reality of its effects. In this sense, the apparently objective call for "clarifying data" and "sharper conceptualizations about human communication and mass audience" was coupled to an interest in controlling the social impact of mass media on behalf of the newly defined democratic order. The pre-war intellectual condescension that characterized research in the field of mass media matched the interests and style of 1930s film censorship. In fact, the words Fearing uses to describe the state of pre-war media research could just as well describe the goals of censorship, concerned as it was with discovering "how harmful the movies were, rather than exploring their possibilities in a democratic society."[38]

Accordingly, Fearing suggested capitalizing on Second World War propensities for a "positive" type of research, embodied in the military uses of film and radio. He admired the military's "frank recognition that film and radio do shape attitudes" and were the "proper media for expressing ideas and values." In part, this issue of the *Journal of Social Issues* was an exercise in social science self-advertising. One of its articles was devoted to dealing with a June 1947 news report about State Department concerns over the disturbing image of American life generated by Hollywood for audiences at home and

37. Ibid., pp. 6–7.
38. Ibid., p. 59.

abroad. In essence, it was proposed that "fundamental ideas in social psychology" could help sort out State Department worries. In another article, Paul Lazarsfeld, one of the intellectual cornerstones of positivist social research, argued that positivist social science could help mass media reduce prejudice toward ethnic minorities. In sum, social science technicians could come to the aid of political policymakers through their ability not only to measure, but to discipline, mass-media effects.

CONCLUSION: THE CHANGED TERMS
OF HOLLYWOOD REGULATION

Such a shift in ideas about sociocultural policing and the mass media's contributions to this effect did not take place overnight. It would be a mistake to argue that changes in the PCA film analysis form reflected a successful completion of a new agenda, a successful co-optation of Hollywood to the interests of liberal consensus. As Fearing's remarks in 1947 acknowledged, the task was one of making up for lost ground in terms of understanding the sociological value of the motion picture. While Fearing may have been patient enough to await the day when social scientists would catch up with their object of study in order to control it, others were more anxious. HUAC's inquisitions, while taking on the character of an anachronistic notion of censorship and media control, actually served to accelerate the conversion of Hollywood into a more effective communicator of liberal consensus ideology.

What the PCA files on the late 1940s gangster film reveal, in conjunction with the expanded format of the censorship form itself, is a profound adjustment in attitudes toward the commercial cinema and its sociocultural value. The period can be characterized as one of transforming rather than completed agendas. The crime film's unique (symbiotic) relationship to the history of censorship meant that it became a key site in the struggle over Hollywood's representations of American life throughout the 1930s and 1940s. As I have argued, the ersatz gangster film was recognized in its own time as a negotiated film form, the product of engagements with the Breen office. At the same time this kind of crime film was also acknowledged as a way to continue to address controversial social issues and to meet audience demand in spite of Code (and later wartime OWI and postwar State Department) strictures.

This codependency between crime and censorship had a generative effect that is overlooked if we limit our notion of censorship to an instrument of prohibition and restriction. In the 1930s the PCA "enjoyed" an awkward divided interest as an agency of industry protection and at the same time guarantor of certain moral prerogatives. While the PCA appeased external pressure groups with a moratorium on gangster films, the Catholic "arrival" as chief arbiters of the Code signaled a breakup of the WASP monopoly as America's moral authority. The PCA granted Catholics a new legitimacy in American culture as the sanctioned policemen of the nation's most significant mass medium. As I have argued, the Code was symptomatic of larger transformations in American ideology and power distribution subsequent to the Wall Street Crash. Yet the Code's denotative and prohibitive character meant it would become increasingly out of step with the sophisticated circumnavigatory products it in some way had helped spawn. In the 1940s the Breen office found itself increasingly unable to enforce its moral mandate. In addition, it underwent internal transformations that changed the goals to which it was committed. This split objective signaled the end of one era and the arrival of something new.

A key moment for this transition was *The Moon Is Blue* controversy in 1953, which spelled the end of old-style Code stipulations about sex and morality. Director Otto Preminger insisted that the film be released independent of Code certification, a demand that necessitated that United Artists resign from the MPAA, which it duly did. The film contained a view of sexuality entirely in contradiction with the Code but in keeping with modern American life. The stakes were clear, and when the New York board of censors tried to ban the film, United Artists took the case to court and won.[39]

The Moon Is Blue controversy is often mistaken for the final victory of anticensorship. What it actually constituted was the inevitable demise of one kind of censorship whose significance has been perhaps overvalued. After all, *The Moon Is Blue* victory did not exactly usher in the most "liberal" period of Hollywood filmmaking. In many ways *The Moon Is Blue* controversy might be better understood as the victory of the new kind of censorship over the old. The appearance of censorship's demise belied the new "affirmative" form it had taken and the new goals to which it had been oriented, goals first established in the late 1940s.

As I shall argue further in the next chapter, the real measure of the

39. See Jack Vizzard, *See No Evil* (New York: Simon and Schuster, 1970), for an insider's account of this moment of transition for the Code.

new order's degree of success in gaining control of Hollywood lay in the demise of a particular kind of socially critical/dysfunctional crime feature filmmaking. Subsequent to HUAC, the appearance of a more liberal regime, prepared to grant the screen new "freedoms," only helped the process of forgetting—the imposition of amnesia—about the violent truth upon which this new liberal consensus order had been built. The intense postwar battle for control of Hollywood was provoked in part by the reemergence of the gangster film and the popularity of the films problematically classified as film noir. The crime feature, with its representation of the violent and corrupt side of American life, was bound to be a profound source of worry to social regulators in the immediate aftermath of the war. The fact that the crime feature and social problem feature rose to a quarter of Hollywood's production in the late 1940s only intensified concerns about Hollywood's social responsibilities.

What made the postwar confrontations over the gangster film all the more significant, however, lay in the film form's twofold power to drag up memories of the New Deal order on one hand and the memory of the Code's first full-scale enforcement on the other. In short, to make a gangster film in the postwar 1940s was to confront the issue of censorship head on and to remind audiences of unsettled scores that had been staved off by the war. The controversial nature of the gangster cycle's past brought to the forefront the realization that any attempt to control Hollywood depended on the control of the movies' relation to collective memory. Key to any attempt to make Hollywood into a vehicle of social affirmation would be the remolding or eradication of the crime film.

The postwar crime film connected itself to a socially antagonistic tradition of filmmaking synonymous with elements of New Deal–era ideology and its demands for social reform, a legacy that McCarthyites and liberal consensus advocates alike wished to eradicate. As a narratively troubled film form, the crime cycle of the 1940s was also structurally ill suited to the task of status quo or power affirmation. In fact, as I have argued, its main propensity was to generate an opposite effect. As such, if Hollywood was to become an effective instrument for the reprogramming of collective memory after the war, this could only be achieved at the cost of the crime film and everything it encoded.

The degree to which this attempt to effect cultural amnesia through mass-media regulation was successful has not been my primary focus. The more significant goal has been to uncover how and why, after the

Wall Street Crash, an apparently vulgar and trivial form of cultural expression came to take on such a high profile in the quest for power. The kinds of pressures the crime film brought to bear on Hollywood's system of representation were not trivial, for the gangster film exemplified a kind of filmmaking that truly troubled political authority. As such, I offer a corrective to a "certain tendency" in Hollywood film theory and historiography. My investigation of how crime was screened throughout the 1930s and 1940s testifies not to the commercial cinema's reactionary function but to its transformative capacities. The battle—from Hays Code to HUAC—to control Hollywood's representation of American life illuminates the extent to which the mass cinema was at odds with power prerogatives. For the latter, the gangster film and 1940s crime cycle constituted the most unacceptable face of the popular culture, a site where memory could be served, where audiences could be reminded of the things power would prefer them to forget. The fact that this "seditious" cycle would become inextricably associated with European filmmakers (especially Germans and Austrians) in exile from fascism only intensifies matters when it comes to evaluating the political significance of the 1940s crime film.

The "Un-American" Film Art

Robert Siodmak, Fritz Lang, and the Political
Significance of Film Noir's German Connection

The route from Babelsberg (site of the major German film studio Universum-Film Aktiengesellschaft, or UFA) to Hollywood had been well traveled before the proclamation of the Third Reich in 1933. Hitler's rise to power, however, triggered a mammoth exodus of film talent for whom the flight to Hollywood became a flight into exile. While these and other central European emigrés spread out into all areas of the American film industry, they left perhaps their most indelible mark on the postwar Hollywood crime film. Directors such as Robert Siodmak, Fritz Lang, Billy Wilder, Kurtis Bernhardt, Wilhelm Dieterle (and Edgar Ulmer, who came to Hollywood before 1933) became synonymous with the creation of a visually dark and thematically pessimistic representation of postwar American life. In conjunction with exiled cameramen such as John Alton, Karl Freund, and Theodore Spahrkuhl, they helped fashion the American crime films that have since been problematically categorized as film noir.[1]

When it comes to addressing the significance of the German exiles' influence on Hollywood's crime film, most scholars will invoke the

---

1. Not only these exile directors, but others, such as Steven Sekely, Otto Preminger, Michael Curtiz, Harry Horner, Boris Ingster, and Max Ophüls, all made significant contributions to this cycle. The contribution to film noir's stylistics is not just limited to directors and cinematographers—the important contribution of central European musicians/composers, such as Miklos Rosza, Franz Waxman, Frederick Hollander, Alfred Newman, and Hans Salter, to the postwar crime cycle's sound is an area that remains remarkably underresearched.

term "Expressionism." The exile's modernist heritage is predominantly used as a prop to argue for the anomalous and exceptional status of something called "film noir." That is, the German exiles' Expressionist filmmaking tradition helps us understand the apparent disjuncture between the 1940s American crime cycle and other Hollywood film forms and traditions. What is needed, however, is a more precise examination of the terms of this transatlantic modernist/formula film conjuncture. There has been a tendency to take a German exile director's Expressionist heritage for granted—its significance limited to its being aesthetically "alien" to the American cinematic tradition. Even if one accepts this as a reasonable premise, it does not help explain why the crime film became the privileged site for this modernist transfusion into the American cinema. Moreover, because there has been no examination of the mitigating circumstances that led to this production of an Expressionist aesthetic within the conventions of the American crime film, no one has connected the "alien" contribution of exiles to the production of an "un-American" cinema in the context of 1940s politics.

My claims for the political significance of film noir's German connection, in the cases of Robert Siodmak and Fritz Lang, rest not on examining whether a given filmmaker's political "intentions" translate onto the screen. Neither am I concerned with establishing an exact causal or teleological relationship between Weimar German cinema and Hollywood. That is, I am not interested in "authenticating" a proper prehistory to what has become known as film noir. This etiological nightmare, as Thomas Elsaesser has warned us, can assume "noir-like" characteristics as we go down endlessly proliferating false paths in search of proof for the existence of a category of film that has itself been disputed.[2] My examination focuses, instead, on how it was the exile's syncretic art in particular that enabled the 1940s American crime film to circumnavigate attempts at its suppression by moral and political censors. My claim for the significance of the German exiles' contribution to the American crime film has everything to do with the way a modernist aesthetic heritage enabled the continued production of a politically troubling film form.

For the task at hand I have isolated two directors as case studies, Fritz Lang and Robert Siodmak. They are perhaps the two exile

2. Thomas Elsaesser, "A German Ancestry to Film Noir? Film History and Its Imaginary," *Iris* 21 (spring 1996), pp. 129–43.

directors most intimately associated with what we call film noir. The majority of their American "oeuvre" took the form of crime thrillers. Robert Siodmak directed some twenty-one feature films in Hollywood between 1939 and 1951, around half of which have been labeled films noirs. Fritz Lang directed twenty-two feature films during his Hollywood sojourn from 1936 to 1956, of which at least fourteen have been included under the noir rubric.[3] In both directors' cases their crime films constitute their best and most profitable undertakings. Moreover, their shared reputation as masters of the postwar crime film's so-called noir aesthetic invites obvious questions about a pervasive Weimar legacy that unifies their work.

The darker and most pessimistic forms of crime film tended to be subsumed under Hollywood's "B" category of filmmaking or under the auspices of independent production companies (see chapter 5 for extenuating reasons). This may explain in part why many exile directors found a vocation here. The B picture was made cheaply and quickly with minimal economic risks, and thus proved attractive to independent producers with small budgets. It served as an American apprenticeship for exile directors anxious to find employment. At the same time the B picture was the area of least top-down studio interference, where the directors' auteurist bents were only limited by the quality of the materials at their disposal and the tight time schedules they had to keep.

Robert Siodmak's story is a case in point. He arrived in Hollywood in 1939, having lived and made films in France since 1933 as an exile from fascism.[4] In America he was to become best known as a master

---

3. Alain Silver and Elizabeth Ward's "encyclopedic" reference lists as films noirs Fritz Lang's *Fury* (1936), *You Only Live Once* (1937), *Woman in the Window* (1945), *Scarlet Street* (1945), *Ministry of Fear* (1945), *Clash by Night* (1952), *The Blue Gardenia* (1953), *The Big Heat* (1953), *Human Desire* (1954), *While the City Sleeps* (1956), and *Beyond a Reasonable Doubt* (1956). To this list could be added crime thrillers that for varying reasons do not fit the rubric of film noir (two spy dramas and a Hitchcock-styled thriller set in England): *Manhunt* (1941), *Cloak and Dagger* (1946), and *Secret Beyond the Door* (1948).

The films of Robert Siodmak that have been categorized as films noirs are the following: *Christmas Holiday* (1944), *Phantom Lady* (1944), *The Strange Affair of Uncle Harry* (1945), *The Killers* (1946), *The Dark Mirror* (1946), *Cry of the City* (1948), *Criss Cross* (1949), and *The File on Thelma Jordan* (1950). To this list could be added two noir-like features that are set in the wrong era or landscape, *The Suspect* (1945) and *The Spiral Staircase* (1945). Alain Silver and Elizabeth Ward, eds., *Film Noir: An Encyclopedic Reference to the American Style*, 3d ed. (Woodstock, N.Y.: Overlook Press, 1992).

4. In France he made eight films: *Le Sexe Faible* (1933), *La Crise est Finie* (1934), *La Vie Parisienne* (1934), *Mr Flow* (1936), *Cargaison Blanche* (1937), *Mollenard* (1937), *Ultimatum* (1938), and *Pieges* (1939).

of the crime film. This was, however, only after he had served a frustrating apprenticeship as a Paramount B-unit director. At Paramount, apart from *Fly By Night* (1942) (a Hitchcockesque propaganda piece about a doctor framed by Nazis for murdering a scientist) and *Son of Dracula* (1943) (which was inspired by his brother Curt, a master of gothic horror), Robert Siodmak churned out highly forgettable fare that did little to attract people's attention and little to tax the skills he had honed in the Weimar cinema.

It was only after he had been fired from Paramount that he started to build a reputation. Starting with *Phantom Lady* in 1944, under the producing auspices of Joan Harrison (a longtime screenwriting associate of Alfred Hitchcock), Siodmak's talents as a metteur-en-scène began to pay dividends. What is important to note is that from this time on Siodmak's most famous and most profitable undertakings were not only crime films, but crime films produced by independent producers and production units—most notably, *The Killers* (1946) and *Criss Cross* (1949), both of which had been sponsored by Mark Hellinger at his independent production company, International Pictures.

It was only in the independent environment that Siodmak was freed from certain aesthetic restrictions he had experienced during his first Hollywood tenure at Paramount. As his brother Curt Siodmak pointed out, he wanted to do "a Siodmak Picture" not "Paramount shit," a sentiment, as we have seen, entirely in keeping with the mood of many directors in the immediate postwar years.[5]

If the B movie was the area most tolerant of experimentation, it was also the area least invested in. The director's innovative talents were thus framed by very practical limitations. Perhaps this also contributed to a unified vision—that is, the crime film's aesthetic experimentalism and its pervasive and uniform "look" are a direct product of common economic and material limitations. The use of the long take and extended dialogue, for example, are precisely part of the pressure of small cutting ratios. Certain of the postwar crime cycle's "experimental" features, such as the approximation of cinematic and real time, can be contextualized under the principle of necessity being the mother of invention. The competing tendency against innovation led to an intense repetition of successful experiments, which encouraged a degree of unity among the B thrillers. This, however, only explains

5. Lee Server, *Screenwriter: Words Become Pictures* (Pittstown, N.J.: The Main Street Press, 1987), p. 217. See chapter 5 for full discussion of the move to independent production companies.

the infrastructural support for a way of filmmaking. An economic argument alone cannot explain why Weimar filmmakers would be best disposed to utilizing this structure to promote such a dark and criminal vision of life. Nor can it explain why such an aesthetic might be considered a recipe for a dissenting cinema.

As exiles who were able to "make it" within the dictates of the studio system, Lang's and Siodmak's cases help us see what enabled an UFA-Hollywood crossover. Their contribution to the Hollywood crime film has been acknowledged as aesthetically significant because of the refinements in terms of lighting techniques, use of mise-en-scène, and camera movement they brought with them from abroad. Yet what makes all this politically interesting is that, among other elements, such German Expressionist devices constitute generic extensions of lighting and mise-en-scène conventions that also characterized the ambience of outlawed American film forms: namely, the 1930s American gangster and fallen woman films.

WEIMAR CRISIS AESTHETICS GO HOLLYWOOD I: THE TRANSCULTURAL DISCOURSE OF CASTRATION

The Weimar cinema's mediations of the modern urban milieu that traveled across the Atlantic could do so not because they were absolutely identical to their American counterparts, but because they could superimpose themselves over the palimpsest of existing generic conventions. More specifically, the 1940s crime cycle revitalized two versions of urban America that had been repressed after the first enforcement of the Production Code in 1935. The most discernible generic predecessors to the films grouped as films noirs are the morally ambivalent pre-Code gangster film and "fallen woman" film.[6] Weimar had its equivalents to America's vamps/femmes fatales and underworld narratives; Marlene Dietrich's Lola in *The Blue Angel* (1930) is a classic example.[7] The similarity of these dramatic encodings of

6. For a full study of the "fallen woman" film's adventure with the censors, see Lea Jacobs, *Wages of Sin: Censorship and the Fallen Woman Film, 1928–1942* (Berkeley and Los Angeles: University of California Press, 1997).

7. Jan-Pieter Barbain's study reveals that women's sexual freedom was also a volatile issue for Weimar's censoring agency, yet with a different emphasis: abortion. This emphasis on the question of reproductive rights was perhaps symptomatic of the Weimar tendency to a more "verist" aesthetic. The most heavily censored women's films dealt with abortion. Two examples are *Muß die Frau Mutter Werden* (Must Woman Become Mother?) (1925) and *Cyankali* (1930). Barbain, "Filme mit Lücken: Die Lichtspielzensur in der Weimarer Republik: von der sozialethischen Schutzmaßnahme zum Politischen Instrument," in *Der Deutsche Film: Aspekte seiner*

modern city life on both sides of the Atlantic points first to the global nature of the transformations brought on by modernization and urbanization after World War I, and, second, to a common body of myths and symbols that have defined a distinctly Western *Weltanschauung*. At the same time there were some crucial differences, ones that made the Weimar versions of street life and urban malaise arguably more applicable to the 1940s American context than existing Hollywood conventions.

The sociohistorical context that framed UFA production in the 1920s and 1930s shared some elements with America. Both cultures were undergoing a profound transformation brought on by the end of the First World War and changes in capitalist modes of production. For Germans the instigation of the Weimar Republic signaled an end to the Wilhelminian era. The post–World War I environment of the United States was marked by the winning of women's suffrage in 1919, the anti-immigration acts of 1921 and 1924, the instigation of Prohibition from 1919 to 1933, and the first Red Scare. It was a period characterized by a contradictory mix of emancipatory, misogynist, reformist, and xenophobic impulses designed to temper the degree of cultural change brought on by the forces of consumer capitalism. It is also the period when the motion picture industry came of age.

The mass cinema played a crucial role in the mediation of these cultural changes. Itself a part of the new consumer capitalist culture, commercial cinema had a vested stake in valorizing moviegoing as a legitimate cultural practice. In the United States, as Lary May demonstrates, the movies were a crucial institution in the regulation of America's shift from a world ruled by the Victorian principles of the producer economy into the world of consumer desire. Role models such as Douglas Fairbanks and Mary Pickford functioned to make the new world of consumption seemingly consonant with older ideals (thereby making leisure safe for bourgeois consumption). Although certain features of consumerism were demonized, this was designed not to erase them but to police the tendencies of consumerism to excess and moral lassitude.[8]

The first years of the war already signaled the signs of things to come. From 1914 to 1916 the figure of "the vamp" enjoyed her highest popularity. The quintessential vamp-star was Theda Bara, who

Geschichte von den Anfängen bis zur Gegenwart, ed. Uli Jung (Trier: WVT Wissenschaftlicher Verlag, 1993).

    8. Lary May, *Screening Out the Past: The Birth of Mass Culture and the Motion Picture Industry* (Chicago: University of Chicago Press, 1983).

encoded women's sexuality as erotic aggression. The sexual vampire was a destroyer of men, using her allure to distract men from their responsibilities to the virtuous moral order (i.e., marriage). Yet, even though this representation of woman as emasculator stigmatized the newfound freedoms of modern women, it also dramatized very real desires of the female audience for emancipation from the Victorian order. The contradiction of Bara's performances was that even as she encoded a masculinist vision of destructive female sexuality, she turned this so-called female aberration into something exciting and appealing. Bara herself commented:

> Women are my greatest fans because they see in my vampire the impersonal vengeance of all their unavenged wrongs . . . they have lacked either the courage or will-power to redress their grievances. Even downtrodden wives write me to this effect.[9]

This alternative vision of the vamp as an avenging angel typifies her later manifestations in such "fallen woman" films of the early 1930s as *Three on a Match* (1932), *Ladies They Talk About* (1933), *Employees Entrance* (1933), and *Baby Face* (1933). The free-living and gold-digging women of such films advance themselves by deliberately cultivating their status as objects of male desire—racy behavior such as sleeping one's way to the top was far easier than "working." If the vamp of the teens in her Cleopatra garb was exotic and alien, her later versions were based in the hurly-burly amorality of the contemporaneous urban milieu.

In the context of the Depression, the sexually empowered woman took on an added edge. In an era of massive unemployment the laissez-faire capitalist order had been brought into disrepute. The out-of-work male symbolized not only a collapse in the economic sense but a collapse in patriarchal definitions of agency. One response was the early 1930s gangster, who represented a desperate attempt at "re-masculinization" as a man who could overcome his milieu and control his destiny. He met his match in the gold-digging woman. The gangster put business before pleasure in an attempt to restore masculine virtue and prowess and "make it" against the distractions of seductive females. The seductive woman, however, turned pleasure into business, embodying the amorality of Depression-era capitalism by using sex as her route to the top. Such representations of female sexuality (where the object becomes subject) typified her contradictory

9. Ibid., p. 106.

function in the patriarchal symbolic economy. No matter how much the dangers of female sexuality were diluted by humor and resolved in the convention of marriage, its representation still proved too much for civic pressure groups and moral guardians. The catalog of peroxide man-eater films—*The Red-Headed Woman* (1932), *Blonde Bombshell* (1933), and *Blondie Johnson* (1933)—fell victim to the censor alongside the gangster.

Across the Atlantic, this prototype of the 1940s and 1950s crime cycle's femme fatale was given more sustained and joylessly candid treatment, occupying a more central place in Weimar cinema than did her American counterpart in Hollywood. She was the central ingredient of the *Straßenfilm* (Street Film), for many the definitive Weimar genre. As Patrice Petro has revealed, the prostitute who roamed Weimar's "joyless streets" encoded the link between sex and the destruction of social order as a potent female attribute. Perhaps the most dramatic encoding of this potential is Fritz Lang's *Metropolis* (1927), where the "duplicity" of woman is split into the "good" (real) woman and her evil robot seducing *doppelgänger* "other." The vamp as robot-destroyer was in some ways the logical misogynist extension of female sexuality. For Petro, the sheer power (albeit destructively encoded) that female sexuality could wield in the Weimar context (of social chaos, inflation, and unemployment) helps explain the contradictory appeal of the *Straßenfilm* for contemporaneous female audiences.[10] In terms of film criticism, Petro's examination of female spectatorship's relation to Weimar vamps echoes the feminist debate about the 1940s and 1950s crime cycle's femme fatale.[11]

The American femme fatale has been discussed as part of the attempt to redomesticate women after the Second World War. In wartime American women had found their desires for autonomy vindicated in the context of staffing the war industry. In the context of peace, however, independent womanhood was considered an obstacle to the reestablishment of bourgeois ideals of homelife. The recasting of female independence in the form of the femme fatale (as home-breaking, avaricious, a sexual predator, and user of men) certainly played a role in the demonization of women's desires for autonomy.

The femme fatale's excesses also signified a desperate attempt to reestablish patriarchal priorities. If we believe that Hollywood has

---

10. Patrice Petro, *Joyless Streets: Women and Melodramatic Representation in Weimar Germany* (Princeton: Princeton University Press, 1989).

11. A starting point for the feminist debate is E. Anne Kaplan, ed., *Women in Film Noir* (London: BFI, 1978).

German exile director Robert Siodmak brings his modernist and deterministic sensibilities to the American screen through careful manipulation of mise-en-scène. The Swede's (Burt Lancaster) inner alienation and sense of entrapment are expressed externally through the careful management of light and shadow in *The Killers* (1946).

always operated on behalf of a masculinist heterosexual order, then the postwar crime film constituted a moment when this order was most under duress. Frank Krutnik's persuasive analysis of Robert Siodmak's *The Killers* (1945), for example, reveals how this male order is seen not only to be most at risk but most contradictory.[12]

Even if the postwar crime film is driven by the command to reestablish male (phallic) order, it is distinguishable as *the* film form that does this most excessively, most visibly, and most ironically. As I shall demonstrate, these films draw attention less to their success as a

---

12. Frank Krutnik, *In a Lonely Street: Film Noir, Genre, Maculinity* (London: Routledge, 1991). Krutnik concludes, however, that film noir is an agent of patriarchal reordering. Yet on the basis of his own argument about the ironic reestablishment of masculine order, we might come to other conclusions.

The (Un-)American nihilism of an exiled director. Sadistic gangster Vince (Lee Marvin) is confronted by the outward manifestation of his own disfiguring behavior in the form of the scarred woman, Debby (Gloria Grahame), in Fritz Lang's *The Big Heat* (1953).

suturing narrative operation that restores patriarchal order than to their repeated failure to accomplish the mission. After all, in the history of Hollywood there have been less desperate and more seamless ways of ratifying patriarchal imperatives than the films categorized as film noir.

Fritz Lang's *The Big Heat* (1953) plays this out to the extreme. At the end of this film order is seemingly restored. Our detective protagonist (Glenn Ford as Dave Bannion) gets his job back and is restored to his desk at homicide. This is an ironically fitting end given the costs of this return to order. Bannion's masculine virtues are ostensibly pitted against the syndicate, which has the police force in its pocket. Bannion's moral rectitude means he can't be bought, and turns him into a vigilante crusader, striving to bring "the big heat" down on the clandestine forces of city corruption. He loses his police job for his meddlesome interference in the police/mob arrangement. Not only this, but his morality costs him his wife's life too (she is blown up by a car bomb intended for him). All told, Bannion's success rides over the corpses of four women. In the end, his victory is truly pyrrhic given the kinds of misogynist mutilations on which it depends. One of the gangster's girls, Debby Marsh (Gloria Grahame) is seen with Bannion and is rewarded by having her face disfigured with scalding coffee. The costs of conforming to the image of the "good" woman ensures death for the prostitute Lucy, who, having conveyed the disturbing truth about the apparent "suicide" of her lover (a corrupt cop) to Bannion, is gruesomely tortured and then murdered. Our knight-crusader's armor depends for its shine on a list of expendable women. The ironic reward for maintaining his moral (phallic) standing is the miserable isolation of the widower and his desk job.

This irony also defines the end of Siodmak's *The Killers* (though less nihilistically for the investigator concerned). Here the insurance investigator, Riordan (played by Edmond O'Brien) is motivated (as a professional maker of sense) to make sense out of the Swede's death. In other words, his is a narrative quest obeying an Oedipal logic. He assumes the posture of the analyst who has to unearth memories and delve into the past in order to explain what initially appears as an aporia. Riordan's search represents an attempt to rationalize that which exceeds the limits of our normative explanatory paradigms. Through the devices of flashback the audience is invited to join Riordan in his act of "reading for the plot." Our task is not to find out "whodunnit," for the film starts out by showing us who "the killers" are. The real quest is to explain why the ex-boxer/gangster Swede took his death so sedately and resignedly (so unlike "a man!").[13] As Krutnik puts it, Riordan's task is one of "masculine reassertion."[14] In the end we undertake a search not of the Swede's psyche but of the detective's (and our own). The motivation for our reading can only

13. Robert Siodmak, in an article entitled "Hoodlums: The Myth," in *Hollywood Directors, 1941–1976,* ed. Richard Koszarski (New York: Oxford University Press, 1977) (originally appearing in *Films and Filming,* June 1959), said this: "In cinema I find the best way of approaching the crime film is to let your audience in on the secret. Not to ask them who did it, but rather to let them follow the story line from one character's point of view . . . a few years ago the director would have asked 'how was [the murder] done.' Today the much more important question is 'why was it done?'" Here Siodmak connects narrative to psychology very explicitly, to the extent that narrative is seen to support subjective exploration.

14. Krutnik, *In a Lonely Street,* p. 123.

stem from a confrontation with the disturbing spectacle of the emasculated man. This leads not to reconfirmation but confrontation with the "normative" masculinist perceptive order.

Riordan's task is to detect the truth about Kitty (Ava Gardner), a classic femme fatale, and to reveal that she is Swede's "castrator." The investigator's praxis of making sense becomes the task of settling on an image of Kitty that will confirm his way of seeing. Riordan's quest must overcome Kitty's power to offer a competing version of herself that confuses the investigator's patriarchal logic. Riordan tries to make Kitty conform to the one-dimensional image of the "bad" woman, but his version must compete against the Swede's more complex acceptance of Kitty's duplicity. Swede's point of view is underscored by the cinematic apparatus's excessive (voyeuristic) indulgence in Ava Gardner's sexually charged performance of her status as an object of male fantasy. The plausibility of Swede's seduction rests concomitantly on Kitty's ability to seduce the audience as well.

Riordan sets in motion a self-defeating logic in trying to get at the truth. To make sense of Swede's seduction, he must precisely grant the agency to Kitty that he so desperately wants to take away from her. Ironically, Riordan's detective work makes it easy for us to see why the Swede could fall victim to this "spider" woman. Riordan's logic necessarily splits the narrative identification between his own point of view and Swede's in order to "understand" Swede's irrational act. This contradiction in terms only renders the whole masculinist enterprise ironic. As the film's end confirms, after all his clashes with the underworld and female vice, Riordan's assertively masculine work results in the grand total of a cut of one-half of one cent on insurance premiums for his company's insureds—and he's given the weekend off by the boss for his efforts.

Thus what Richard W. McCormick describes as a "discourse of castration" in the German cinema typifies not only the Weimar vamp, but the women of Siodmak's and Lang's American postwar crime classics: *The Killers, Criss Cross* (1949), *Scarlet Street* (1945), *Woman in the Window* (1945), and *The Big Heat*.[15] This paranoid psychosexual mediation of sociohistorical change rooted in Weimar cinema grafts itself onto less candid and more humorous pre-Code American traditions. Lang's *Scarlet Street* and *Woman in the Window* star Edward G.

15. Richard W. McCormick: "From Caligari to Dietrich: Sexual, Social, and Cinematic Discourses in Weimar Film," *Signs* (spring 1993).

Robinson as the gullible male who is exploited in both films by the seductress Joan Bennett (as Kitty March and Alice Reed, respectively). This is an interesting intertextual twist on both the pre-Code gangster and "fallen woman" film.

Robinson's star appeal had been built on his 1930s gangster portrayals originating in his characterization of *Little Caesar,* in 1930. His roles in Lang's 1940s films constituted a disturbance of audience expectations. Where his Little Caesar character and his later Johnny Rocco character in *Key Largo* (1948) manifest a strong masculinist misogyny, his roles as Chris Cross and Richard Wanley in Lang's films signify an end to this power (*Key Largo* confirming this, as it is all about the end of this ethnic typology's cultural relevance). As his characters' names betray in *Scarlet Street* and *Woman in the Window,* Robinson no longer embodies the ethnic underworld type fighting his sociological limits. Now he is trapped in a different ghetto: the prison of bourgeois rectitude where any transgression of bourgeois morality leads one into a realm of psychotic self-punishment. It is no longer the state that brings Robinson / Little Caesar down in an old-fashioned shoot-out, but something more faceless and internally regimented. This transformation of type is played out against the established expectations of Robinson's star appeal. These crime films rely in part on this antagonistic intertext for their dramatic impact. Robinson as Chris Cross is Little Caesar "double-crossed," stripped of agency. The actor associated so strongly with the 1930s gangster, the man of action, is now "emasculated" and condemned to bourgeois anonymity.

For Siodmak, the intertext of the 1930s was not grafted onto the star system but onto formula. *The Killers,* for example, was a gangster film but not in the mold of its American predecessors. Siodmak's generic revisions depended on introducing a different kind of gangster type to the American screen. The star of *The Killers* was an unknown, Burt Lancaster. This quality of anonymity was underscored by the kind of gangster he protrayed. Unlike previous gangster types like Robinson and Cagney, Lancaster played the small guy antihero in the "organization." Lancaster's characterization of the Swede, for example, constituted a shift of gangster portrayal from that which stood out to that which blended in. This change (as demonstrated in chapter 5) was a function of the general postwar trend both to shift the site of crime from the realm of the ethnic "underclass" to a bourgeois milieu, and to recast gangsterdom as a "syndicate," a dark parody of the faceless corporation that determined the fate of the average person. As I shall contend, to a director trained in Weimar Germany, this attention to the anonymity and alienation of modern life was nothing new. The presence of Weimar film exiles such as Siodmak and Lang only helped to accelerate the transformation of the American gangster film. No longer was gangsterdom a ghetto or backdrop to individuation; rather, it was a faceless system that could stand in for the corporate totality that robbed one of his autonomy.

In the 1930s the gangster came from a nameable social space, the Lower East Side. The first talking gangster stars, James Cagney, Edward G. Robinson, and Paul Muni, were all discernibly ethnic East Side natives. Their accents, slang, and streetwise body gestures betrayed their actual proximation to their roles and made them distinctively new stars in Hollywood. This ethnic marking made the 1930s gangster an easy object of imitation. The ethnic gangster stars inscribed their "otherness" as a positive attribute, as that which bestowed identity and autonomy.

In stark contrast, Lancaster's power lay in his ability to pass for the average Joe, the fall guy and patsy. This was less concomitant with the American gangster tradition of nameable cult heroes like Al Capone than with a Weimar concern for the criminal character of normative institutions. The passivity Lancaster encodes in the opening of *The Killers* is all the more troubling because of his past. He turns out to be the ex-boxer who cannot counterpunch anymore, the ex-gangster who has lost his desire for upward mobility and craves anonymity. In this sense, the past that catches up with the Swede is an intertextual one of now redundant masculine (phallic) tropes.

WEIMAR CRISIS AESTHETICS GO HOLLYWOOD II: THE EXPRESSIONIST LEGACY

Most critical reviews of these exile directors' contributions to Hollywood note but do not develop their disproportional presence in crime feature filmmaking. Such critical reviews comment on the legacy of "Expressionism," which those trained in Berlin and Vienna brought with them and which was somehow remolded to the requirements of Hollywood's system of representation. The problem with such accounts is that they do little to unravel the full permutations of this modernist aesthetic impulse in the Hollywood context. J. P. Telotte, for example, describes German Expressionism as a "language of heightened expression, one that would let [the filmmaker] give external shape and substance to inner, subjective experiences, feelings and attitudes, in effect turning the psyche inside out." [16] Yet he is satisfied to conclude that the German connection's value is essentially technical: it paved the way for the 1940s and early 1950s crime film's subjective camera narration. We are left with somewhat inadequate observations that German Expressionism helped produce the most "experimental" film style in the history of American cinema. [17]

Such broad technical accounts of German Expressionism override the very specific sociohistorical context to which this aesthetic was bound. The period of German Expressionism extends from 1903 to 1933, covering the transformation (catalyzed by the trauma of the First World War) from Wilhelminian authority into the modern and chaotic world of the Weimar Republic (1919–1933), Germany's first democratic government. What is more, much of what we all too loosely call film noir's Expressionist heritage is actually something derived from very specific and different Expressionist offshoots. This is particularly apparent in the cases of Siodmak and Lang. Siodmak made his name as a pioneer of the intimate and verist *Milieutonfilm* ("milieu talkie"), derived from the silent *Kammerspielfilm*. This stood in stark contrast to Fritz Lang, who demonstrated a more spectacular and auteurist proclivity for apocalyptic and underworld conspiracy epics.

Siodmak articulated a notion of the "hoodlum myth," which thematically played on a Hollywood crime film intertext. [18] His stated preference for the studio over location shooting, however, is testament to the Weimar legacy to which his style is most indebted, the *Kammerspielfilm*. While this preference obviously enabled Siodmak to fit into the American studio system, it was born out of his Weimar investment in finding an aesthetic appropriate to the intimate and interior crisis features of modern urban life. The influence of this modernist approach to social contradictions came to determine not only Siodmak's recharacterization of the American gangster type, but the

16. J. P. Telotte, *Voices in the Dark: The Narrative Patterns of Film Noir* (Urbana and Champaign: University of Illinois, 1989), pp. 17–18.

17. For example, in their comprehensive work on film noir, Alain Silver and Elizabeth Ward, J. P. Telotte, and Frank Krutnik all limit film noir's German connection to a question of style. Yet in doing this they still do not give a precise enough account of what they mean by "Expressionism." Even though Krutnik (in a footnote) makes this very point, he states that "such questions will not receive much attention here" (pp. 235–36). Silver and Ward, eds., *Film Noir: An Encyclopedic Reference to the American Style;* Krutnik, *In a Lonely Street;* Telotte, *Voices in the Dark.*

18. See Siodmak, "Hoodlums: The Myth," in *Hollywood Directors, 1941–1976,* pp. 283–88.

visual and narrative repatterning of the formula itself. *The Killers* and *Criss Cross* are marked by a range of Expressionist codes—a compact use of mise-en-scène featuring chiaroscuro lighting, minimalist sets, mobile camera, and extreme angle shots, and the use of narrative fragmentation through flashback—all to underscore the subjective telling of a determinist tale.

Strictly speaking, the *Kammerspielfilm* was a "silent" film art championed by the Austrian author, dramaturge, and screenwriter Carl Mayer (also an exile). Regarded as one of the most significant variations of the Expressionism defining the Weimar silent era, the archetypes of this film form were *Hintertreppe* (1921), *Scherben* (1921), *Sylvester* (1923), and *Der Letzte Mann* (1924), all written and conceived by Mayer. The *Kammerspielfilm* transferred the apocalyptic declarations that characterized earlier Expressionist films, such as *Das Kabinett des Dr. Caligari* (1919), into closed and more "naturalistic" settings. The *Kammerspielfilm* mediated the lower-middle- to middle-class milieu as hermetic and impenetrably pessimistic. Life obeyed the logic of the vicious circle, and to sustain this determinist ambience this film form maintained a classic unity between time, space, and plot.

The *Kammerspielfilm* pioneered the use of the *entfesselte kamera*— the unchained or mobile camera. Cameramen like Karl Freund developed means such as cranes and body-holsters to free the camera from the tripod. This was the technological underpinning for the aesthetic desire to realize an intensely subjective drama. The subjective camera projected the intimate psychology of individuals onto a world of external objects. As such, the mise-en-scène became a prime bearer of meaning. In the context of Weimar Berlin, this externalized subconscious was hemmed in by the milieu of run-down apartments. The combined effect, characteristically, was pessimistic, sparse, dark, and claustrophobic. This compact determinist subjectivity was serviced by an uninterrupted visual flow. Unusually for the silent era, the *Kammerspielfilm* had little to no intertitles because these were deemed redundant features that disturbed the rhythm and unity of the film: the camera told the story.

Siodmak was hailed as one of the first directors to make a "sound" *Kammerspielfilm*, the first *Milieutonfilm* or "milieu talkie," *Abschied*, in 1930. Siodmak's attraction to this film aesthetic grew from his first film, *Menschen am Sonntag* (1929), a "film without stars" covering, in documentary fashion, the petty dramas of a group of Berliners on a Sunday outing. Siodmak's uncompromising view of the mundane blends Expressionist concerns with a Weimar verist aesthetic—*Neue Sachlichkeit* or New/Neo-Objectivity. While the latter was constituted in opposition to certain forms of Expressionism (especially in its celebration rather than fear of the new technology), even this documentary-realist treatment of big-city life was permeated by an Expressionist concern for the vicious circles people get enmeshed in daily. In many ways, then, a "noir disposition" was in the making. Although it could be argued that almost all Siodmak's Weimar films betray this propensity, I shall limit my discussion to the two that best embody it: *Abschied* (1930) and *Brennendes Geheimnis* (1932).

The tension in *Abschied* (Farewell/Departure) depends on "a day in the life of" unfolding of time and an extremely minimalist use of set, limited to the rooms in one apartment. The characters are seemingly faceless and their troubles banal. Two lovers, Peter and Hella, cannot afford to get married. Peter has his eyes on a new job but wants to surprise his partner with it. Hella misinterprets his apparent secrecy as a sign of mistrust. She has just ordered a new hat and dress but cannot bring herself to ask her lover for the money. She borrows the money from a rich Russian friend and refuses to tell Peter, her partner, where she's going that evening (she only wants to pick up the clothes). Peter, suspecting betrayal, is consumed by jealousy and after Hella has gone out, he storms off. He forgets, however, the ring that Hella once gave him. The Russian friend returns to the empty apartment and, always on the lookout for valuables, pockets the ring. He takes pity on Hella when she breaks down and cries on hearing the news that Peter has walked out. He gives her the ring without knowing of its history, claiming that Peter had asked him to do so. She can only interpret this as her lover's final rejection, and what little happiness she has changes into a lamentable "farewell."

Aesthetically, Emmerich Pressburger (screenwriting collaborator on the film) proclaimed *Abschied* to be the first "milieu talkie," with its unpretentious slice-of-life approach. "The plot begins at 7 and is over by 9. The chronological order is never interrupted. And neither is the unity of the milieu. Not once does the camera leave the apartment. Its empire extends from corridor door to the bathroom." The "unity of the milieu" is even preserved by the "verist" use of music, which bridges the plot's dead time. The film score doesn't emanate from some space outside the film's diegesis, but is produced by another actor (albeit unseen): namely, an unemployed pianist who lives elsewhere in the apartment (trapped within the same milieu, as it were), and who withdraws into a fantasy world by practicing aimlessly on his piano for hours on end.[19] *Abschied* extends the *Kammerspiel-film*'s metaphorical journeys through Berlin's real urban spaces, where the *Hinterhof, Hintertreppe,* and *Gasse* functioned as gateways into the "backyard" of the average person's psyche.[20]

Brennendes Geheimnis (Burning Secret) tells the story of a mother and son on holiday. The set is essentially limited to a railway carriage compartment and a couple of hotel rooms. During the journey to the hotel a handsome man joins the pair in their railway carriage. He is attracted to the boy's mother and seeks to gain her attentions by be-friending the child. The son gets the impression he is in the way. Through his hotel-room window the boy sees, to his horror, the man and his mother disappear together into the shadows of the hotel grounds. Hysterically upset, he runs out and tries to prevent the couple from going on their way. He then disappears into the shadows and flees to his grandmother in Zurich. His worried mother is in-formed of his whereabouts and sets off to get him. On her arrival, she finds her husband is also waiting. He wants to know why their son ran away. The son is faced with a terrible decision—to reveal his mother's indiscretions to his father or to keep quiet and thus condemn himself in the eyes of his father as having acted out of stubborn and selfish immaturity. He takes the latter option.

Once again the maintenance of intimate and realist space-time co-ordinates is essential in generating a sense of repression and pessi-mism. Where set design is minimal, claustrophobic, and sparsely populated by mainly anonymous characters, visual style and camera movement are granted the starring roles in communicating the the-matic interest. This emphasis on subjective camera movement, high contrast lighting, minimalist set design and music—all used as vehi-cles for a pessimistic mediation of modern urban life and its everyday psychic ills—was appropriate to the problems of Weimar city culture and became generically characteristic of much of the German cinema of this period.

The challenge to find ways to adequately represent the problems of the urban milieu in Weimar cinema, however, was inflected by a fac-tional political controversy over mass film's ideological function. The

19. Emmerich Pressburger, "*Abschied,* der erste Milieutonfilm," *Licht-Bild-Bühne* (Au-gust 19, 1930) (my translation).

20. Hans Feld, in *Film Kurier* (August 26, 1930), noted *Abschied*'s use of space-time coor-dinates that were once the exclusive preserve of the *Kammerspiel* theater. Another contempora-neous review praised it as the first worthwhile venture in sound, turning sound into the "new actor." *Filmwelt* 35 (August 31, 1930).

most public debate over this issue developed over the popularity of so-called Zille films, such as *Dirnentragödie* (1927). The latter were essentially commercial street films, which played on a middle-class fascination with the illicit features of street life, especially with the figure of the prostitute. Middle-class (mainly male) protagonists are burned by their temptations to cross the moral and class frontier within the city, while the denizens of the city's dark lower-class side are deemed to be trapped or beyond redemption.

These films were named after Heinrich Zille, a Berlin artist famed for his sketches and drawings of everyday city life. Zille, however, did not regard himself as "a romantic of the back alleys" and "often cursed the so-called Zille films which were making their way through the theaters." [21] As a remedy to the misappropriation of his art by the commercial film industry, Zille approved an attempt by a socialist film collective (Prometheus) to make an "authentic" Zille film, *Mutter Krausen's Fahrt ins Glück* (1929). To socialists, the classical Zille film indulged in "poverty painting" and was a reactionary endorsement of the status quo. In sentimentalizing social misery, films like *Dirnentragödie* were accused of reversing art's obligation to the social. Aesthetically, the social and political content of urban life and its associated problems had been co-opted to the requirements of modernist experimentation—the malfunctioning referent urban milieu was seen to be subordinated to the needs of art. [22]

I have framed Siodmak's *Milieutonfilme* in this light, not to make a

21. Frank D. Hirschbach, ed., *Germany in the Twenties: The Artist as Social Critic* (Minneapolis: University of Minnesota Press, 1980), p. 79.

22. In fact, the question of how to make the "proper" Zille film was just one part of a rich popular frontist debate over the relationship of aesthetics to politics "in the age of mechanical reproduction" (to cite Walter Benjamin). The cornerstones of Marxist cultural theory in Weimar Germany (and later in exile), Walter Benjamin, Ernst Bloch, Berthold Brecht, and Theodor Adorno were split over the revolutionary possibilities of mass culture. This debate was triggered by Georg Lukacs' concern for the reactionary political nature of "Expressionist" aesthetics. To Lukacs, Expressionism's nihilistic subjectivism and tendency to solipsism avoided the proper function of art to represent reality objectively. To Bloch, Expressionism was a valid response to the crises of an epoch of radical transition, and the mode of representation most appropriate to a stage of modernity in which bourgeois paradigms were disintegrating but proletarian consciousness remained dormant. The cultural nihilism and apparent elitism of Expressionism could be counteracted by attending to the popular fascination or empathy for this modernist way of representing social life's fragmentary nature. In this sense, Bloch insisted that Expressionism was underpinned by an historically authentic experience. See Fredric Jameson, *Aesthetics and Politics* (London: Verso, 1980) and Andreas Huyssen, *After the Great Divide: Modernism, Mass Culture, Postmodernism* (Bloomington: Indiana University Press, 1986) for extended treatments of this issue.

decision about the political value of Siodmak's films but to highlight how commercial representations of modern urban life in Weimar cinema provoked strong and polemical political responses. The question of the mass mediation of urban social realities was a politically loaded one at all levels in the Weimar Republic as defenders and proponents assumed sectarian positions about the conjunction of modernist aesthetics with the new mass communications technology. In this climate Siodmak's films could have been understood as "counterrevolutionary" by one group and great works of art by another. Such polarized positions, however, overlooked the more interesting way in which his aesthetic experiments, as part of a commercial film industry, were audience-directed. That is, Siodmak's recourse to modernist aesthetic devices was part of a quest to better address the historically authentic experience of Weimar filmgoers. In a different cultural and historical context this means of dramatizing social crisis for a mass audience would be received quite differently by political monitors.

In many ways Siodmak's attention to the prosaic and profane features of modern urban life could not be further removed from Fritz Lang's auteurist and apocalyptic epics. Lang's late Weimar films— *Metropolis* (1927), *Spione* (1928), *M* (1931), and *Das Testament des Dr. Mabuse* (1932)—share in a grand and encapsulating vision of the social realm. In *Metropolis* the totality is split into overworld and underworld, and the narrative turns on the problem of how to make these spheres work together. Likewise in *M*, the underworld's organizational capacities are pitted against those of the legal institutions in a collective quest to root out a serial murderer. In *Spione* the world is seen to be ultimately at the mercy of a great puppet master—the Haghi—a criminal mastermind whose spy network enables him to control entire national economies. The Haghi is another manifestation of Lang's ur-criminal genius, Dr. Mabuse. *Das Testament des Dr. Mabuse* is the last of this supernatural agent's Weimar incarnations. Here Mabuse dies in the asylum, only to have his spirit live on in the body of his psychoanalyst! The idea that the evil doctor can continue to control our destinies from beyond the grave only helps increase Lang's paranoid vision. The question of who is really the inmate of the asylum is prescient in a world on the verge of total collapse.

Lang's totalizing visions stem more from the apocalyptic Expressionist tradition. Clearly influenced by Max Reinhardt's theater of the spectacle (rather than Reinhardt's "other" intimate theater, the *Kammerspiel*), Lang believed that film was the "Esperanto for the entire world." Idealistically, he conceived of film as a medium that could facilitate intercultural understanding.[23] His own films, however, point to a different propensity: an international discourse on global social chaos. Perhaps, in the shared context of economic catastrophe, this aspect of film-as-Esperanto allowed Lang to move relatively easily from Weimar dissolution into Depression-era Hollywood. As Alain Silver argues, Lang's initial Hollywood contribution, *Fury* (1936), is an adaptation of "the fateful visual style of his earlier German Expressionism, full of Freudian and cryptoreligious symbolism, to the more prosaic reality of the American depression."[24]

The working titles of *Fury* were "Mob" and "Mob Rule," and in many ways the film is an extension of his most "prosaic" mediation of Weimar life, *M*. The latter's crucial last scene—the kangaroo court— is concerned precisely with the problems of mob justice. At the same time it brings up a *Dr. Mabuse*–like scenario in asking questions about the degree to which we can be responsible for our actions and the degree to which our actions are predetermined. The child murderer claims he cannot control his urges to kill. Here what Lang elsewhere attributes to a criminal mastermind is instead imposed on the agentless and uncontrollable workings of a pathological psyche. It is this feature of Lang's deterministic bias that best translates into Hollywood's more "prosaic" representational codes.

Most of Lang's postwar crime films, such as *Scarlet Street, Woman in the Window, Clash by Night* (1952), and *Human Desire* (1954), inherit more from the psychologically intimate Weimar generic tradition of *Milieutonfilm* and *Straßenfilm* than from his own more auteurist epic spectacles. (Furthermore, *Scarlet Street* and *Human Desire* were remakes of French dramas and films concerned with sexual obsession: Georges de la Fouchardiere's *La Chienne* and Jean Renoir's *La Bête Humaine*, respectively.) This turning inward to the intimacies of bourgeois psychosexual retardation was probably a function of changed working conditions. In Weimar, Lang ruled. In Hollywood, he was just another cog in the machine who had to downscale his aspirations to suit the requirements of the studio system (a position to which Siodmak was more accustomed). Two films, however, seem to have particular recourse to his dominant Weimar vision—*The Ministry of Fear* (1945) and *The Big Heat*. Here the apocalyptic view of the conspiring milieu gets aired again: in one film the innocent is

23. Fritz Lang, quoted in Hirschbach, ed., *Germany in the Twenties*, p. 84.
24. Silver and Ward, eds., *Film Noir*, p. 110.

caught in a spy ring; in the other the city and its governing institutions are run by a corrupt mobster-puppeteer.

Why these less prosaic visions could reemerge has everything to do with the legitimating circumstances of both films. *The Ministry of Fear* was made in the last year of the Second World War and concerned a Nazi espionage ring. The atmosphere of intrigue is enhanced by the spy ring's recourse to supernatural trickery—the fortune teller at the parish bazaar is an agent, and the séance group functions as a spiritualistic front to the entire enterprise. *The Big Heat* has no supernatural symbolism, but it has a far more apocalyptic plot than most of Lang's American work. The film reveals how an entire community is in the grip of a corrupt administration, and carries the futile logic of one man's attempt to fight the system through to its extreme consequences. It is probably stretching it to argue that *The Big Heat* is an allegory of McCarthyism. Yet, the film's retrograde recourse to Lang's Weimar apocalyptic tendencies has to be contextualized. Lang had always been an outspoken opponent of ideological and moral intervention in the film industry. The House Committee on Un-American Activities (HUAC) must have reminded him of a Nazi-styled attempt at culture control.[25] As a syndicate-crime film made in the immediate fallout of HUAC's last hearings, *The Big Heat* echoes the totalizing view of Lang's Weimar films. One cannot help but think that it reflects Lang's own pessimism about America's future. *The Big Heat* was undeniably culled out of the paranoid residues of the Red Scare—and received in that context too.[26] However, it drew as much on Lang's experience in the last years of the Weimar cinema for its aesthetic expression.

25. For exiles, the HUAC/Hollywood relation must have awakened some disturbing memories of the Hugenberg (and later Goebbels)/UFA relation. Hugenberg, an ultraconservative publishing magnate, saved UFA from bankruptcy in 1927. This Nazi ally was strongly attracted to the power of the mass cinema as a nationalist propaganda weapon.

26. In many ways film noir's relationship to McCarthyism echoes the relationship of German Expressionism to fascism. Siegfried Kracauer argued that the Weimar aesthetic paved the way for a leadership cult. *From Caligari to Hitler: A Psychological History of German Film* (Princeton: Princeton University Press, 1947). It could equally be argued that what we term film noir played its role in cultivating a collective willingness to the subjection of the postwar political order. Given the aporias that characterize both cinemas and their attention to the deterioration of the phallic order, such arguments certainly cannot be dismissed. However, such a view overlooks the way these variations on a determinist discourse are structurally incompatible with the needs of political authority. After all, the fascist's first task was not to praise Expressionism but to condemn it as decadent and against the national interest. These proclamations echo uncannily the desires of the OWI, the State Department, HUAC, and Eric Johnston in creating a Hollywood after their own image.

In spite of their different investments in Expressionist devices, Lang and Siodmak shared a deterministic bias, which was probably only heightened by the experience of exile, the horror of Nazi fascism, and the atmosphere of McCarthyism. In both Lang's and Siodmak's American work we see a continuation of a Weimar critique of the key institutions of modern life. Marriage, the legal system, and bourgeois mores in general foster intolerable contradictions. For both Lang and Siodmak, the best mediation of the problems that beset Weimar citizenry was an aporia-driven cinema of disillusionment, characterized by a pessimistic psychosocial ambience. Each was an exponent of Expressionist vision: one was part of an auteurist apocalyptic tradition, the other extended the generic codes of the *Kammerspielfilm*. Both shared in the development of a cinematic *Angstkomplex* regarding subject-power relations in modern society. In the context of postwar America, they found that this sociopsychological aesthetic could address their new culture's conditions as well.

A POLITICALLY DYSFUNCTIONAL CINEMA: NOIR'S DIFFERENCE IN REPETITION

In accounting for what exiled German filmmakers brought to Hollywood's crime film, I wish to do more than affirm film noir's exceptionalism to some American norm, for we need to account for how this ostensibly "alien" presence was integrated into "more of the same." In their time, Siodmak and Lang's American films were appreciated less for their aesthetic "difference" than for their revival and refinement of an established American crime cycle or tradition. Moreover, the political significance of the work by exiles such as Siodmak and Lang can only be revealed when it is recognized that their Weimar-derived stylistic innovations took place within the regime of American crime film conventions and thus against the political interest of movie censors.

The kind of crime film that was fostered by such filmmakers did not necessarily advance a "progressive" political line. It did, however, trouble political and moral authorities that crime films could continue to be made. As I have documented, after the war the crime film was viewed by the State Department as counterproductive to the national interest. Those films we call films noirs all possess modernist stylistic attributes that enabled them successfully to negotiate attempts at their exorcism from the Hollywood system.

What often attracts film scholars to the postwar crime film cycle is its apparent departure from Hollywood norms. The presence of foreign directors only exacerbates a tendency to separate so-called film noir from other Hollywood film cycles. Not only does this do damage to our aesthetic appreciation of how the postwar generation of crime movies is intimately tied to the prewar generation, but it also impedes our understanding of these films' political status, for it was the perception by moral and political monitors that the postwar crime film was connected to a subversive past that concerned them.

Theorists arguing for the existence of something called film noir have necessarily been forced to advance its exceptionalism to the lore of "classical" narrative. Film noir is deemed to gain its distinction as a form that deviates from the conventions that dictated the narrative patterns and style of Hollywood's Golden Age, the 1930s. Implicit in this kind of argument is the notion that film noir's formal deviations constitute the first radical challenge to an endemically conservative Hollywood. Such structural accounts, however, truncate the postwar crime film from the pre-war period and in the process encourage a somewhat mechanical understanding of the cycle's sociohistorical significance: film noir is read as springing from the isolated problems that characterize the 1940s and early 1950s.

Two difficulties emerge from this way of accounting for the postwar crime cycle's significance under the rubric of film noir. First, it grants (very statically and ahistorically) a normative (and ideologically reactionary) status to something called "classical" Hollywood narrative. Second, such an approach, in "decading off" the films grouped under the label film noir, encourages critical amnesia about how this film cycle leans on an informing prehistory, both intertextual and extratextual, for its mediation of America's postwar sociocultural crisis.

As Frank Krutnik reminds us, a key fact often overlooked in discussions of film noir is that it was not known as such in 1940s America. Film noir is a posthumous nomenclature that gained critical currency among French postwar film critics. In the summer of 1946, five American thrillers made in the wartime 1940s were exhibited in Paris—*The Maltese Falcon* (1941), *Double Indemnity* (1944), *Laura* (1944), *Murder, My Sweet* (1944), and *Woman in the Window* (1945). The films having been isolated from the original context of their release (in terms of both time and space) and exhibited as a group, critics writing for *L'Ecran Français*, *Revue du Cinema*, and *Nouvelle Critique* were able to see distinct trends that connected these films and that distinguished them from prewar screen crime typology. The films were linked to *série noir* American detective fiction.[27] While I agree that this link to literature is important, it has fostered the general trend to isolate this crime cycle from its cinematic predecessors at home and abroad. The French critics who noted the films' connections to detective fiction authors (three of the films were based on novels by Dashiell Hammett, Raymond Chandler, and James M. Cain) overlooked the equally distinctive fact that three of the five films—*Laura, Double Indemnity,* and *Woman in the Window*—were made by Austro-German exiles, Otto Preminger, Billy Wilder, and Fritz Lang, respectively.

As I have documented in the preceding chapters, those who had an investment in policing Hollywood after World War II detected something antithetical to their interests in the 1940s criminal thriller but could not name it other than in terms already in use. To censors, federal monitors, and ideologues, such films represented not something new, but a return of the repressed prewar gangster narrative and its negative representation of American life.

Similarly, HUAC's inquisitions between 1947 and 1953 were not about detecting something new in Hollywood. The committee failed to find much evidence of Communist infiltration in the films themselves.[28] The purging from Hollywood of Communism (an alien infiltration) functioned as a pretext for the expurgation of things closer to home. As Albert Maltz, a screenwriter and one of the famous Hollywood Ten (the ten suspected Communists called before HUAC who initially refused to testify and name names), pointed out, HUAC was really about the expurgation of the Rooseveltian vision and the New Deal era from American history and collective memory:

> HUAC was made up of highly conscious political people of the right. . . . And their general attitude, I would say, would be semi-fascist, and if there were a fascist government in the United States,

27. Krutnik, *In a Lonely Street,* pp. 15–17. He further elaborates that while in 1955 Raymonde Borde and Etienne Chaumeton produced the first full study of film noir—*Panorama du Film Noir Américain, 1941–1953* (Paris: Editions de Minuit, 1955)—the term "noir" only gained critical currency in Anglo-American film criticism in the 1960s and 1970s.

28. Dorothy Jones, "Communism and the Movies," in *Report on Blacklisting I: Movies,* ed. John Cogley (New York: Fund for the Republic, 1956). In her study of the films of the Hollywood Ten, Jones found no evidence of Communist propaganda. She points instead to the high quality war films they made as positive contributions to the war effort. See also Philip Kemp, "From the Nightmare Factory: HUAC and the Politics of Noir," *Sight and Sound* 55, no. 4 (autumn 1986).

fully fascist. Because bear in mind, here you had an outfit that had considered Roosevelt a fellow traveler of the Communist Party—this was the mentality you were dealing with. They said it, I'm not inventing it. This was said by Parnell Thomas, who was chairman of the Committee.[29]

As Zheutlin and Talbot conclude, "HUAC was intent on branding New Deal thought subversive."[30] The real "enemy within" was not Soviet-style Communism per se but the memory of the New Deal.[31]

Of even more significance, perhaps, is the fact that exiled German (and Austrian) filmmakers underwent their Americanization during the more open political era of the New Deal. For exiles, the pull factors of America's plural and populist possibilities must have been intensified in the light of fascist push factors back home. While many exiles had problems adjusting to their host culture and were plagued by strong feelings of *Heimweh* (homesickness), many others overcame initial obstacles (language barriers, unemployment, rootlessness) and became enthusiastic American citizens. Driven by their own experience of political tyranny, exiles formed the core of many liberal-left causes throughout the Depression and the war. Directors such as Wilder, Lang, and Preminger were at the forefront of the Anti-Nazi League during the war, and following the war were prominent members of the Committee for the First Amendment (CFA), which attempted to defend the rights of Hollywood workers against HUAC's inquisition and its attack on civil liberties. The shifts in the political landscape that led up to HUAC were terribly disconcerting to exiles. Not only were such changes nightmare reminders of the very things exiles thought they had left behind, but they were regarded as

---

29. Interview with Albert Maltz in Barbara Zheutlin and David Talbot, "Albert Maltz: Portrait of a Hollywood Dissident," *Cineaste* 8, no. 3 (winter 1977–78), p. 14.

30. Ibid.

31. As Gary Gerstle has argued, the particular "subversions" of the New Deal lay in its more open and accessible power structure, its tripartite politics of coalition between government, unions, and big business. During the Depression big business had not only suffered financial loss, but a more damaging collapse in public confidence. Big business's loss was the worker's gain, as unions capitalized on the situation and won a bargaining seat alongside the government and corporate leadership in the making of policy. The economic mobilization for war spelled an end to this power arrangement, as workers were asked to put their demands on ice in the name of nationhood and fighting the common enemy. At the same time, big business won back its brokering position as the war machine revitalized not only its financial fortunes but its public image. Gary Gerstle, *Working Class Americanism: The Politics of Labor in a Textile City, 1914–1960* (Cambridge: Cambridge University Press, 1989). See Part IV, "The Crucial Decade—and After, 1941–1960."

truncations of the political possibilities (or fantasies) America seemed to stand for during the Depression period—precisely, that period of the exile's Americanization.[32]

The postwar 1940s signaled a return to the unsettled prewar disputes between government, unions, and big business, but the power positions had been substantially altered.[33] The result was a highly volatile period in which rival interests competed for control of America's postwar destiny. The era is thus notable not only as that of McCarthyism and the birth of the liberal consensus, but as the most strike-ravaged period in American history. It is in this context that the rhetoric of Americanism played a crucial role in the battle to legitimate the new and desanction the old. The postwar crime film was at the heart of this struggle to refashion the political language.[34]

The abstruse nature of HUAC's Hollywood witch hunt functioned not so much to identify a particular enemy than to produce paranoia and collective mistrust about ruling American paradigms. It could be argued that what has come to be called film noir certainly had a role

32. Elsewhere I have given this more extended treatment in the case of Austrian-Jewish exiles, Billy Wilder, Otto Preminger, and Edgar Ulmer, all of whom Americanized during the 1930s both inside and outside the Hollywood "hash machine" (Ulmer's words), and who, as staunch defenders of the ideals their adopted nation stood for during the Depression (and the war), were particularly disappointed by Hollywood's acquiescence to political conservatism after the war. "Heimat Hollywood: Billy Wilder, Otto Preminger, Edgar Ulmer and the Criminal Cinema of Austrian-Jewish Diaspora," in *From World War to Waldheim: Culture and Politics in Austria and the United States,* ed. David Good and Ruth Wodak (Berghahn, forthcoming).

33. The most significant change in the political landscape was secured through the Taft-Hartley Act, a response to the strike wave of 1946–1947. The Republican senator Robert Taft, chair of the Senate Committee on Labor and Public Welfare, strove to rewrite the nation's labor law on behalf of managerial interests. His specific target was to quell the general strikes and mass disruptions, calling them rank-and-file "abuses." His rhetorical justification for his antiunion move was that labor law as it had been shaped by the Wagner Act (1935) allowed for "practices incompatible with traditional American freedoms." This was symptomatic of the postwar exploitation of American/un-American rubric to demonize New Deal legacies. Taft-Hartley did herald in an era of relatively peaceful labor-capital relations, but this came at the cost of suppressing more militant (and arguably more socially democratic) mandates in favor of the liberal consensus. See Steve Fraser and Gary Gerstle, eds., *The Rise and Fall of the New Deal Order, 1930–1980* (Princeton: Princeton University Press, 1989) and George Lipsitz, *A Rainbow at Midnight: Labor and Culture in the 1940s* (Urbana and Champaign: University of Illinois Press, 1994).

34. For lengthier exegesis on the relation of Hollywood to the ideological struggle that typified the Cold War era (especially on Hollywood's relation to the postwar liberal consensus), see Lary May, ed., *Recasting America: Culture and Politics in the Age of Cold War* (Chicago: University of Chicago Press, 1989); Richard Maltby, *Harmless Entertainment: Hollywood and the Ideology of Consensus* (Metucheon: Scarecrow Press, 1983); Lipsitz, *Rainbow at Midnight;* and Brian Neve, *Film and Politics in America: A Social Tradition* (London: Routledge, 1992). See also chapter 6 for fuller discussion of the general politics of liberal consensus.

in fostering this climate of fear. Anti-Communist films predominantly took the form and style of gangster-syndicate films—for example, *Red Menace* (1949), *The Woman on Pier 13* (1949), *The Whip Hand* (1951), and *I Was a Communist for the FBI* (1951). The postwar crime film was suited to this because it was sceptical of authoritarianism. Because of the overarching thematic preoccupations of the postwar crime cycle with the deterministic relation between power and subject, it could function as a weapon in the demonization of totalitarian force. This, however, did not mean that it could function, conversely, to valorize an alternative authority. As Frank McConnell highlights in his examination of Samuel Fuller's ostensibly anti-Communist (small-time gangster) film, *Pick-Up on South Street* (1953), these crime films were ill suited to top-down didacticism:

> In making a conventional anti-Communist thriller in the midst of the McCarthy era, Fuller was lucky and brilliant enough to forge a parable about liberation and love that abrogates the twin economics of Communism and capitalism both. The final politics of Fuller's film is the politics of the brain-cage, of the individual trapped and all but lost in an inhospitable system.[35]

As I have demonstrated, the attributes of style and theme that could be deployed against Communism in one instance could also service a liberal-left critique of xenophobia, as in *Crossfire* (1947), or dramatize fears about subservience to the tyranny of corporate organizations, as in *Force of Evil* (1948) (see chapter 5). Paradoxically, it is precisely the dark and determinist qualities that made the postwar crime cycle available to Red Scare–mongers that could also function for an anticorporatist and antifascist discourse. This returns us to the exiles.

I have advanced two assertions here—that the postwar crime cycle is fundamentally antiauthoritarian and antididactic. The crime film / exile relation was one of mutual attraction where the exiled party saw in the existing conventions of the American crime film an opportunity to dramatize his own experience of "deracination." That this view should find a mass audience had everything to do with the coincidence of both personal and general experience. Translated into the mass language of the crime film, the themes of paranoia, alienation, and rootlessness that obtained to the particularity of the exiles came to resonate with a general postwar sociocultural condition.

This having been said, there are two key facts that complicate

---

35. Frank McConnell, *The Spoken Seen: Film and the Romantic Imagination* (Baltimore: Johns Hopkins University Press, 1975), p. 35.

matters. First, much of the despondency with the postwar order of things manifest in the 1940s and 1950s crime films of Siodmak, Lang, Wilder, Preminger, Ulmer, and Dieterle (to name a few) is predicated less on the experience of exile than on a distinctively *American* dissatisfaction with the deferment of New Deal–era promises. That is, by the war's end most of these directors considered themselves Americans (emigrés not exiles). Having Americanized during the Depression (an era of relatively radical political promise) and having contributed considerably to the anti-Nazi war effort, these directors had a vested stake in preventing their adopted homeland from departing from the values and ideals that had defined it as a positive asylum from fascism. Second, as I have illustrated, the exile/emigré's recourse to a determinist aesthetic treatment of postwar authority is indebted to a modernist Weimar German film heritage that predates the actuality of the Nazi triumph and the experience of exile. To this extent, we have to understand the postwar crime film's German connection almost independently of the mitigating influence of exile. In fact, it is notable how well the exile filmmakers I deal with here adjusted and fitted in to the Hollywood studio system during the 1930s. The question to ask, then, is why does the modernist German heritage come to bear most fully on the emigré's representations of American life after the war?

In providing invaluable insights into what makes the 1940s crime cycle symptomatic of a particularly "modern" moment of crisis, Dana Polan and J. P. Telotte provide two of the best treatments of the 1940s crime cycle. Like most film scholars, they tend to take the term film noir too much for granted. Unlike most scholars of this cycle, they have defined film noir less through its visual style and thematic preoccupations than through its structural engagement with narrative as a disciplining (tyrannical and quasi-totalitarian) force. Polan places film noir within the larger contexts of wartime and postwar Hollywood production and the issue of writing history. Filmic narrative and historical narrative production are seen to be intertwined and mutually dependent. In this sense, Polan is invested in writing a social history through film, given the role the mass narrative cinema has played in mediating subject-power relations in society. For Telotte, film noir's narrative experimentations are less specifically located in history. Film noir is read as a unique moment in cinema—or rather a moment only possible in the mass cinema—where reason's epistemological limit is reached. In articulating the contradictions of the "human situation" or the discontinuities of the modern subject's experience, film noir conveys the disenfranchised feeling of trying to speak in a world that's already narrated, already patterned and ordered.[36]

For both Polan and Telotte, then, film noir is part of a distinctively modern crisis in subject-power relations where individuals find themselves disenfranchised of any agency before the machinations of some abstract sense of fate. This fate's mercilessly deterministic character takes its force from the dynamics of narrative movement itself. That is, film noir "foregrounds" its own constructed nature as a narrative mediation of everyday life, and it does so not to liberate us from such ordering procedures, but to emphasize the extent to which we are trapped and administered by them.

This definitive feature is often deducible from the titles of films noirs alone. Titles such as *Roadblock* (1951), *Detour* (1945), *Destination Murder* (1950), *Caught* (1949), *Woman on the Run* (1950), *Where the Sidewalk Ends* (1950), *Sunset Boulevard* (1950), *The Set-Up* (1949), *Railroaded* (1947), *Pitfall* (1948), *Pushover* (1954), *Out of the Past* (1947), *Nightmare Alley* (1947) signify that they are films noirs in their self-conscious foreshadowing of problems with narrativity, either through the metaphor of the road or street or through metaphors of traumatic memory. All are ways of mediating subject-power relations fatalistically. The term "film noir" has served one clarifying function above all others: it emphasizes the postwar crime film's solipsistic and modernist preoccupation with the laws of aesthetic mediation and narrativity. It is this that is deemed to set film noir apart from the 1930s gangster film and other American crime prototypes, and it is this that remains the exile's most identifiable contribution to the American cinema. As Paul Schrader articulates:

> Film noir attacked and interpreted its sociological conditions and, by the close of the noir period, created a new artistic world that went beyond a simple sociological reflection, a nightmarish world of American mannerism. . . . Because film noir was first of all a style, because it worked out its conflicts visually rather than thematically, because it was aware of its own identity, it was able to create artistic solutions to sociological problems. And for these reasons films like *Kiss Me Deadly*, *Kiss Tomorrow Goodbye*, and *Gun Crazy* can be works of art in a way that gangster films like *Scarface*, *The Public Enemy*, and *Little Caesar* can never be.[37]

36. Dana Polan, *Power and Paranoia: History, Narrative and the American Cinema, 1940–1950* (New York: Columbia University, 1986) and Telotte, *Voices in the Dark.*

37. Paul Schrader, "Notes on Film Noir," in *The Film Genre Reader*, ed. Barry Keith Grant (Austin: University of Texas Press, 1986), p. 182.

This having been said, the postwar crime film's status as something emblematic of a politically dysfunctional Hollywood was, as I have argued throughout, equally dependent not on its difference from the 1930s gangster film but its reinvocation of that cycle. This reinvocation reproduced more than the gangster film per se. The three gangster films Schrader mentions above were the prime cause for the first prohibition resolution against the gangster film in 1931 and fueled the moratorium of 1935. As we have seen, the postwar reemergence of the gangster film brought up old memories of the antagonistic relationship between Hollywood and civic pressure groups. By finding their métier in the crime film, the exile directors and cameramen wittingly or unwittingly stirred up an old controversy and gave it new life and new form.

CONCLUSION: POLITICAL CONSEQUENCES

The 1940s crime film's characteristic use of flashback, as in *The Killers*, underpinned a characteristic concern for memory, for the problem of overcoming amnesia and correctly remembering the past. In turn, this underscored both an abstract epistemological concern for getting at the truth and a more concrete postwar concern about historical recollection. The establishment of postwar political hegemony was to depend on the divestment of Depression-era cultural capital. As I have documented, central to this cultural reprogramming was the film industry.

The crime film, however, was in the way. Its underworld themes and femmes fatales exhumed precisely a collective memory of the prewar order, an unusable past for those interested in recasting America after the war. The postwar crime film's generic extensions also serviced a tradition of narrative discontinuity. Both the pre-Code 1930s gangster cycle and the "fallen woman" film were structurally "open" texts that resisted easy accommodation to teleology. The irony of the gangster's death and the emancipated woman's succumbing to wedlock turned narrative closure into a problem, an imposition.

A film like *The Killers* intensified the crime film's subversive capacity to defamiliarize narrative's ordering oppressions—to expose narrative's work on behalf of a particular sociocultural order. This was a function of the crime film's endemic ability to demonize a full range of (narrative) regimes (political, psychological, moral, nationalist). Censors and ideologues had always viewed this kind of film form as a potential social menace. Hollywood had to be brought into line, and that meant narrative realignment. As Eric Johnston, head of the MPAA, put it in 1946:

> It is no exaggeration to say that the modern motion picture industry sets the styles for half the world. There is not one of us who isn't aware that the motion picture industry is the most powerful medium for the influencing of people that man has ever built . . . we can set new styles of living and the doctrine of production must be made completely popular.[38]

Johnston's liberal consensus desires for a Hollywood dedicated to manufacturing affirmative images of the American way aligned all too easily with the more overtly sinister desires of HUAC. Following his second interview with HUAC in 1947, Johnston proclaimed:

> I want to see it become a joke to be a Communist in America. I want it to be fashionable to radiate conviction and pride in our democratic capitalism.[39]

Johnston's ideas for Hollywood as an agent of postwar democratic capitalism were entirely consonant with those of the State Department, which shared his deep concern for the postwar reinvigoration of antithetical film forms such as the gangster film (see chapters 5 and 6). That exiles happened to be prime agents in this reinvigoration of something deemed "seditious" was bound to have negative consequences.

The fact that the prime years of what we call film noir coincide with HUAC's, however, has led to some symptomatic theses about HUAC and the crime film's symbiosis. Philip Kemp, for example, maintains:

> The last and darkest phase of film noir . . . coincides with the height of the anti-Communist obsession, and the decline of the cycle follows closely on the fall of McCarthy. As the hysteria loosened its grip, the national psyche no longer needed the countervailing subconscious fantasies—or at least, not that particular kind.[40]

This perpetuates a somewhat mechanical theory of the postwar crime film's relationship to society and to history—that it "mirrors" its times or it "reflects" the climate of McCarthyism. I have tried to emphasize a more dialectical understanding of the postwar crime film's

---

38. Eric Johnston, "Utopia Is Production," *Screen Actor* 14 (April 1946), p. 7. This text is the centerpiece of Lary May's invaluable article, "Movie Star Politics: The Screen Actors' Guild, Cultural Conversion, and the Hollywood Red Scare," in *Recasting America*.

39. Zheutlin and Talbot, "Albert Maltz," p. 13.

40. Kemp, "From the Nightmare Factory," p. 270.

contentious relation to political authority. By placing this film cycle not only in the context of the postwar 1940s, but in a contextualizing (intertextual) history of reception that predates the war, we can see how what has been called film noir is not a mechanical reflection of one time or era.

The story I have tried to tell here is one where filmmakers such as Lang and Siodmak associated with a pre-war Weimar cinema found that their modernist sensibilities were entirely appropriate to the task of representing the nature of the changes American culture and society had undergone during and after the war. Given this pre-war aesthetic legacy, they found themselves in an advantageous position to address contemporaneous issues of middle-class malaise and maladjustment. This investigation, however, could only take place in the cinematic space within the American system that was most open to it—the crime film. In order to exploit this privileged site for a critique of postwar conditions, the exiles worked over the palimpsest of illicit/taboo 1930s Hollywood formulas and cycles (the gangster film and the "fallen woman" film). To use a suitably gruesome metaphor, the exiles put the flesh back on the skeleton of suppressed (New Deal–associated) conventions in order to feed ongoing desires for adequate representations of everyday life, desires that did not go away just because the censors brought down the boom.

To this extent, the dark and paranoid visions of 1940s and 1950s crime films were not simply responses to HUAC. In the context of HUAC rhetoric, the crime film could only have been perceived as an already existing "un-American" symptom, a New Deal hangover that fostered detrimental images of the American way. The fact that crime film production dropped off after HUAC's last Hollywood hearings in 1953 (and that Siodmak and Lang would soon after find their Hollywood careers truncated) is no coincidence. It is testament less to the "loosening of hysteria" (in Kemp's language) than to the combined triumph of the ideologues over Hollywood and the disappearance of the crime film's prime venues (through the financial collapse of the independent movement and the breakup of the studio monopolies that signified the death of the B crime feature).[41]

In December 1947, Fritz Lang wrote an article entitled "The Freedom of the Screen," which polemicized against censorship (in defense of *Scarlet Street,* which had been banned in New York State,

41. See chapter 5 for full exposition.

Milwaukee, and Memphis). It was ostensibly an appeal to the new Johnston office to sweep Breen's and Hay's ghosts out of the closet and "relinquish the censorship of films which it now applies." The article's timing, however, coincided with the aftermath of HUAC's first hearings in October. Lang's critique suddenly found that it obtained to a new object: the political "big heat" that threatened Hollywood freedoms. Ironically, he predicted much of what was yet to come:

> Censorship, whether of books, of plays or of motion pictures, is never effective in combatting social ills. . . . It can to a limited extent . . . prevent the spread of ideas or suggestions which might evoke a dangerous response among the immature, illiterate or irresponsible. However, people do not encounter such ideas in literature, theatre and film alone; they are constantly exposed to them in the normal course of life. To pretend that such ideas do not exist and to deny them an honest treatment in the arts is to treat the public as children. But perhaps this is the idea of censorship: to keep the public in a state of immaturity so that it can be the more easily influenced and imposed upon.[42]

After he completed *Clash by Night* (appropriately enough, a film noir) in February 1952, Lang was offered no more projects for almost nine months. This must have seemed like an interminable hiatus at the height of the McCarthyist Hollywood purge. Eventually, it was disclosed to him that he had indeed been blacklisted. His affiliations with New Deal–era and wartime antifascist activities (including contributions to the Anti-Nazi League) were deemed reason enough to indict him as someone with pro-Communist potential.[43]

While Lang's outspoken views may have singled him out for HUAC's attention, this cannot account for the fate of Robert Siodmak. In fact, Siodmak's case points to the more significant effect of HUAC's inquisition as it came to influence postwar Hollywood: the suffocation of aesthetic as well as political possibilities. One could read the effect of HUAC's Hollywood purge as instigating an antimodernist move. The committee's investigation certainly aided those who castigated the industry for a lack of political commitment, such as the Motion Picture Alliance for the Preservation of American Ideals. While it encouraged Hollywood to support the prerogatives of nationalist affirmation, HUAC discouraged "un-American"

---

42. Fritz Lang, "Freedom of the Screen," in *Hollywood Directors, 1941–1976*. Article originally appeared in *Theatre Arts* (December 1947).

43. See Janet Bergstrom, "The Mystery of The Blue Gardenia," in *Shades of Noir: A Reader*, ed. Joan Copjek (London: Verso, 1993), pp. 98–100.

tendencies to provide candidly dark views of the American way. For Robert Siodmak, a man who had deployed his skills in the making of innovative crime films, yet who was not of seditious political persuasion, the consequence was to set his exile route into reverse. Associated with an increasingly censurable film form, he found himself without an American métier. In 1954, after the second HUAC Hollywood hearings of 1953, he returned via France to Germany.

Epilogue

From Gangster to Gangsta

Against a Certain Tendency of Film Theory and History

In accounting for the transformation of the gangster film in the period from 1929 to 1958, all too little has been done to connect the postwar crime cycle with its prewar antecedents. The emphasis has fallen, instead, on how what we posthumously call film noir constitutes a break with traditional generic conventions. Hailed as the most experimental and transgressive of Hollywood's film forms, film noir's apparent "exceptionalism" to established aesthetic and narrative norms has encouraged a tendency to view the 1940s and early 1950s crime cycle as indicative of an anomalous period in Hollywood filmmaking. Ironically, this has actually enabled the imposition of narrative coherence on Hollywood's history. The postwar crime film cycle is the exception that proves the rule—the aleatory element that assumes the status of "classical" Hollywood's "other."

Critics like J. P. Telotte and Dana Polan have argued eloquently that what unifies the crime features they group under the term film noir is their collective undermining of one of power's fundamental prerequisites: the establishment of a stable narrative structure and coherent logic (the basis for any authority's effective rationalization).[1] While Telotte and Polan are content to discuss film noir within the boundaries of the 1940s and 1950s, the effect is to sever this crime

1. Dana Polan, *Power and Paranoia: History, Narrative, and the American Cinema, 1940–1950* (New York: Columbia University Press, 1986) and J. P. Telotte, *Voices in the Dark: The Narrative Patterns of Film Noir* (Urbana and Champaign: University of Illinois Press, 1989).

221

cycle from its shaping history. We get a picture of a film form that effectively reproduces the paradox of modernity, but that seems strangely isolated from both an intertextual tradition and from the extratextual terrain of political investments in Hollywood as a narrative machine. Such renditions screen out how 1940s cinematic deviation was connected to a dissenting tradition. They are unable to situate the 1940s crime cycle in terms of an ongoing fight to establish a Hollywood that would conform to power's demands, a fight whose roots lie in the 1930s gangster film.

Film scholarship's tendency to neatly "decade off" film history has only exacerbated this rupture, aided and abetted by the fact of World War II, a traumatic event that clearly separated 1930s from 1940s culture. Film noir, however, did not magically arrive fully formed from nowhere. In terms of their contemporaneous reception, these films were understood as reinvocations of existing (albeit taboo) genres and forms that reinvoked the collective memory of the pre-war era and its unfulfilled promises. My task has been not to deny that the 1940s crime film was different than its forebears, but to reframe this difference in terms of the mitigating influences of historical change and the pressures of moral and political censorship. The postwar crime film's meaning was dependent on the degree to which it invoked contentious past film forms. In the process, these 1940s films conjured up a particular kind of Depression memory that was regarded as extremely seditious by those postwar power groups seeking to regulate Hollywood on behalf of their own interests.

There has been a recent movement to correct our ahistorical vision of the 1940s crime cycle. Frank Krutnik and Marc Vernet, for example, have pointed out how what we call film noir is not unique. To Krutnik, film noir represents only a pseudo-difference from the system of "classical" Hollywood narrative economy, a duplicitous mask that hides the cycle's continuity with preexisting film forms and the order (masculinist/heterosexual/bourgeois) they affirm.[2] To Vernet, those aspects of theme and style that are regarded as definitive of film noir can be found in myriad other film forms that predate the 1940s.[3] The problem with both these accounts is that while they effectively engage the theoretical ruse the term film noir executes in disengaging

2. Frank Krutnik, *In a Lonely Street: Film Noir, Genre, Masculinity.* (London: Routledge, 1991).

3. Marc Vernet, "*Film Noir* on the Edge of Doom," in *Shades of Noir: A Reader,* ed. Joan Copjek (London: Verso, 1993), pp. 1–32.

the past from the present, they tend to reaffirm the critical consensus on "classical" Hollywood.

By contrast, Thomas Elsaesser has argued that to search for a pre-history of film noir is a hopelessly labyrinthine task, and one that seeks only to resubject film history to the tyranny of teleology. To conceive of film noir as the product of singular or ultimate causes is to do violence to its overdetermined nature. He argues instead for an archaeology of film noir, one that looks laterally as much as backwards.[4] While I am in agreement with this and Joan Copjek's proviso that film noir is a "positivist fiction,"[5] I hope to have emphasized the degree to which the transatlantic prehistory of film noir is constructed out of definitively discontinuous film forms. To this extent, I have argued that the 1940s crime film cycle represents not so much disengagement from the system as the *continuity of discontinuity*—the endurance of a dissenting tradition. It is this that has proven most disconcerting, not only for those trying to make Hollywood subservient to particular political agendas but to those of us trying to write coherent histories of Hollywood.

Only by remembering the crime film's forgotten antagonistic history can one properly account for why the makers and stars of postwar gangster films such as *Force of Evil* and *Asphalt Jungle* would come to be blacklisted. The combined effect of HUAC's external investigations and the internal pressures being brought to bear on the industry by representatives (such as Eric Johnston) of the new political order was a major factor in bringing about this crime cycle's demise. The production conditions of *Touch of Evil* (1957–1958) serve to confirm the extent to which Hollywood's politically antagonistic possibilities had shrunk by the late 1950s. Orson Welles, long regarded as an anti-establishment filmmaker of dubious political affiliation, and who constantly sought autonomy from the studio system, was under FBI investigation when he was "allowed" to direct *Touch of Evil*. Paradoxically, he had only gained the right to direct through the film's star, Charlton Heston—a right-wing anti-Communist—who had threatened to pull out of the project if Welles didn't direct.[6]

Welles had been responsible for a number of aesthetically innovative crime films, such as *Lady from Shanghai* (1948) and *Mr. Arkadin*

4. Thomas Elsaesser, "Towards a Pre-History of *Film Noir*," New Histories of *Film Noir* Panel Presentation, Society for Cinema Studies Conference (New York 1995).

5. Joan Copjek, introduction to *Shades of Noir*, pp. vii–xii.

6. James Naremore, "The Trial: The FBI vs. Orson Welles," *Film Comment* 27, no. 1 (January–February 1991).

(1955), which extended his work on *Citizen Kane* (1941). While the latter was not a crime film, its visual style and elliptical and fragmented narrative configurations are definitive of much of what is regarded as film noir. It is regarded as one of the first films to combine the use of the long take, deep focus, and chiaroscuro lighting with a concern for recovering the past through complex multiple flashback narration. While both *Citizen Kane* and *Mr. Arkadin* constituted intriguing critiques of wealth and power, and *Lady from Shanghai* concerned the duping of a naive young man by a fraudulent trial lawyer and a scheming femme fatale, Welles's most "political" of films over this period was *The Stranger* (1946), the least extravagant and experimental of his postwar films.

Consistent with Welles's belief in artistic autonomy, however, *The Stranger* was made for International Pictures, the quasi-independent wing of Universal Studios responsible for many successful postwar crime thrillers (see chapter 5, especially the discussion of Mark Hellinger). The film concerned the uncovering of a prominent Nazi (played by Orson Welles) in postwar hiding in a small New England college. The atmosphere of international intrigue and an ongoing Nazi underworld hiding behind the mask of small-town New England respectability contributed to the larger postwar concerns about a world out of order and subject to perverse political maneuvering. Welles's personal political commitments to left-liberal and anti-Nazi causes throughout the Depression only exacerbated his image as a liability to studio bosses and ideologues alike.

The controversy over Welles exemplified what I have discussed at length—the extent to which the filmmakers who were identified as politically contentious were also synonymous with a certain kind of crime filmmaking. *Touch of Evil* represented the end of the line. The discouraging atmosphere of the Red Scare was corroborated by the disintegration of the monopoly structure of the majors in the wake of the anti-trust suit, signaling the decline of the B feature—the crime film's primary venue. *Touch of Evil*'s production conditions revealed how it had become a liability to make a socially critical crime film in this period of economic restructuring and political restraint.

Touch of Evil concerned the passing of two distinguishing postwar crime types: the morally ambivalent rogue cop and the femme fatale, played by Welles and Marlene Dietrich, respectively. At the same time, it incorporated something new, the Juvenile Delinquency film (the "JD" film), embodied in *City across the River* (1949), *Rebel without a Cause* (1955), *Crime in the Streets* (1956), and *The Purple Gang*

(1960). In many ways the latter would usurp the place of traditional gangster narratives, changing the focus of the gang film from critiques of corporate-styled power abuse and universal corruption to generational conflict and youthful deviancy. The gang in *Touch of Evil*, while ethnically encoded as Hispanic, are also young and bored, and fans of drugs, modern jazz, and popular music. Youth music and narcotics are, in fact, the prime devices of torture in the film, and are used to scare and intimidate Susan Vargas (Janet Leigh), the kidnapped wife of Mike Vargas (Charlton Heston).

In many ways it is arguable that after *Touch of Evil* only neo-noir has been possible. The postwar crime cycle that gave birth to the term film noir had been put out of business. Since then the term noir has gained popular currency as a vague, ahistorical, catchall aesthetic marker—a label for a form of dark or violent camp. The label has become applicable to virtually everything. While this may be symptomatic of the term's cross-generic pertinence, it is also testament of the degree to which we have forgotten the historically specific ramifications of the postwar crime film's stylistic and thematic attributes. That is, the term has been disengaged from its anchorage in the topical issues of 1940s and 1950s America. *Touch of Evil* was a temporary epitaph to a dissenting cinematic tradition first nurtured by the early 1930s talking gangster genre.

As the recent controversy surrounding "gangsta" rap reminds us, the gangster has been revived as a seditious site in the struggle for self-representation against inequitous and prejudicial forces. Amid the overblown and distracting rhetoric about riots, black male character assassination, misogyny, cop killing, drug abuse, juvenile delinquency, and moral turpitude lies the continuing fact that the inner-city ghetto still exists. The ghetto as a space both real and imagined also continues to be a "raced" space, an uncomfortable reminder of the racist nature of economic and spatial destitution. The different demands to censor gangsta rap (the confrontational image and voice of the ghetto) by groups external to the black community such as Parents Music Resource Center and those within it (Dolores Tucker and Calvin Butts), as well as the concern over the release of films like *Boyz 'n the Hood* (1991), echo uncannily the complex battle in the 1930s over urban ethnic representation and the early talking gangster film.

Today the stakes are different. To be black and unemployed in a deindustrializing post–Civil Rights society is not the same as being ethnic and working class in Prohibition and Depression USA. Ghettoization for 1990s black Americans is not the precursor to eventual

"Americanization" and *embourgeoisement*, as it was for ethnic whites earlier in the century, but rather a way to continue to incarcerate a group of Americans who do not even function as the reserve army of industrial labor. Yet the black recourse to the gangster image is part of a long history of struggle, both black and white, to use the weapons of confinement against the grain and communicate (visibly and audibly) across race and class lines—to dramatize an enduring collective sense of grievance. The black gangster tradition (1930s Harlem race films, the fiction of Rudolf Fisher, Chester Himes, Robert Beck, and Donald Goines, the "blaxploitation" films of the early 1970s) is a different part of the seditious tradition I have documented here. In "remembering" the classic Hollywood gangster's history of struggle with authority I ask us to think again about the significance this part of mass culture has held for *all* rebels with a cause.

Appendix
Production Code Administration Film Analysis Forms, 1934–1957

The forms of the Motion Picture Association of America / Production Code Administration (MPAA / PCA) were gleaned from sample gangster texts researched at the Margaret Herrick Library Special Collections, Academy for Motion Picture Arts and Sciences (AMPAS), Los Angeles. I have designated these as "Film Analysis Forms" in the absence of any official Production Code Administration title.

These forms were used in final screening sessions to help detect areas likely to cause controversy with censors and civic interest groups. The first form was found in the file on *Angels with Dirty Faces* (1938). Because the Code film analysis form was instigated to aid the issuing of a Code Seal of Approval, we may assume that this form was in use at least from 1938, if not earlier (e.g., 1934, the first year of the Code Seal). In 1941 the file on *Bullets for O'Hara* contains a revised film analysis form. This form was apparently in use until 1949, when a radically altered form came into existence. Shifting from a one-page format to a multipage document divided into seven parts, the new film analysis form expanded the scope and nature of censorship interest in Hollywood's films. It was used on *The Asphalt Jungle*, but not *White Heat*, which indicates that the new form was initiated in late 1949. Research in the PCA file on *Al Capone*, the 1959 film starring Rod Steiger, unearthed a revised and less detailed version of the 1949 form.

PRODUCTION CODE ADMINISTRATION FILM ANALYSIS FORM 1934–1940

Title: _____

Producer: _____

Story summary: _____

_____

_____

What country: _____ What city (state) identified: _____

Type: Social problem [ ] _____ Biographical [ ] _____ Musical drama [ ] ___ Farce [ ] _____

Crime [ ] _____ Historical [ ] _____ Musical comedy [ ] ___ Western [ ] _____

War [ ] _____ Juvenile [ ] _____ Comedy [ ] _____ Cartoon [ ] _____

	ROLE		CHARACTERIZATION				
	Prom.	Minor	Straight	Comic	Sym.	Unsym.	Indif.
Clergyman:							
Catholic	[ ]	[ ]	[ ]	[ ]	[ ]	[ ]	[ ]
Protestant	[ ]	[ ]	[ ]	[ ]	[ ]	[ ]	[ ]
Other _____	[ ]	[ ]	[ ]	[ ]	[ ]	[ ]	[ ]
Banker	[ ]	[ ]	[ ]	[ ]	[ ]	[ ]	[ ]
Children	[ ]	[ ]	[ ]	[ ]	[ ]	[ ]	[ ]
Doctor	[ ]	[ ]	[ ]	[ ]	[ ]	[ ]	[ ]
Judge	[ ]	[ ]	[ ]	[ ]	[ ]	[ ]	[ ]
Justice of peace	[ ]	[ ]	[ ]	[ ]	[ ]	[ ]	[ ]
Lawyer	[ ]	[ ]	[ ]	[ ]	[ ]	[ ]	[ ]
Public officials	[ ]	[ ]	[ ]	[ ]	[ ]	[ ]	[ ]
Policeman	[ ]	[ ]	[ ]	[ ]	[ ]	[ ]	[ ]
Reporter	[ ]	[ ]	[ ]	[ ]	[ ]	[ ]	[ ]
Editor	[ ]	[ ]	[ ]	[ ]	[ ]	[ ]	[ ]
Publisher	[ ]	[ ]	[ ]	[ ]	[ ]	[ ]	[ ]
Negro	[ ]	[ ]	[ ]	[ ]	[ ]	[ ]	[ ]
Italian	[ ]	[ ]	[ ]	[ ]	[ ]	[ ]	[ ]
Chinese	[ ]	[ ]	[ ]	[ ]	[ ]	[ ]	[ ]
Mexican	[ ]	[ ]	[ ]	[ ]	[ ]	[ ]	[ ]
Others _____	[ ]	[ ]	[ ]	[ ]	[ ]	[ ]	[ ]

Drinking: None _____ Little _____ Much _____

Court scenes? _____ How treated? Dignified _____ Comic _____

Type of crime(s) _____ No. of killings, if any? _____

Type of criminal(s) _____ Violence? _____

Military angle? _____ Political? _____ Religious? _____ Foreign? _____ Racial? _____

What religious ceremonies? _____ How handled? _____

Settings: Bedrooms _____ Beach _____ Gambling rooms _____ Prison _____

Nightclub _____ Bars _____ Saloons _____ Church _____ Hospital _____

Adultery _____ Illicit Sex _____ Gambling _____ Marriage _____ Divorce _____ Suicide _____

PRODUCTION CODE ADMINISTRATION FILM ANALYSIS FORM 1941–1949

Title: _____ Date reviewed: _____ Footage: _____ No. _____

Producer: _____ Feature: _____ Short: _____ Domestic: _____ Foreign: ____

Type: _____

Country: _____ City (state): _____

Angle: Foreign _____ Political _____ Racial _____ Religious _____ Scientific _____ Military _____

Settings: _____

Locale of note: _____

	ROLE		CHARACTERIZATION				
	Prominent	Minor	Straight	Comic	Sympathetic	Unsympathetic	Indiff.
Leads: _____	[]	[]	[]	[]	[]	[]	[]
_____	[]	[]	[]	[]	[]	[]	[]
_____	[]	[]	[]	[]	[]	[]	[]
Profession/business:							
Banker	[]	[]	[]	[]	[]	[]	[]
Doctor	[]	[]	[]	[]	[]	[]	[]
Lawyer	[]	[]	[]	[]	[]	[]	[]
Journalist	[]	[]	[]	[]	[]	[]	[]
_____	[]	[]	[]	[]	[]	[]	[]
_____	[]	[]	[]	[]	[]	[]	[]
Public officials:							
Judge	[]	[]	[]	[]	[]	[]	[]
Justice of peace	[]	[]	[]	[]	[]	[]	[]
Police	[]	[]	[]	[]	[]	[]	[]
D.A.	[]	[]	[]	[]	[]	[]	[]
Sheriff	[]	[]	[]	[]	[]	[]	[]
_____	[]	[]	[]	[]	[]	[]	[]
_____	[]	[]	[]	[]	[]	[]	[]
Religious workers:							
Catholic	[]	[]	[]	[]	[]	[]	[]
Protestant	[]	[]	[]	[]	[]	[]	[]
Jewish	[]	[]	[]	[]	[]	[]	[]
_____	[]	[]	[]	[]	[]	[]	[]
_____	[]	[]	[]	[]	[]	[]	[]
Races or nationals:							
_____	[]	[]	[]	[]	[]	[]	[]
_____	[]	[]	[]	[]	[]	[]	[]
_____	[]	[]	[]	[]	[]	[]	[]
Miscellaneous:							
_____	[]	[]	[]	[]	[]	[]	[]
_____	[]	[]	[]	[]	[]	[]	[]

Liquor: Shown at: Night club _____ Bar _____ Saloon _____ Home _____ Other _____

Drinking: None _____ Little _____ Much _____

Type of crime(s) _____ No. killings _____

Other violence: _____

Fate of criminal(s): _____

Court scenes: _____ How treated? Dignified _____ Comic _____

Religious ceremonies? _____ How handled? _____

Adultery _____ Illicit sex _____ Divorce _____ Marriage _____ Suicide _____ Gambling _____

PRODUCTION CODE ADMINISTRATION FILM ANALYSIS FORM 1949

ANALYSIS OF FILM CONTENT PART ONE— GENERAL

Title: _____

PCA approval date: _____

PCA seal number: _____

Footage: _____

Type: _____

Feature [ ]   Short [ ]

Domestic [ ]   Foreign [ ]

B&W _____ Color _____ Toned _____

Producer (company): _____

Producer (indiv'l): _____

Director: _____

Screenwriter: _____

Where filmed: _____

Distributor: _____

Material Source:

Biography _____

Comic strip _____

Folklore _____

Novel _____

Original screen story _____

Radio program _____

Short story _____

Stage play _____

Other: _____

Significant Story Elements/Angles:

Foreign _____ Political _____

Historical _____ Psychological _____

Juvenile _____ Racial _____

Medical _____ Religious _____

Military _____ Scientific _____

Educational _____ Family life _____

Ending:

Happy _____ Unhappy _____ Moral _____

Other: _____

Period: _____

Major locales (A): _____

_____

Major locales (B):

City _____ Rural _____

Suburban _____ Undeveloped areas _____

Small town ___ Not clear _____

Other: _____

Settings (A): _____

_____

Settings (B):

Very wealthy _____ Moderate _____

Well-to-do _____ Poor _____

Not clear _____

Foreign language(s) in addition to English:

_____

_____

Foreign countries treated:

	Sym.	Unsym.	S&U	Indif.
Canada	[ ]	[ ]	[ ]	[ ]
China	[ ]	[ ]	[ ]	[ ]
England	[ ]	[ ]	[ ]	[ ]
France	[ ]	[ ]	[ ]	[ ]
Germany	[ ]	[ ]	[ ]	[ ]
Italy	[ ]	[ ]	[ ]	[ ]
Japan	[ ]	[ ]	[ ]	[ ]
Mexico	[ ]	[ ]	[ ]	[ ]
Russia	[ ]	[ ]	[ ]	[ ]

Others: _____

Key: Sym. = Sympathetic
Unsym. = Unsympathetic
S&U = Sym. and Unsym.
Indif. = Indifferent

PART TWO—PORTRAYAL OF PROFESSIONS

Profession:	ROLE			CHARACTERIZATION								
	Prom	Min	Inci	Str	Com	S&C	Sym	Unsym	S&U	Indif	Dishon*	For**
————————	[]	[]	[]	[]	[]	[]	[]	[]	[]	[]	[]	[]
————————	[]	[]	[]	[]	[]	[]	[]	[]	[]	[]	[]	[]
————————	[]	[]	[]	[]	[]	[]	[]	[]	[]	[]	[]	[]
————————	[]	[]	[]	[]	[]	[]	[]	[]	[]	[]	[]	[]
————————	[]	[]	[]	[]	[]	[]	[]	[]	[]	[]	[]	[]
————————	[]	[]	[]	[]	[]	[]	[]	[]	[]	[]	[]	[]
————————	[]	[]	[]	[]	[]	[]	[]	[]	[]	[]	[]	[]
————————	[]	[]	[]	[]	[]	[]	[]	[]	[]	[]	[]	[]
————————	[]	[]	[]	[]	[]	[]	[]	[]	[]	[]	[]	[]
————————	[]	[]	[]	[]	[]	[]	[]	[]	[]	[]	[]	[]
————————	[]	[]	[]	[]	[]	[]	[]	[]	[]	[]	[]	[]

*Check this column if professional character is inefficient or dishonest in the performance of his professional duties.
**Check this column if character is both of foreign birth and, in all probability, not a citizen of the United States.

PART THREE—PORTRAYAL OF "RACES" AND NATIONALS

"Race" or National	ROLE			CHARACTERIZATION							U.S. CITIZEN		
	Prom	Min	Inci	Str	Com	S&C	Sym	Unsym	S&U	Indif	Yes	No	N.C.
————————	[]	[]	[]	[]	[]	[]	[]	[]	[]	[]	[]	[]	[]
————————	[]	[]	[]	[]	[]	[]	[]	[]	[]	[]	[]	[]	[]
————————	[]	[]	[]	[]	[]	[]	[]	[]	[]	[]	[]	[]	[]
————————	[]	[]	[]	[]	[]	[]	[]	[]	[]	[]	[]	[]	[]
————————	[]	[]	[]	[]	[]	[]	[]	[]	[]	[]	[]	[]	[]
————————	[]	[]	[]	[]	[]	[]	[]	[]	[]	[]	[]	[]	[]
————————	[]	[]	[]	[]	[]	[]	[]	[]	[]	[]	[]	[]	[]
————————	[]	[]	[]	[]	[]	[]	[]	[]	[]	[]	[]	[]	[]

Key: Prom = Prominent, Min = Minor, Inci = Incidental, Str = Straight,
Com = Comic, Sym = Sympathetic, Unsym = Umsympathetic, Indif = Indifferent

PART FOUR—LIQUOR

Title: _____

Treatment of liquor: None shown or consumed [ ] Shown only [ ] Consumed [ ]

If liquor consumed, amount of drinking: Very little [ ] Little [ ] Much [ ]

Where liquor shown or consumed:

	Shown Only	Con-sumed		Shown Only	Con-sumed
Bar	[]	[]	Saloon	[]	[]
Cafe-restaurant	[]	[]	Night club	[]	[]
Club (other than night club)	[]	[]	Hotel-inn-tavern	[]	[]
Home and/or apartment	[]	[]	Castle-palace	[]	[]
Office	[]	[]	Out-of-doors	[]	[]
Ship, plane, or train	[]	[]	Automobile	[]	[]
Other: _____	[]	[]			

What does character(s) drink? Wine [ ] Beer [ ] Hard liquor [ ] Unident. [ ]
Drinking engaged in by: Men [ ] Women [ ] Both [ ]
Drinking engaged in by: Prominent character(s) [ ] Minor [ ] Incidental [ ]

If prominent character(s) drinks, is treatment of character(s):
  Sympathetic [ ] Unsympathetic [ ] Indifferent [ ] Mixed [ ]
If minor character(s) drinks, is treatment of character(s):
  Sympathetic [ ] Unsympathetic [ ] Indifferent [ ] Mixed [ ]
If incidental character(s) drinks, is treatment of character(s):
  Sympathetic [ ] Unsympathetic [ ] Indifferent [ ] Mixed [ ]

Is social acceptability of drinking indicated? Yes [ ] No [ ] Indecisive[ ]
If drinking is socially acceptable, is it so for: Men [ ] Women [ ] Both [ ]
If drinking is socially acceptable, is it so in:
  Common man settings [ ] Well-to-do settings [ ] Both [ ] Not clear [ ]

Is actual drunkenness portrayed: Yes [ ] No [ ]
If drunkenness portrayed, is character(s): Men [ ] Women [ ] Both [ ]
If drunkenness portrayed, is character(s): Prominent [ ] Minor [ ] Incidental [ ]
Is feigned drunkenness portrayed? Yes [ ] No [ ]

PART FIVE— CRIME
Title: _____

Does picture contain one or more crimes? Yes [ ] Yes, very incidental [ ] No [ ]
If "yes," into which of the following classifications does picture basically fall (check one only):

Western	[ ]	Social problem (drama)	[ ]
Mystery (whodunnit)	[ ]	Literary or dramatic classic	[ ]
War, spy or sabotage	[ ]	Biographical or historical	[ ]
Musical	[ ]	Story involving political wrong-doing	[ ]
Comedy	[ ]	Story involving financial wrong-doing	[ ]
Farce	[ ]	Story involving professional criminals	[ ]
Romance	[ ]	Story involving non-prof. criminals	[ ]
Psychological	[ ]	Story of lust or passion	[ ]
Social problem (melodrama)	[ ]	Other: _____	[ ]

If "yes," specify types of crime: _____

Is crime: The major element (core) in this picture [ ]
         An important story point [ ] Incidental [ ]
Does story tend to enlist the sympathy of the audience for the criminal(s)?
Yes [ ] No [ ] Yes & no [ ] If other than "no" explain: _____

If audience sympathy is enlisted, are these criminals basically seeking to further justice?
Yes [ ] No [ ] Not clear [ ]

Fate of criminals:	CRIMINAL #1		CRIMINAL #2		CRIMINAL #3		CRIMINAL #4		CRIMINAL GROUPS	
	Tr	Ind	Tr	Ind	Tr	Ind	Tr	Ind	Tr	Ind
Killed by law	[ ]	[ ]	[ ]	[ ]	[ ]	[ ]	[ ]	[ ]	[ ]	[ ]
Killed by criminal	[ ]	[ ]	[ ]	[ ]	[ ]	[ ]	[ ]	[ ]	[ ]	[ ]
Killed by other	[ ]	[ ]	[ ]	[ ]	[ ]	[ ]	[ ]	[ ]	[ ]	[ ]
Death through accident	[ ]	[ ]	[ ]	[ ]	[ ]	[ ]	[ ]	[ ]	[ ]	[ ]
Punished by law	[ ]	[ ]	[ ]	[ ]	[ ]	[ ]	[ ]	[ ]	[ ]	[ ]
Suicide	[ ]	[ ]	[ ]	[ ]	[ ]	[ ]	[ ]	[ ]	[ ]	[ ]
Reform	[ ]	[ ]	[ ]	[ ]	[ ]	[ ]	[ ]	[ ]	[ ]	[ ]
Mental suffering	[ ]	[ ]	[ ]	[ ]	[ ]	[ ]	[ ]	[ ]	[ ]	[ ]
Aims not achieved	[ ]	[ ]	[ ]	[ ]	[ ]	[ ]	[ ]	[ ]	[ ]	[ ]
None	[ ]	[ ]	[ ]	[ ]	[ ]	[ ]	[ ]	[ ]	[ ]	[ ]
Other: _____	[ ]	[ ]	[ ]	[ ]	[ ]	[ ]	[ ]	[ ]	[ ]	[ ]

Professional screen name of criminal #1 _____

#2 _____

#3 _____

#4 _____

Group: _____

Does justice triumph primarily through the efforts of: Agents of the law [ ]
Private citizens [ ] Both [ ] Not clear [ ] Question irrelevant [ ]

PART SIX—SOCIOLOGICAL FACTORS

Title: _____

Does gambling occur during the picture? Yes [ ] No [ ] Not clear [ ]
What gambling setting? Common man [ ] Well-to-do [ ] Both [ ] Not clear [ ]

Violence? None [ ] Shooting [ ] Stabbing [ ] Strangling [ ] Clunking [ ]
Isolated punches, slaps [ ] Prolonged fist fights [ ] Kicks [ ] Lashings [ ]
War [ ] Torture (other than above) [ ] Other: _____

Is courtroom scene shown during the picture? Yes [ ] No [ ]
How is courtroom scene(s) portrayed? Dignified [ ] Otherwise [ ]

Is burial shown during the picture? Yes [ ] No [ ]
How is burial portrayed? Dignified [ ] Otherwise [ ]
Is the burial: Religious [ ] Lay [ ] Both [ ] Not clear [ ]

Is prayer(s) said during the picture? Yes [ ] No [ ]
How is prayer(s) portrayed? Dignified [ ] Otherwise [ ]
Is prayer(s) said by: Clergy [ ] Layman [ ] Both [ ] Not clear [ ]

Does marriage(s) occur during the picture? Yes [ ] No [ ]
Are the characters: Prominent [ ] Minor [ ] Incidental [ ]
Does marriage ceremony occur during the picture? Yes [ ] No [ ]

How is wedding ceremony portrayed? Dignified [ ] Otherwise [ ]
Is wedding ceremony conducted by: Clergy [ ] Justice of the Peace [ ] Both [ ] Other [ ] Not clear [ ]

Is divorce a dramatic element in the picture? Yes [ ] No [ ]
Does divorce occur during the picture? Yes [ ] No [ ] Not clear [ ]
Are the characters: Prominent [ ] Minor [ ] Incidental [ ]
Is divorce: The major element (core) of the picture [ ]
An important story point [ ] Incidental [ ]

Is adultery a dramatic element in the picture? Yes [ ] No [ ]
Are the characters: Prominent [ ] Minor [ ] Incidental [ ]
Is adultery: The major element (core) of the picture [ ]
An important story point [ ] Incidental [ ]

Is illicit sex a dramatic element in the picture? Yes [ ] No [ ] Not clear [ ]
Are the characters: Prominent [ ] Minor [ ] Incidental [ ]
Is illicit sex: The major element (core) of the picture [ ]
An important story point [ ] Incidental [ ]

Is romance a dramatic element in the picture? Yes [ ] No [ ] Not clear [ ]
Is romance: The major element (core) of the picture [ ]
An important story point [ ] Incidental [ ]

Does picture end with promise of marriage or continued love? Yes [ ] No [ ] Not clear [ ]
Does the picture concern family relationships or problems? Yes [ ] No [ ]
Are family relationships or problems: The major element (core) of the picture [ ] An important story point [ ] Incidental [ ]

PART SEVEN— OTHER SOCIOLOGICAL FACTORS

Title: _____

	MAJOR CHARACTER				SUB. MAJOR CHARACTER			
Character number	[1]	[2]	[3]	[4]	[1]	[2]	[3]	[4]
Economic status:								
Poor	[ ]	[ ]	[ ]	[ ]	[ ]	[ ]	[ ]	[ ]
Moderate means	[ ]	[ ]	[ ]	[ ]	[ ]	[ ]	[ ]	[ ]
Well-to-do	[ ]	[ ]	[ ]	[ ]	[ ]	[ ]	[ ]	[ ]
Very wealthy	[ ]	[ ]	[ ]	[ ]	[ ]	[ ]	[ ]	[ ]
Not clear	[ ]	[ ]	[ ]	[ ]	[ ]	[ ]	[ ]	[ ]
Marital status:								
Single	[ ]	[ ]	[ ]	[ ]	[ ]	[ ]	[ ]	[ ]
Married	[ ]	[ ]	[ ]	[ ]	[ ]	[ ]	[ ]	[ ]
Divorced	[ ]	[ ]	[ ]	[ ]	[ ]	[ ]	[ ]	[ ]
Widowed	[ ]	[ ]	[ ]	[ ]	[ ]	[ ]	[ ]	[ ]
Not clear	[ ]	[ ]	[ ]	[ ]	[ ]	[ ]	[ ]	[ ]

	MAJOR CHARACTER				SUB. MAJOR CHARACTER			
Character number	[1]	[2]	[3]	[4]	[1]	[2]	[3]	[4]
Social age:								
Child	[]	[]	[]	[]	[]	[]	[]	[]
Adolescence	[]	[]	[]	[]	[]	[]	[]	[]
Young adult	[]	[]	[]	[]	[]	[]	[]	[]
Independent adult	[]	[]	[]	[]	[]	[]	[]	[]
Middle-aged	[]	[]	[]	[]	[]	[]	[]	[]
Past middle-aged	[]	[]	[]	[]	[]	[]	[]	[]
Not clear	[]	[]	[]	[]	[]	[]	[]	[]
Motivations:								
Success in love	[]	[]	[]	[]	[]	[]	[]	[]
Acquisition of wealth	[]	[]	[]	[]	[]	[]	[]	[]
Luxurious living	[]	[]	[]	[]	[]	[]	[]	[]
Pleasure as the chief goal	[]	[]	[]	[]	[]	[]	[]	[]
Social prestige	[]	[]	[]	[]	[]	[]	[]	[]
Political prestige or success	[]	[]	[]	[]	[]	[]	[]	[]
Public Service	[]	[]	[]	[]	[]	[]	[]	[]
Obedience to duty or job	[]	[]	[]	[]	[]	[]	[]	[]
Professional or artistic achievement	[]	[]	[]	[]	[]	[]	[]	[]
Idealism for way of life	[]	[]	[]	[]	[]	[]	[]	[]
Marital happiness	[]	[]	[]	[]	[]	[]	[]	[]
Protection of self from harm	[]	[]	[]	[]	[]	[]	[]	[]
Protection of others from harm	[]	[]	[]	[]	[]	[]	[]	[]
Winning or holding confidence, respect	[]	[]	[]	[]	[]	[]	[]	[]
Desire for adventure or excitement	[]	[]	[]	[]	[]	[]	[]	[]
Thwarting wrong-doing	[]	[]	[]	[]	[]	[]	[]	[]
Power for its own sake	[]	[]	[]	[]	[]	[]	[]	[]
Establ. and maintenance of happy home	[]	[]	[]	[]	[]	[]	[]	[]
Psychological adjustment/peace of mind	[]	[]	[]	[]	[]	[]	[]	[]
Help others to be happy, succeed	[]	[]	[]	[]	[]	[]	[]	[]
Revenge	[]	[]	[]	[]	[]	[]	[]	[]
Other: _____	[]	[]	[]	[]	[]	[]	[]	[]

Code for motivations:

Sympathetic-Achieved = 1	Unsympathetic-Achieved = 4	Sym and Unsym-Achieved = 7
Sym-Not Achieved = 2	Unsym-Not Achieved = 5	Sym and Unsym-Not Achieved = 8
Sym-Not Clear = 3	Unsym-Not Clear = 6	Sym and Unsym-Not Clear = 9

PRODUCTION CODE ADMINISTRATION FILM ANALYSIS FORM 1959

ANALYSIS OF FILM CONTENT PART ONE— GENERAL

Title: _____

PCA approval date: _____

PCA seal number: _____

Footage: _____

Type: _____

Feature [ ]   Short [ ]

Domestic [ ]   Foreign [ ]

B&W _____ Color _____ Toned _____

Producer (company): _____

Producer (indiv'l): _____

Director: _____

Screenwriter: _____

Where filmed: _____

Distributor: _____

Material Source:

Biography _____

Comic strip _____

Folklore _____

Novel _____

Original screen story _____

Radio program _____

Short story _____

Stage play _____

Other: _____

Significant Story Elements/Angles:

Foreign _____ Political _____

Historical _____ Psychological _____

Juvenile _____ Racial _____

Medical _____ Religious _____

Military _____ Scientific _____

Educational _____ Family life _____

Ending:

Happy _____ Unhappy _____ Moral _____

Other: _____

Period: _____

Major locales (A): _____

_____

Major locales (B):

City _____ Rural _____

Suburban _____ Undeveloped areas _____

Small town ___ Not clear _____

Other: _____

Settings (A): _____

_____

Settings (B):

Very wealthy _____ Moderate _____

Well-to-do _____ Poor _____

Not clear _____

Foreign language(s) in addition to English:

_____

_____

Foreign countries treated:

	Sym.	Unsym.	S&U	Indif.
Canada	[ ]	[ ]	[ ]	[ ]
China	[ ]	[ ]	[ ]	[ ]
England	[ ]	[ ]	[ ]	[ ]
France	[ ]	[ ]	[ ]	[ ]
Germany	[ ]	[ ]	[ ]	[ ]
Italy	[ ]	[ ]	[ ]	[ ]
Japan	[ ]	[ ]	[ ]	[ ]
Mexico	[ ]	[ ]	[ ]	[ ]
Russia	[ ]	[ ]	[ ]	[ ]

Others: _____

Key: Sym. = Sympathetic
Unsym. = Unsympathetic
S&U = Sym. and Unsym.
Indif. = Indifferent

PART TWO—PORTRAYAL OF PROFESSIONS

Profession:	ROLE			CHARACTERIZATION								
	Prom	Min	Inci	Str	Com	S&C	Sym	Unsym	S&U	Indif	Dishon*	For**
_____	[]	[]	[]	[]	[]	[]	[]	[]	[]	[]	[]	[]
_____	[]	[]	[]	[]	[]	[]	[]	[]	[]	[]	[]	[]
_____	[]	[]	[]	[]	[]	[]	[]	[]	[]	[]	[]	[]
_____	[]	[]	[]	[]	[]	[]	[]	[]	[]	[]	[]	[]
_____	[]	[]	[]	[]	[]	[]	[]	[]	[]	[]	[]	[]
_____	[]	[]	[]	[]	[]	[]	[]	[]	[]	[]	[]	[]
_____	[]	[]	[]	[]	[]	[]	[]	[]	[]	[]	[]	[]
_____	[]	[]	[]	[]	[]	[]	[]	[]	[]	[]	[]	[]
_____	[]	[]	[]	[]	[]	[]	[]	[]	[]	[]	[]	[]
_____	[]	[]	[]	[]	[]	[]	[]	[]	[]	[]	[]	[]
_____	[]	[]	[]	[]	[]	[]	[]	[]	[]	[]	[]	[]

*Check this column if professional character is inefficient or dishonest in the performance of his professional duties.
**Check this column if character is both of foreign birth and, in all probability, not a citizen of the United States.

PART THREE—PORTRAYAL OF "RACES" AND NATIONALS

"Race" or National	ROLE			CHARACTERIZATION							U.S. CITIZEN		
	Prom	Min	Inci	Str	Com	S&C	Sym	Unsym	S&U	Indif	Yes	No	N.C.
_____	[]	[]	[]	[]	[]	[]	[]	[]	[]	[]	[]	[]	[]
_____	[]	[]	[]	[]	[]	[]	[]	[]	[]	[]	[]	[]	[]
_____	[]	[]	[]	[]	[]	[]	[]	[]	[]	[]	[]	[]	[]
_____	[]	[]	[]	[]	[]	[]	[]	[]	[]	[]	[]	[]	[]
_____	[]	[]	[]	[]	[]	[]	[]	[]	[]	[]	[]	[]	[]
_____	[]	[]	[]	[]	[]	[]	[]	[]	[]	[]	[]	[]	[]
_____	[]	[]	[]	[]	[]	[]	[]	[]	[]	[]	[]	[]	[]
_____	[]	[]	[]	[]	[]	[]	[]	[]	[]	[]	[]	[]	[]

Key: Prom = Prominent, Min = Minor, Inci = Incidental, Str = Straight,
Com = Comic, Sym = Sympathetic, Unsym = Umsympathetic, Indif = Indifferent

PART FOUR—LIQUOR

Title: _____

Treatment of liquor: None shown or consumed [ ] Shown only [ ] Consumed [ ]

If liquor consumed, amount of drinking: Very little [ ] Moderate [ ] Much [ ]

Where liquor consumed:

Cafe, restaurant	[ ]	Dwelling place	[ ]
Saloon, bar	[ ]	Office or business place	[ ]
Night club	[ ]	Other: _____	[ ]

What does character(s) drink? Wine [ ] Beer [ ] Hard liquor [ ] Unidentified [ ]

Is actual drunkenness portrayed? Yes [ ] No [ ]

PART FIVE—CRIME

Title: _____

Does picture depict crime? Yes [ ] No [ ] Important story point [ ]
Incidental [ ]

Describe crimes depicted: _____
_____
_____

Does story tend to enlist the sympathy of the audience for the criminal(s)?
Yes [ ] No [ ] Both yes and no [ ]

Fate of Criminal(s)

Killed	[ ]	_____
Death by accident	[ ]	_____
Punished by law	[ ]	_____
Suicide	[ ]	_____
Reform	[ ]	_____
Mental suffering	[ ]	_____
Other	[ ]	_____
No punishment	[ ]	_____

PART SIX—SOCIOLOGICAL FACTORS

Title: _____

Is violence depicted? Yes [ ] No [ ]
If so in which form? Shooting [ ] Knifing [ ] Swordplay [ ] Strangling [ ]
Torture [ ] Punch [ ] Fist fight [ ] Flogging [ ] War [ ] Other: _____
_____

Remarks: _____

Is gambling depicted? Yes [ ] No [ ] Important story point [ ] Incidental [ ]
If depicted, describe: _____

Is courtroom depicted? Yes [ ] No [ ] Dignified [ ] Otherwise [ ]
If depicted, describe: _____

Are prayers said or religious ceremonies performed? Yes [ ] No [ ]
If so, describe: _____

Is wedding ceremony shown in picture? Yes [ ] No [ ] Dignified [ ] Other [ ]
If so, by whom is ceremony performed? Clergyman [ ] Justice of the Peace [ ]
Judge [ ] Other [ ]

Is divorce an element in the picture? Yes [ ] No [ ]
Does divorce occur in the picture? Yes [ ] No [ ]
Is divorce: An important story point [ ] Minor [ ] Incidental [ ]
Are characters involved: Important [ ] Minor [ ] Incidental [ ]

Is adultery an important element in the picture? Yes [ ] No [ ]
Does adultery occur in the picture? Yes [ ] No [ ]
Is adultery: An important story point [ ] Minor [ ] Incidental [ ]
Are characters involved: Important [ ] Minor [ ] Incidental [ ]

Is illicit sex an element in the picture? Yes [ ] No [ ]
Does illicit sex occur in the picture? Yes [ ] No [ ]
Is illicit sex: An important story point [ ] Minor [ ] Incidental [ ]
Are characters involved: Important [ ] Minor [ ] Incidental [ ]

Is illegitimacy: Shown [ ] Indicated [ ] Not shown [ ]
Is seduction: Shown [ ] Indicated [ ] Not shown [ ]
Is rape: Shown [ ] Indicated [ ] Not shown [ ]

Bibliography

Adorno, T. W., and Max Horkheimer. *The Dialectic of Enlightenment*. Translated by John Cummings. New York: Seabury Press, 1972.

Althusser, Louis. *Lenin and Philosophy*. Translated by Ben Brewster. New York: Monthly Review Press, 1971.

Bakhtin, Mikhail. *The Dialogical Imagination*. Translated by Carl Emerson and Michael Holquist. Edited by Michael Holquist. Austin: University of Texas Press, 1981.

Balio, Tino, ed. *The American Film Industry*. Madison: University of Wisconsin Press, 1985.

———. *The Grand Design: Hollywood as a Modern Business Enterprise, 1930–1939*. Berkeley and Los Angeles: University of California Press, 1995.

Ball, Terence. "The Politics of Social Science in Postwar America." In *Recasting America*, edited by Lary May. Chicago: University of Chicago Press, 1989.

Ball-Rokeach, Sandra J., and Muriel Cantor, eds. *Media, Audience, and Social Structure*. Beverly Hills: SAGE, 1986.

Barbain, Jan-Pieter. "Filme mit Lücken: Die Lichtspielzensur in der Weimarer Republik: von der sozialethischen Schutzmaßnahme zum Politischen Instrument." In *Der Deutsche Film: Aspekte seiner Geschichte von den Anfangen bis zur Gegenwart*, edited by Uli Jung. Trier: WVT Wissenschaftler Verlag, 1993.

Barrett, James R. "Americanization from the Bottom Up: Immigration and the Remaking of the Working Class in the United States, 1880–1930." *The Journal of American History* 79, no. 3 (December 1992).

Barthes, Roland. *Mythologies*. New York: Hill and Wang, 1972.

Behlmer, Rudy. *Inside Warner Bros., 1935–1951*. New York: Viking Penguin, 1985.

Benjamin, Walter. *Illuminations*. Edited by Hannah Arendt. New York: Shocken Books, 1969.

Bercovitch, Sacvan. *The American Jeremiad*. Madison: University of Wisconsin Press, 1978.

Bergman, Andrew. *We're in the Money: Depression America and Its Films*. New York: Harper & Row, 1972.

Bergstrom, Janet. "The Mystery of *The Blue Gardenia*." In *Shades of Noir: A Reader*, edited by Joan Copjek. London: Verso, 1993.

Black, Gregory D. *Hollywood Censored: Morality Codes, Catholics, and the Movies.* Cambridge: Cambridge University Press, 1994.

Borde, Raymonde, and Etienne Chaumeton. *Panorama du Film Noir Américain, 1941–1953.* Paris: Editions de Minuit, 1955.

Bordwell, David, Janet Staiger, and Kristin Thompson. *The Classical Hollywood Cinema: Film Style and Mode of Production to 1960.* London: Routledge, 1985.

Brinkley, Alan. "The New Deal and the Idea of the State." In *The Rise and Fall of the New Deal Order, 1930–1980,* edited by Steve Fraser and Gary Gerstle. Princeton: Princeton University Press, 1989.

Burner, David. *The Politics of Provincialism: The Democratic Party in Transition, 1914–1932.* New York: Knopf, 1967.

Burnett, W. R. "The Outsider." Interview by Ken Mate and Pat McGilligan. In *Backstory: Interviews with Screenwriters of Hollywood's Golden Age,* edited by Pat McGilligan. Berkeley and Los Angeles: University of California Press, 1986.

Cagney, James. *Cagney by Cagney.* Garden City, N.Y.: Doubleday, 1976.

Carey, Gary. *All the Stars in Heaven: The Story of Louis B. Mayer and M.G.M.* London: Robson Books, 1982.

Cargnelli, Christian, and Michael Omasta, eds. *Aufbruch ins Ungewisse.* Vienna: Wespennest, 1993.

Ceplair, Larry, and Steven Englund. *The Inquisition in Hollywood: Politics in the Film Community, 1930–1960.* Berkeley and Los Angeles: University of California Press, 1983.

Chaney, David. *Fictions of Collective Life: Public Drama in Late Modern Culture.* London: Routledge, 1993.

Cogley, John, ed. *Report on Blacklisting: I, Movies.* New York: Fund for the Republic, 1956.

Cohen, Lizabeth. *Making a New Deal: Industrial Workers in Chicago, 1919–1939.* Cambridge: Cambridge University Press, 1990.

Collier, John. "Censorship and the National Board." *Survey* 35 (October 1915).

Copjek, Joan, ed. *Shades of Noir: A Reader.* London: Verso, 1993.

Davis, Mike. *Prisoners of the American Dream: The Failure of the American Left.* London: Verso, 1990.

de Certeau, Michel. *The Practice of Everyday Life.* Translated by Steven Redall. Berkeley and Los Angeles: University of California Press, 1984.

de Lauretis, Teresa. *Alice Doesn't: Feminism, Semiotics, Cinema.* Bloomington: Indiana University Press, 1984.

Dick, Bernard F. *The Star-Spangled Screen: The American World War II Film.* Lexington: University Press of Kentucky, 1985.

Doane, Mary Ann. "Ideology and the Practice of Sound Editing and Mixing." In *Film Sound: Theory and Practice,* edited by Elisabeth Weis and John Belton. New York: Columbia University Press, 1985.

Dyer, Richard. *Stars.* London: British Film Institute, 1979.

Eisner, Lotte H. *The Haunted Screen.* Translated by Roger Greaves. Berkeley and Los Angeles: University of California Press, 1973. Originally published as *L'Ecran Démoniaque* (1952).

Elsaesser, Thomas. "A German Ancestry to Film Noir? Film History and Its Imaginary." *Iris: A Journal of Theory on Image and Sound* 21 (spring 1996).

Erenberg, Lewis. *Steppin' Out: New York Night Life and the Transformation of American Culture*. Chicago: University of Chicago Press, 1984.

Erenberg, Lewis, and Susan E. Hirsch, eds. *The War in American Culture: Society and Consciousness during World War II*. Chicago: University of Chicago Press, 1996.

Eyles, Allen. "The Films of ENTERPRISE, A Studio History." *Focus on Film* 35 (April 1980).

Fearing, Franklin, ed. "Special Edition: Mass Media Analysis." *Journal of Social Issues* 3, no. 3 (summer 1947).

Feld, Hans. *"Abschied." Film Kurier* (August 1930).

Forgacs, David, ed. *An Antonio Gramsci Reader: Selected Writings 1916–1935*. New York: Schocken Books, 1988.

Foucault, Michel. *The Archaelogy of Knowledge*. Translated by A. M. Sheridan Smith. New York: Pantheon, 1972.

———. *Discipline and Punish: The Birth of the Prison*. Translated by Alan Sheridan. New York: Vintage, 1979.

Fraser, Steve, and Gary Gerstle, eds. *The Rise and Fall of the New Deal Order, 1930–1980*. Princeton: Princeton University Press, 1989.

Geist, Kenneth L. *Pictures Will Talk: The Life and Films of Joseph L. Mankiewicz*. New York: Charles Scribner's Sons, 1978.

Gerstle, Gary. *Working Class Americanism: The Politics of Labor in a Textile City, 1914–1960*. Cambridge: Cambridge University Press, 1989.

Gomery, Douglas. "The Coming of Sound: Technological Change in the American Film Industry." In *Film Sound: Theory and Practice*, edited by Elisabeth Weis and John Belton. New York: Columbia University Press, 1985.

Gramsci, Antonio. *Selections from the Prison Notebooks*. Translated and edited by Quentin Hoare and Geoffrey Nowell Smith. New York: International Publishers, 1971.

Grant, Barry Keith, ed. *The Film Genre Reader*. Austin: University of Texas Press, 1986.

Gusfield, Joseph R. *Symbolic Crusade: Status Politics and the American Temperance Movement*. Urbana and Champaign: University of Illinois Press, 1963.

Habermas, Jürgen. *Legitimation Crisis*. Translated by Thomas McCarthy. Boston: Beacon Press, 1975.

Hall, Stuart. "Encoding/Decoding." In *Culture, Media, Language*, edited by Stuart Hall, Dorothy Hobson, Andrew Lowe, and Paul Willis. London: Hutchinson, 1980.

———. "Notes on Deconstructing the Popular." In *People's History and Socialist Theory*, edited by Raphael Samuel. London: Routledge, 1981.

Hall, Stuart, Dorothy Hobson, Andrew Lowe, and Paul Willis, eds. *Culture, Media, Language*. London: Hutchinson, 1980.

Hamby, Alonzo. *Liberalism and Its Challengers*. New York: Oxford University Press, 1985.

Heale, Michael. *American Anti-Communism*. Baltimore: Johns Hopkins University Press, 1990.

Heath, Stephen. "Film and System." *Screen* 16, no. 1 (spring 1975) and no. 2 (summer 1975).

Henry, Ralph L. "The Cultural Influence of the 'Talkies.'" *School and Society* (February 1929). Reprinted in *The Movies in Our Midst: Documents in the Cultural History of Film in America*, edited by Gerald Mast. Chicago: University of Chicago Press, 1982.

Hesse, Barnor. "Black to Front and Black Again: Racialization through Contested Times and Spaces." In *Place and Politics of Identity*, edited by Michael Keith and Steven Pile. London: Routledge, 1993.

Hilfer, Tony. *The Crime Novel: A Deviant Genre*. Austin: University of Texas Press, 1990.

Hirschbach, Frank D., ed. *Germany in the Twenties: The Artist as Social Critic*. Minneapolis: University of Minnesota, 1980.

Hobsbawm, E. J. *Bandits*. Second Edition. Harmondsworth: Penguin, 1985.

Hobsbawm, E. J., and Terence Ranger, eds. *The Invention of Tradition*. Cambridge: Cambridge University Press, 1983.

Hodgson, Godfrey. *America in Our Time: America from World War II to Nixon*. New York: Random House, 1976.

Huyssen, Andreas. *After the Great Divide*. Bloomington: Indiana University Press, 1986.

Jacobs, Ruth. *Wages of Sin: Censorship and the Fallen Woman Film, 1928–1942*. Berkeley and Los Angeles: University of California Press, 1997.

James, C. L. R. *American Civilization*. Edited by Anna Grimshaw and Keith Hart. Oxford: Blackwell, 1993.

Jameson, Fredric. *The Political Unconscious: Narrative as Socially Symbolic Act*. Ithaca: Cornell University Press, 1981.

Johnston, Eric. *America Unlimited*. Garden City, N.J.: Doubleday, 1944.

———. "Utopia Is Production." *Screen Actor* 14 (April 1946).

Jones, Dorothy B. "Communism in the Movies." In *Report on Blacklisting: I, Movies*, edited by John Cogley. New York: Fund for the Republic, 1956.

Jung, Uli, ed. *Der Deutsche Film: Aspekte seiner Geschichte von den Anfängen bis zur Gegenwart*. Trier: WVT Wissenschaftler Verlag, 1993.

Kaplan, E. Anne, ed. *Women in Film Noir*. London: British Film Institute, 1978.

Karasek, Helmuth. *Billy Wilder: Eine Nahaufnahme*. Munich: Wilhelm Heyne Verlag, 1994.

Karpf, Stephen L. *The Gangster Film: Emergence, Variation, and Decay of a Genre, 1930–1940*. Salem, N.H.: Ayer, 1973.

Keith, Michael, and Steven Pile, eds. *Place and Politics of Identity*. London: Routledge, 1993.

Kemp, Philip. "From the Nightmare Factory: HUAC and the Politics of Noir." *Sight and Sound* 55, no. 4 (autumn 1986).

Klinger, Barbara. "'Cinema/Ideology/Criticism' Revisited: The Progressive Genre." In *The Film Genre Reader*, edited by Barry Keith Grant. Austin: University of Texas Press, 1986.

Koppes, Clayton R., and Gregory D. Black. *Hollywood Goes to War: How Profits Shaped World War II Movies*. London: I. B. Tauris, 1987.

Koszarski, Richard, ed. *Hollywood Directors, 1941–1976*. Oxford: Oxford University Press, 1977.

Kracauer, Siegried. *From Caligari to Hitler: A Psychological History of the German Film*. Princeton: Princeton University Press, 1947.

Krutnik, Frank. *In a Lonely Street: Film Noir, Genre, Masculinity*. London: Routledge, 1991.

Lang, Fritz. "Freedom of the Screen." In *Hollywood Directors, 1941–1976*, edited by Richard Koszarski. Oxford: Oxford University Press, 1977. Originally in *Theatre Arts* (December 1947).

Lears, Jackson. *No Place of Grace: Antimodernism and the Transformation of American Culture, 1880–1920*. New York: Pantheon, 1981.

Leff, Leonard J., and Jerold L. Simmons. *The Dame in the Kimono: Hollywood Censorship and the Production Code, from the 1920s to the 1960s*. New York: Grove Weidenfeld, 1990.

Lichtenstein, Nelson. "From Corporatism to Collective Bargaining: Organized Labor and the Eclipse of Social Democracy in the Postwar Era." In *The Rise and Fall of the New Deal Order, 1930–1980*, edited by Steve Fraser and Gary Gerstle. Princeton: Princeton University Press, 1989.

Lichtman, Allan J. "Critical Election Theory and the Reality of American Presidential Politics, 1916–40." *American Historical Review* 18, no. 1 (February 1976).

Linkh, Richard. *American Catholicism and European Immigrants, 1900–1924*. New York: Center for Migration Studies, 1976.

Lipsitz, George. *Rainbow at Midnight: Labor and Culture in the 1940s*. Urbana and Champaign: University of Illinois Press, 1994.

———. *Time Passages: Collective Memory and American Culture*. Minneapolis: University of Minnesota Press, 1990.

Lubell, Samuel. *The Future of American Politics*. New York: Harper, 1952.

Lyotard, Jean-François. *The Postmodern Condition: A Report on Knowledge*. Translated by Geoff Bennington and Brian Massumi. Minneapolis: University of Minnesota Press, 1984.

Maltby, Richard. "*Film Noir*: The Politics of the Maladjusted Text." *Journal of American Studies* 18, no. 1 (April 1984).

———. *Harmless Entertainment: Hollywood and the Ideology of Consensus*. Metucheon: Scarecrow Press, 1983.

———. "The Production Code and the Hays Office." In *The Grand Design: Hollywood as a Modern Business Enterprise*, edited by Tino Balio. Berkeley and Los Angeles: University of California Press, 1995.

———. "Tragic Heroes? Al Capone and the Spectacle of Criminality, 1947–1931." In *Screening the Past: The Sixth Australian History and Film Conference*, edited by John Benson, Ken Berryman, and Wayne Levy. Melbourne: La Trobe University Press, 1995.

Mast, Gerald, ed. *The Movies in Our Midst: Documents in the Cultural History of Film in America*. Chicago: University of Chicago Press, 1982.

May, Lary. "Movie Star Politics: The Screen Actor's Guild, Cultural Conversion, and the Hollywood Red Scare." In *Recasting America: Culture and Politics in the Age of Cold War*, edited by May. Chicago: University of Chicago Press, 1989.

———. *Screening Out the Past: The Birth of Mass Culture and the Motion Picture Industry*. Chicago: University of Chicago Press, 1983.

————. *Recasting America: Culture and Politics in the Age of Cold War.* Chicago: University of Chicago Press, 1989.

McArthur, Colin. *Underworld USA.* London: Secker and Warburg, 1972.

McClure, Arthur. "Censor the Movies! Early Attempts to Regulate the Content of the Motion Pictures in America, 1907–1936." In *The Movies: An American Idiom; Readings in the Social History of the American Motion Picture,* edited by McClure. Rutherford, N.J.: Fairleigh Dickinson University Press, 1971

McClure, Arthur F., ed. *The Movies: An American Idiom; Readings in the Social History of the American Motion Picture.* Rutherford: Fairleigh Dickinson University Press, 1971.

McConnell, Frank. *The Spoken Seen: Film and the Romantic Imagination.* Baltimore: Johns Hopkins University Press, 1975.

McCormick, Richard W. "From *Caligari* to Dietrich: Sexual, Social and Cinematic Discourses in Weimar Film." *Signs* (spring 1993).

McGilligan, Pat. *Backstory: Interviews with Screenwriters of Hollywood's Golden Age.* Berkeley and Los Angeles: University of California Press, 1986.

Miller, Don. *B Movies.* New York: Ballantine Books, 1973.

Motion Picture Producers and Distributors of America. "The Don'ts and Be Carefuls." Federal Trade Commission Hearing (October 1927). Reprinted in *The Movies in Our Midst: Documents in the Cultural History of Film in America,* edited by Gerald Mast. Chicago: University of Chicago Press, 1982.

————. "The Production Code." Originally published in 1930. Reprinted in *The Movies in Our Midst: Documents in the Cultural History of Film in America,* edited by Gerald Mast. Chicago: University of Chicago Press, 1982.

Munby, Jonathan. "*Manhattan Melodrama*'s 'Art of the Weak': Telling History from the Other Side in the 1930s Talking Gangster Film." *Journal of American Studies* 30, pt. 1 (April 1996).

————. "The 'Un-American' Film Art: Robert Siodmak and the Political Significance of Film Noir's German Connection." *Iris: A Journal of Theory on Image and Sound* 21 (spring 1996).

Naremore, James. "The Trial: The FBI vs Orson Welles," *Film Comment* 27, no. 1 (January–February 1991).

National Board of Review. *State Censorship of Motion Pictures.* New York: National Board of Review, 1921. Reprinted in *The Movies in Our Midst: Documents in the Cultural History of Film in America,* edited by Gerald Mast. Chicago: University of Chicago Press, 1982.

Neale, Stephen. *Genre.* London: British Film Institute, 1980.

Neve, Brian. *Film and Politics in America: A Social Tradition.* London: Routledge, 1992.

Newcomb, Horace. "On the Dialogical Aspects of Mass Communication." *Critical Studies in Mass Communication* 1, no. 1 (1984).

Nichols, Bill, ed. *Movies and Methods: An Anthology.* Berkeley and Los Angeles: University of California Press, 1976.

————. *Movies and Methods: An Anthology, Volume II.* Berkeley and Los Angeles: University of California Press, 1985.

Noble, David. *The End of American History: Democracy, Capitalism, and the Metaphor of Two Worlds in Anglo-American Historical Writing, 1880–1980*. Minneapolis: University of Minnesota Press, 1985.

O'Brien, David J. *American Catholics and Social Reform: The New Deal Years*. New York: Oxford University Press, 1968.

Parker, James J. "The Organizational Environment of the Motion Picture Sector." In *Media, Audience, and Social Structure*, edited by Sandra Ball-Rokeach and Muriel Cantor. Beverly Hills: SAGE, 1986.

Peiss, Kathy. *Cheap Amusements: Working Women and Leisure in Turn-of-the-Century New York*. Philadelphia: Temple University Press, 1985.

Pells, Richard. *Radical Visions and American Dreams: Culture and Social Thought in the Depression Years*. Middletown, Conn.: Wesleyan University Press, 1973.

Petro, Patrice. *Joyless Streets: Women and Melodramatic Representation in Weimar Germany*. Princeton: Princeton University Press, 1989.

Pichel, Irving. "Areas of Silence." *Hollywood Quarterly* 3 (fall 1947).

Poffenberger, A. T. "Motion Pictures and Crime." *Scientific Monthly* 12 (April 1921). Reprinted in *The Movies in Our Midst: Documents in the Cultural History of Film in America*, edited by Gerald Mast. Chicago: University of Chicago Press, 1982.

Polan, Dana. *Power and Paranoia: History, Narrative, and the American Cinema, 1940–1950*. New York: Columbia University Press, 1986.

Pressburger, Emmerich. "*Abschied*, der Erste Milieutonfilm." *Licht-Bild-Bühne* (August 19, 1930).

Quart, Leonard and Albert Auster. *American Film and Society since 1945*. 2d ed. New York: Praeger, 1991.

Rabinowitz, Peter. *Before Reading: Narrative Conventions and the Politics of Interpretation*. Ithaca: Cornell University Press, 1987.

Radway, Janice. *Reading the Romance: Women, Patriarchy and Popular Literature*. Chapel Hill: University of North Carolina Press, 1984.

Ray, Robert B. *A Certain Tendency of the Hollywood Cinema, 1930–1980*. Princeton: Princeton University Press, 1985.

Robinson, Edward G., with Leonard Spigelgass. *All My Yesterdays: An Autobiography*. New York: Hawthorn, 1973.

Roffman, Peter, and Jim Purdy. *The Hollywood Social Problem Film: Madness, Depair, and Politics from the Depression to the Fifties*. Bloomington: Indiana University Press, 1981.

Rosenzweig, Roy. *Eight Hours for What We Will*. Cambridge: Cambridge University Press, 1985.

Rosow, Eugene. *Born to Lose: The Gangster Film in America*. New York: Oxford University Press, 1978.

Ruth, David. *Inventing the Public Enemy: The Gangster in American Culture, 1918–1934*. Chicago: University of Chicago Press, 1996.

Rutland, J. R., ed. *The Reference Shelf Series: State Censorship of Motion Pictures*. New York: Wilson, 1923. Reprinted in *The Movies in Our Midst: Documents in the Cultural History of Film in America*, edited by Gerald Mast. Chicago: University of Chicago Press, 1982.

Samuel, Raphael, ed. *People's History and Socialist Theory*. London: Routledge, 1981.

Sayer, Derek. *Capitalism and Modernity: An Excursus on Marx and Weber*. London: Routledge, 1991.

Schatz, Thomas. *Hollywood Genres: Formulas, Filmmaking and the Studio System*. New York: Random House, 1981.

Schindler, Colin. *Hollywood in Crisis: Cinema and American Society, 1929–1939*. London: Routledge, 1996.

Schrader, Paul. "Notes on Film Noir." In *The Film Genre Reader*, edited by Barry Keith Grant. Austin: University of Texas Press, 1986.

Schumach, Murray. *The Face on the Cutting Room Floor: The Story of Movie and Television Censorship*. New York: William Morrow and Company, 1964.

Schwartz, Nancy Lynn. *The Hollywood Writer's Wars*. New York: Knopf, 1972.

Server, Lee. *Screenwriter: Words Become Pictures*. Pittstown, N.J.: Mainstreet Press, 1987.

Silver, Alain, and Elizabeth Ward, eds. *Film Noir: An Encyclopedic Reference to the American Style*. 3d ed. Woodstock, N.Y.: Overlook Press, 1992.

Siodmak, Robert. "Hoodlums: The Myth." *Films and Filming* (June 1959). Reprinted in *Hollywood Directors, 1941–1976*, edited by Richard Koszarski. Oxford: Oxford University Press, 1977.

Sklar, Robert. *City Boys: Cagney, Bogart, Garfield*. Princeton: Princeton University Press, 1992.

———. *Movie-Made America: A Cultural History of the American Movies*. New York: Random House, 1975.

Slotkin, Richard. *Gunfighter Nation: The Myth of the Frontier in Twentieth Century America*. New York: Harper Collins, 1993.

Smith, Paul. *Discerning the Subject*. Minneapolis: University of Minnesota Press, 1988.

Steinberg, Stephen. *The Ethnic Myth: Race, Ethnicity, and Class in America*. Boston: Beacon Press, 1989.

Susman, Warren. *Culture as History: The Tranformation of American Society in the Twentieth Century*. New York: Pantheon, 1984.

———. "Did Success Spoil the United States? Dual Representations in Postwar America." In *Recasting America: Culture and Politics in the Age of Cold War*, edited by Lary May. Chicago: University of Chicago Press, 1989.

Taves, Brian. "The B Film: Hollywood's Other Half." In *The Grand Design: Hollywood as a Modern Business Enterprise*, edited by Tino Balio. Berkeley and Los Angeles: University of California Press, 1995.

Telotte, J. P. *Voices in the Dark: The Narrative Patterns of Film Noir*. Urbana and Champaign: University of Illinois Press, 1989.

Todorov, Tzvetan. *Mikhail Bakhtin: The Dialogical Principle*. Translated by Wlad Godzich. Minneapolis: University of Minnesota Press, 1984.

Tuska, Jon. *Dark Cinema: American Film Noir in Cultural Perspective*. Westport, Conn.: Greenwood Press, 1984.

Vasey, Ruth. *The World According to Hollywood, 1918–1939*. Exeter: University of Exeter Press, 1997.

Vaughn, Stephen. "Morality and Entertainment: The Origins of the Motion Picture Production Code." *Journal of American History* (June 1990).

Vernet, Marc. "*Film Noir* on the Edge of Doom." In *Shades of Noir: A Reader*, edited by Joan Copjek. London: Verso, 1993.

Vizzard, Jack. *See No Evil*. New York: Simon and Schuster, 1970.

Walsh, Andrea. *Women's Film and Female Experience, 1940–1950*. New York: Praeger, 1984.

Warren, Douglas, with James Cagney. *James Cagney: The Authorized Biography*. New York: St. Martin's Press, 1983.

Warshow, Robert. "The Gangster as Tragic Hero." *Partisan Review* 15, no. 2 (February 1958).

———. *The Immediate Experience*. New York: Atheneum, 1975.

Weis, Elisabeth, and John Belton, eds. *Film Sound: Theory and Practice*. New York: Columbia University Press, 1985.

Whitfield, Stephen J. *The Culture of the Cold War*. Baltimore: Johns Hopkins University Press, 1991.

Wright, Judith Hess. "Genre Films and the Status Quo." In *The Film Genre Reader*, edited by Barry Keith Grant. Austin: University of Texas Press, 1986.

Zheutlin, Barbara, and David Talbot. "Albert Maltz: Portrait of a Hollywood Dissident." *Cineaste* 8, no. 3 (winter 1977–78).

Film Index

Subject Index

actors: ethnic, 39, 41, 44, 55, 63, 106; silent, 33, 41–42 n.4
Adorno, Theodor W., 14, 80–81, 204 n.22
African Americans, 2, 3, 225–26
Alger, Horatio. *See* Horatio Alger myth
Alton, John, 122, 186
American Academy of Dramatic Arts, 107
"Americanism": and immigration, 26–27, 90, 95; and the movies, 90, 150; nativist vs. "new," 27–28 n.11, 30 n.16, 89, 144–45; postwar, 150, 212
"Americanization," 26–30, 49, 107; and Catholicism, 94–96; in classic gangster films, 48–51, 52–53, 56–58, 62; of emigré filmmakers, 211–12, 214; and film censorship, 90, 98
Americanness: "authentic," 26, 27, 29–30, 40–41, 45, 106–7; and censorship, 85, 89, 90, 93, 94; inclusive, 32, 96, 132. *See also* melting pot theory
"American way of life," 119, 149, 155, 163, 174, 217, 220
anglicization: of names, 41, 107, 161; of voices, 58, 59, 73, 83
Anglo-Saxon Protestants: and censorship, 4–5, 6, 24, 83, 93, 106, 144–45; hegemony of, 26–27, 38, 44, 62, 94–97; and leisure industries, 31, 33–34; in movies, 53–54, 59, 61, 73, 75 n.9, 111; and Prohibition, 32–34; and Roosevelt, 35, 97. *See also* nativism
anti-Communism: during the 1920s, 21, 30, 191; postwar, 9, 77, 133, 148, 149–50, 167, 210–11, 213, 224. *See also* House

Committee on Un-American Activities; McCarthyism
anti-Communist films, 133 n.22, 213
Anti-Nazi League, 211, 219
antitrust suit (Paramount suit), 123, 126, 224
assimilation. *See* "Americanization"
Association of Motion Picture Producers, 19, 66
audience: demand, 55, 86, 102–3, 104–5, 106, 120, 122, 182; female, 192, 193; heterogeneity, 88, 91; identification with 1930s gangster film, 13, 50, 54, 58, 68, 69, 70, 106; identification with postwar crime films, 116, 132–33, 139, 165, 170, 178, 205, 213; reception, 15, 55, 62–63, 81–82, 119, 180; research, 172, 175–77, 180–81
Ayres, Lew, 100

Bakhtin, Mikhail, 62 n, 64 n
Ball, Terence, 174, 175
Bandits' Roost, 22, 23–24
Bara, Theda, 191–92
Barbain, Jan-Pieter, 190 n.7
Barrett, James R., 27
Beard, Charles, 85, 86
Beck, Robert, 226
Benjamin, Walter, 204 n.22
Bennett, Joan, 198
Bercovitch, Sacvan, 45
Bergman, Andrew, 12–13, 16, 43 n, 53 n
Bergman, Ingrid, 75 n.9
Berkeley, Martin, 127 n.15
Berlin, 201, 203

255